THE ORIGINS AND EVOLUTION OF ISLAMIC LAW

Long before the rise of Islam in the early seventh century, Arabia had come to form an integral part of the Near East. This book, covering more than three centuries of legal history, presents an important account of how Islam developed its own law while drawing on ancient Near Eastern legal cultures, Arabian customary law and Quranic reform. The development of the judiciary, legal reasoning and legal authority during the first century is discussed in detail as is the dramatic rise of Prophetic authority, the crystallization of legal theory and the formation of the all-important legal schools. Finally, the book explores the interplay between law and politics, explaining how the jurists and the ruling elite led a symbiotic existence and mutual dependency that – seemingly paradoxically – allowed Islamic law and its application to be uniquely independent of the "state."

Wael B. Hallaq is a James McGill Professor of Islamic Law, teaching at the Institute of Islamic Studies, McGill University. He is the author of *Ibn Taymiyya Against the Greek Logicians* (1993), *A History of Islamic Legal Theories* (1997) and *Authority, Continuity and Change in Islamic Law* (2001).

THEMES IN ISLAMIC LAW 1

Series editor: Wael B. Hallaq

Themes in Islamic Law offers a series of state-of-the-art titles on the history of Islamic law, its application and its place in the modern world. The intention is to provide an analytic overview of the field with an emphasis on how law relates to the society in which it operates. Contributing authors, who all have distinguished reputations in their particular areas of scholarship, have been asked to interpret the complexities of the subject for those entering the field for the first time.

THE ORIGINS AND EVOLUTION OF ISLAMIC LAW

WAEL B. HALLAQ
McGill University

CAMBRIDGE
UNIVERSITY PRESS

CAMBRIDGE UNIVERSITY PRESS
Cambridge, New York, Melbourne, Madrid, Cape Town, Singapore, São Paulo

Cambridge University Press
The Edinburgh Building, Cambridge, CB2 8RU, UK

Published in the United States of America by Cambridge University Press

www.cambridge.org
Information on this title: www.cambridge.org/9780521803328

First Published 2005
Third printing 2007

Printed in the United Kingdom at the University Press, Cambridge

A catalogue record for this book is available from the British Library

Library of Congress Cataloging-in-Publication Data

Hallaq, Wael B., 1955–
The origins and evolution of Islamic law / Wael B. Hallaq.
p. cm. – (Themes in Islamic law; 1)
Includes bibliographical references and index.
ISBN 0 521 80332 2 – ISBN 0 521 00580 9 (pb.)
1. Islamic law – History – To 1500. I. Title. II. Series.
KBP55.H35 2004
340.5′9′09 – dc22 2004049739

ISBN-13 978-0-521-80332-8 hardback
ISBN-13 978-0-521-00580-7 paperback

To Charry

Contents

Maps

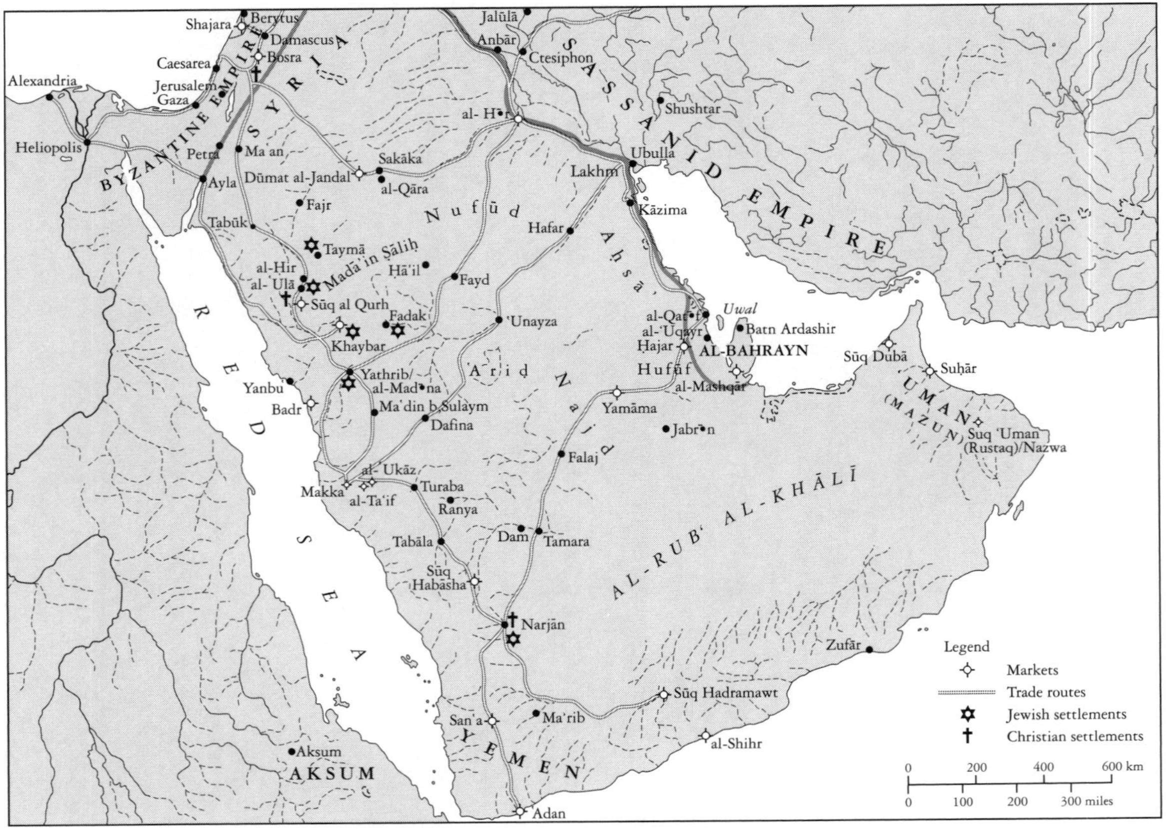

1 Arabia ca. 622 AD

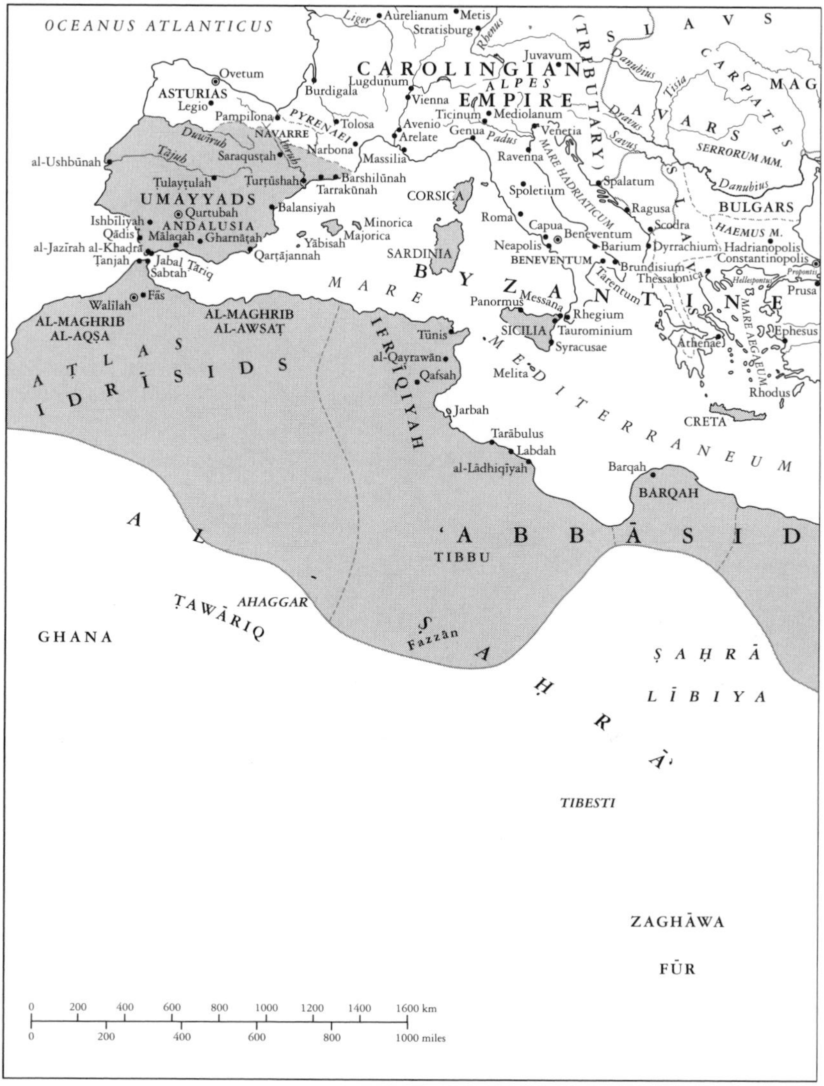

2 Muslim lands in the third/ninth century

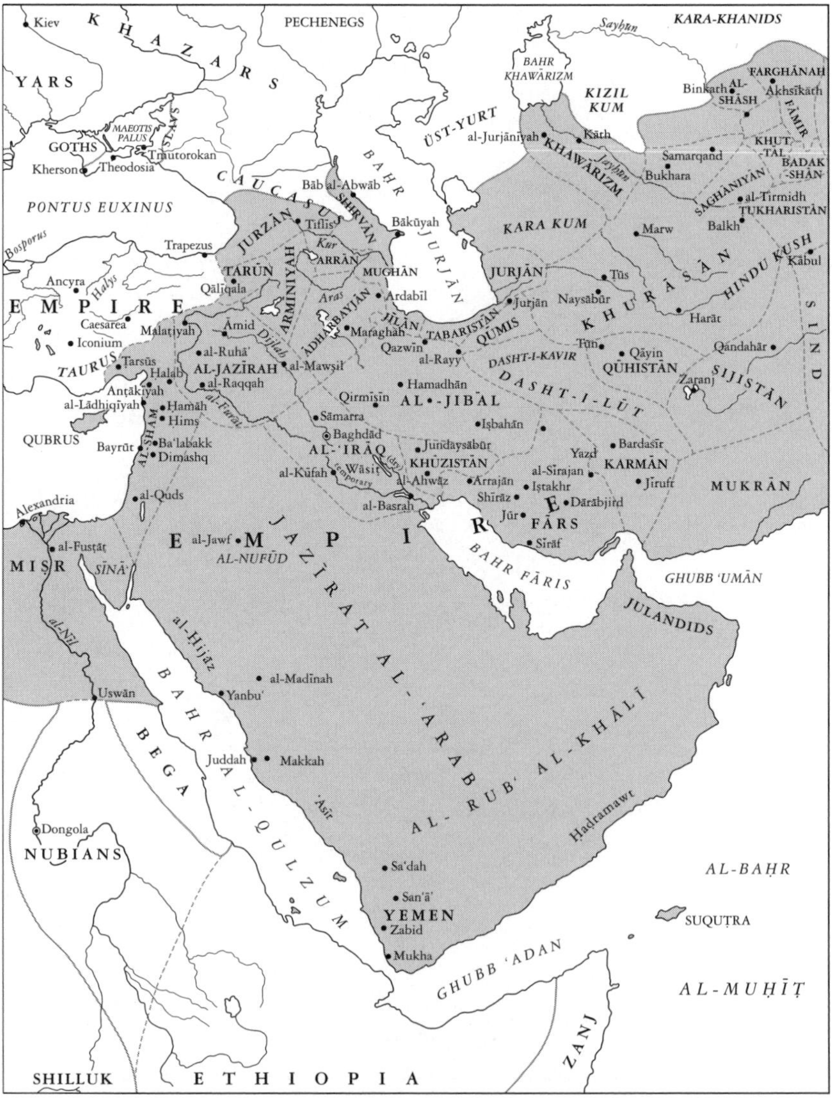

Kiev
KHAZARS
PECHENEGS
KARA-KHANIDS
Sayhūn
YARS
BAHR KHAWĀRIZM
KIZIL KUM
FARGHĀNAH
Binkath
AL-SHĀSH
Akhsīkath
FĀMIR
MAEOTIS PALUS
SLAVS
GOTHS
Tmutorokan
Kherson
Theodosia
ÜST-YURT
al-Jurjāniyah
Kāth
KHAWĀRIZM
Jayhūn
Samarqand
KHUT-TAL
BADAK-SHĀN
Bukhara
CAUCASUS
BAHR JURJĀN
Bāb al-Abwāb
SHIRVĀN
SAGHĀNIYĀN
al-Tirmidh
TUKHARISTĀN
PONTUS EUXINUS
Bosporus
Tiflis
Bākūyah
KARA KUM
Marw
Balkh
Trapezus
JURZĀN
Kur
ARRĀN
ARMINIYAH
KHURĀSĀN
HINDU KUSH
Kābul
TARŪN
MUGHĀN
JURJĀN
Tūs
Ancyra
Halys
Qālīqala
Aras
Ardabīl
Jurjān
Naysābūr
SIND
EMPIRE
JĪLĀN
TABARISTĀN
QŪMIS
Harāt
Caesarea
Malaṭiyah
Āmid
ĀDHARBAYJĀN
Maraghah
Qazwīn
al-Rayy
Iconium
Dijlah
Tūn
Qāyin
Qandahār
TAURUS
Tarsūs
al-Ruhā'
DASHT-I-KAVIR
QŪHISTĀN
AL-JAZĪRAH
al-Mawṣil
Halab
al-Raqqah
Hamadhān
DASHT-I-LŪT
Zaranj
SIJISTĀN
Anṭākiyah
al-Lādhiqīyah
al-Furāt
Qirmīsīn
AL-JIBĀL
Ḥamāh
Ḥimṣ
AL-SHĀM
Sāmarra
Iṣbahān
QUBRUS
Baghdād
Bayrūt
Ba'labakk
Dimashq
AL-'IRĀQ
Jundaysābūr
Bardasīr
Yazd
(dry)
KHŪZISTĀN
KARMĀN
al-Kūfah
Wāsiṭ
temporary
al-Ahwāz
Arrajān
al-Sīrajan
Jīruft
MUKRĀN
al-Quds
Shīrāz
Iṣṭakhr
Dārābjird
Alexandria
al-Baṣrah
Jūr
FĀRS
al-Fusṭāṭ
EMPIRE
al-Jawf
Sīrāf
AL-NUFŪD
MIṢR
SĪNĀ'
BAHR FĀRIS
GHUBB 'UMĀN
JAZĪRAT AL-'ARAB
JULANDIDS
al-Nīl
al-Ḥijāz
al-Madīnah
Uswān
Yanbu'
BAHR AL-QULZUM
BEGA
Juddah
Makkah
AL-RUB' AL-KHĀLĪ
'Asīr
Ḥaḍramawt
Dongola
NUBIANS
AL-BAḤR
Sa'dah
San'ā'
SUQUṬRA
YEMEN
Zabīd
Mukha
GHUBB 'ADAN
AL-MUḤĪṬ
ZANJ
SHILLUK
ETHIOPIA

Introduction

One of the fundamental features of the so-called modern Islamic resurgence is the call to restore the Sharīʿa, the religious law of Islam. During the past two and a half decades, this call has grown ever more forceful, generating religious movements, a vast amount of literature, and affecting world politics. There is no doubt that Islamic law is today a significant cornerstone in the reaffirmation of Islamic identity, not only as a matter of positive law but also, and more importantly, as the foundation of a cultural uniqueness. Indeed, for many of today's Muslims, to live by Islamic law is not merely a legal issue, but one that is distinctly psychological.

The increasing importance of Islamic law in the Muslim world since the late 1970s and early 1980s has generated in western academia a renewed interest in this field, which had attracted only peripheral scholarly interest during the preceding decades. And even though the formative and modern periods were, and continue to be, two of the most studied epochs in the history of Islamic law, they remain comparatively unexplored. Worse still is the state of scholarship on the intervening periods, which continue to be a virtual *terra incognita*.[1]

An index of the state of scholarship on the formative period is the fact that, to date, there has not been a single volume published that offers a history of Islamic law during the first three or four centuries of its life. At least three works have thus far appeared bearing titles that contain the designation "Origins," in one way or another associated in these same titles with "Islamic law" or "Islamic jurisprudence."[2] None, however, can boast

1 For analysis of the selective interests of modern scholarship and their political implications, see Wael Hallaq, "The Quest for Origins or Doctrine? Islamic Legal Studies as Colonialist Discourse," *UCLA Journal of Islamic and Near Eastern Law*, 2, 1 (2002–03): 1–31. See also the introduction in Wael Hallaq, ed., *The Formation of Islamic Law*, in Lawrence I. Conrad, ed., *The Formation of the Classical Islamic World*, vol. XXVII (Aldershot: Ashgate Publishing, 2003).

2 Joseph Schacht, *The Origins of Muhammadan Jurisprudence* (Oxford: Clarendon Press, 1950); Harald Motzki, *Die Anfänge der islamischen Jurisprudenz: Ihr Entwicklung in Mekka bis zur Mitte*

content that truly reflects what is implied in these titles, all three volumes being specialized studies that – however meritorious some of them may be – endeavor to study the formative period through a rather narrow lens.

Although the main contours of legal development during the formative period can be culled from existing primary sources, there is much that remains unexplored. The quality of the sources from the first centuries of Islam is historiographically problematic, but even if this problem did not exist, we would still find that these sources remain quantitatively insufficient. For example, we possess no court records or any other source that can inform us of how the judiciary operated during the formative period, or what went on in courts of law. We have no clear idea of the types of problems that were litigated, how they were resolved, what legal doctrines were applied, how the parties represented themselves, how accessible courts were for women, how the judges used social and/or tribal ties to negotiate and solve disputes, and so forth. Thus, none of these issues can be addressed here in a comprehensive fashion, if at all. In line with the introductory nature of the present series, I attempt in this volume to sketch the outlines of the formative period, presenting a general survey of the main issues that contributed significantly to the formation of Islamic law. And it is in this general coverage that the present work differs from its above-mentioned predecessors, which offer topical or partial treatments rather than a synthesized picture of formative legal development.

Crucial to the present endeavor is the definition of a formative period. What is it that distinguishes a formative era from other historical periods? More specifically in our context, what are the criteria through which we can identify the formative period in Islamic law? Until recently, it has been thought that this period ended around the middle of the third century H (ca. 860 AD), when, following Joseph Schacht's findings, we thought that the all-important legal schools, as personal juristic entities, had come into existence and that, again after Schacht, Islamic law and legal theory had come of age. More recent research, however, has shown that Schacht's findings were largely incorrect and that the point at which Islamic law came to contain all its major components must be dated to around the middle of the fourth/tenth century, an entire century later than had originally been assumed. For our purposes, I define the "formative period" as that historical period in which the legal system arose from rudimentary beginnings

des 2./8. Jahrhunderts (Stuttgart: Franz Steiner, 1991), trans. Marion H. Katz, *The Origins of Islamic Jurisprudence: Meccan Fiqh before the Classical Schools* (Leiden: Brill, 2002); and Y. Dutton, *The Origins of Islamic Law: The Qur'an, the Muwaṭṭa' and Medinan 'Amal* (Richmond: Curzon, 1999).

and then developed to the point at which its constitutive features had acquired an identifiable shape.

I say "identifiable" because all that is needed in the context of "formation" is the coming into existence of those attributes that distinguish and make unmistakably clear the constitutive features of that system. The notion of "formation," therefore, would have to be restricted to the evolution of the general features of the system, since the details – or what we might, philosophically speaking, call "accidental attributes" – endured constant movement and change. Thus, and to continue with our philosophical terminology, formation must be defined in terms of "essential attributes" which make a thing what it is; or, conversely, the absence of any essential attribute would alter the very nature of the thing, rendering it qualitatively different from another in which that attribute does exist. In the case of Islamic law, the essential attributes – those that gave it its shape – were four: (1) the evolution of a complete judiciary, with a full-fledged court system and law of evidence and procedure; (2) the full elaboration of a positive legal doctrine; (3) the full emergence of a science of legal methodology and interpretation which reflected, among other things, a large measure of hermeneutical, intellectual and juristic self-consciousness; and (4) the full emergence of the doctrinal legal schools, a cardinal development that in turn presupposed the emergence of various systemic, juristic, educational and practice-based elements. (Any other essential attribute, such as, e.g., the religious character of the law, must ultimately and derivatively fall under one or more of these four.)

By the middle of the third/ninth century, the third and fourth attributes had not yet developed into anything like their complete form. By the middle of the fourth/tenth century, however, all of them had. And this is the cut-off point. All later developments, including change in legal doctrine or practice, were "accidental attributes" that – despite their importance for legal, social and other historians – did not affect the constitution of the phenomenon we call Islamic law. With or without these changes, Islamic law, for our present purposes, would have remained Islamic law, but without the legal schools or the science of legal theory, Islamic law cannot be deemed, in hindsight, complete.

Far more complex than plotting the end-point of the formative period is the determination of its beginning. It is no exaggeration to say that of all the major questions in Islamic legal history, the issues involved in studying these beginnings have proved the most challenging. The problems associated with "beginnings" have for long stemmed more from unproven assumptions than from any real historical evidence. Hence, the classic

Orientalist creed that the Arabia of the Prophet was a culturally impoverished region, and that when the Arabs built their sophisticated cities, empires and legal systems, they could not have drawn on their own vacuous cultural resources. Instead, it is maintained, they freely absorbed the cultural elements of the societies they eventually conquered, including (but especially) the Byzantino-Roman and Sasanid civilizations. In this account, Syria and Iraq become the loci of legal transmission.

These assumptions have consistently failed to stand the test of scrutiny, as recent research has shown. Except in a few cases, attempts to demonstrate genetic links with these cultures have proved futile, if only because Arabia has provided an equally, if not more, convincing source for much of the law that Islam came to adopt. Chapter 1, therefore, attempts to provide a more balanced account of pre-Islamic Arabia as a region that was an integral part of the general culture of the Near East. Through intensive contacts with the northern Arabs who dominated the Fertile Crescent during the centuries before the rise of Islam, the Peninsular Arabs maintained forms of culture that were closely linked to those prevailing in the north. The Bedouins themselves were to some extent part of this cultural map, but the sedentary and agricultural settlements of the Hejaz were even more dynamic participants in the commercial and religious activities of the Near East. Through trade, missionary activities, and northern tribal connections (and hence the constant shifting of demographic boundaries), their inhabitants knew Syria and Mesopotamia as well as the inhabitants of the latter did the Hejaz. When Muhammad embarked on his mission of establishing a new religion and building a state, he and his collaborators were well acquainted not only with the political and military problems of the Fertile Crescent, but also with its cultures and much of its law. While law as a doctrine and legal system does not appear to have been on the Prophet's mind during most of his career, the elaboration of a particularly Islamic conception of law did begin to emerge a few years before his death. The legal contents of the Quran, viewed in the larger context of already established Jewish law and the ancient Semitic–Mesopotamian legal traditions, provide plentiful evidence of this rising conception.

During the first decades after the Prophet's death, an Islamic polity took shape, guided by both the Quranic legal ethic and the customary laws of the Peninsular Arabs – laws that underwent a gradual transformation under the influence of emerging religious values. Chapter 2 provides a sketch of the evolving legal culture as reflected in the transformations that took place in the office of the proto-*qāḍīs*, the earliest quasi-judges of Islam. The increasing specialization of this office as a judicial function represents an index of the evolution of an Islamic legal ethic, signified by the concomitant rise of Prophetic authority. Chapter 3 continues this theme by exploring the emergence of the so-called legal specialists, a group of men who in their private lives elaborated a legal doctrine that became the juristic foundation of legal practice. With the rise of the class of legal specialists at the end of the first century H and the beginning of the next (ca. 700–40), there again occurred a concomitant development in the construction of Prophetic authority, represented by the emergence of *ḥadīth*, the verbal expression of the Prophetic model. Chapters 2 and 3 thus explain, among other things, how Prophetic authority was to emerge out of the ideas of social consensus and the model behavior (*sunna*; pl. *sunan*) of the tribal and garrison societies that contributed to the first stage of empire-building.

Chapter 4, which takes up the next stage of judicial development, describes the process through which the Muslim court, as part of the empire's structure, acquired its final shape, in which all its essential features came into existence in developed forms. Chapter 5 treats jurisprudential changes that occurred parallel to the developments in the judiciary described in the previous chapter. Here, we return to the changing dynamics of legal authority, which marked a further, but still gradual, shift from what we have called sunnaic practice to a staggering proliferation of Prophetic *ḥadīth*. In this chapter, we also describe the relationship between these competing sources of the law and the positive concepts of consensus, *ijtihād* and *ra'y*. A discussion of the changing relationship between the latter two also illustrates the evolving dynamic of legal reasoning toward stricter and more systematic procedures.

By the end of the second/eighth century, all essential features of the judiciary and positive legal doctrine had clearly acquired a highly developed form, only to undergo further refinements, *mutatis mutandis*, throughout the centuries thereafter. But legal theory, the so-called *uṣūl al-fiqh*, remained in embryo, still struggling to take shape. Indeed, the competing movements of the rationalists and the traditionalists (initially discussed in chapter 3, section 4) would have to settle on a compromise before such a theory – which ultimately came to define Sunnite Islam itself – could emerge. Chapter 6 examines what I have called the Great Rationalist–Traditionalist Synthesis, and how legal theory emerged out of it. The remainder of this chapter offers an outline of this theory as it stood during the second half of the fourth/tenth century.

Chapter 7 offers an account of the rise of doctrinal legal schools (*madhhabs*), the last feature of Islamic law to develop. These schools originally emerged out of the scholarly circles of legal specialists, going through a middle stage dominated by what I have termed "personal schools" (a designation mistakenly used by some scholars to refer to what I in this monograph have characterized as doctrinal schools). In this chapter, I also attempt to explain why only four legal schools survived, and why the others failed to do so. It will become obvious that the success of the four schools, as well as their evolution to the final stage of doctrinal schools, was partly connected with a particular relationship that existed between law and the legal profession, on the one hand, and the political, ruling elite, on the other. Although this chapter completes the account of the formation of Islamic law in all its constitutive elements, this relationship between law and politics remains in want of further analysis, and this I take up in the eighth and final chapter. Here, I discuss the relative independence of positive law from government, and the symbiotic relationship that existed on the basis of mutual interests between the legal profession and those wielding political power. Despite all of the attempts of the latter to manipulate the law, classical Islam, in my view, offered a prime case of the rule of law. To say that the caliphs, rulers and their proxies ultimately fell under the imperatives of the religious law is merely to state the obvious. Yet, it is undeniable that political authority and power did affect the evolution of certain aspects of law, especially the direction in which the legal schools developed and were shaped. The reader, therefore, may find it beneficial to review chapter 7 after having read chapter 8. Finally, the conclusion offers a summary of the main issues raised in this volume, with a view to providing a synthetic account of how these issues contributed to the formation of Islamic law.

One further remark about calendars. This book uses a dual system of dating: one is the Muslim Hijri calendar, the other Gregorian (e.g., 166/782). To omit the former would deprive the reader of the sense of relativity of time in Muslim history; and to omit the latter would probably aggravate the problem even further (and in other ways to boot). I have therefore thought it judicious to use both calendars. But this method has its own problems, hence the following caveat: In this work, it is often stated that this or that event occurred, for example, "at the end of the second/eighth century." In fact, the end of that Hijri century, say 190–200, corresponds to 805 to 815 AD, i.e., the beginning of the ninth century AD. Stylistically, it would be awkward consistently to render the Gregorian equivalent of the approximate Hijri date numerically. So the reader is advised that in such contexts, the Gregorian dates in this book are provided merely as guidelines, whereas the Hijri calendar reflects the more accurate dating. However, the reader will do well to keep in mind that the ends of the first three Hijri centuries roughly correspond to an average of a decade and a half in the beginning of each of the eighth, ninth and tenth centuries AD.

CHAPTER 1

The pre-Islamic Near East, Muḥammad and Quranic law

1. THE GENERAL NEAR EASTERN BACKGROUND

It was in the Hejazi cities of Mecca and Yathrib – later renamed Medina – that a man called Muḥammad came forward to proclaim a new religion with a political order at its center. By the time of his death in 11/632, he had left behind a small state and clear notions of justice, but with underdeveloped ideas of law and an even less developed judiciary. Soon, however, Islam was to conquer lands east and west, ranging from western China to the Iberian peninsula. Along with this territorial expansion, the new religion generated a full-fledged, sophisticated law and legal system in the short span of the three-and-a-half centuries that followed its inception.

By the time of Muḥammad, Mecca and its northern neighbor Yathrib had known a long history of settlement and were largely a part of the cultural continuum that had dominated the Near East since the time of the Sumerians. True, the two cities were not direct participants in the empire cultures that prevailed elsewhere in the Near East, but they were tied to them in more ways than one. Prior to the Arab expansion in the name of Islam, Arabian society had developed the same types of institutions and forms of culture that were established in the imperial societies to the south and north, a development that would later facilitate the Arab conquest of this region. This conquest, as one historian put it, "helped to complete the assimilation of the conquering peoples, begun in Arabia, into general Middle Eastern society."[1] It was these societies and cultures that provided the larger context in which Islam, as a legal phenomenon, was to grow. This context, however, was only to become relevant much later, as we shall see in due course.

[1] Ira M. Lapidus, "The Arab Conquests and the Formation of Islamic Society," in G. H. A. Juynboll, ed., *Studies on the First Century of Islamic Society* (Carbondale and Edwardsville: Southern Illinois University Press, 1982), 50.

In the century or so before the rise of Islam, there existed three centers of empire: the Byzantine in the north-west, the Sasanid in the north-east and the Yemenite in the south. This latter was subsidiary to the former two by virtue of being, at different times, either a vassal state of the Ethiopian kingdom – which in turn was a constant ally of the Eastern Roman Empire – or under the direct occupation of the Sasanids. But early on the Yemen had experienced a long history of independent kingdoms that attained a high level of civilization. It possessed a strategic commercial position, lying on the ancient trade route from the Indonesian Archipelago and India to Syria. Spices, incense, leather, silk, ivory, gold, silver, glue and precious stones were among the many items that made their way through the Yemen to Pharaonic Egypt and later to the Greek, Roman and Byzantine Empires. The Maʿīnite, Sabaʾite and Ḥimyarite kingdoms that flourished in the Yemen developed a sedentary style of life and governance, and an elaborate urban existence complete with markets, palaces and imposing houses, supported by sophisticated agrarian and commercial networks.

In 525 AD, eight decades before the rise of Islam, the Abyssinians occupied the Yemen and brought an end to the Ḥimyarite kingdom, ruled at the time by the Jewish monarch Dhū Nuwās. On the surface, and probably for propaganda reasons, the occupation was made to appear as a retaliatory measure against the oppressive religious policies of this king, who persecuted the Christians of the Yemen, especially those at Najrān. However, underlying this conquest were the commercial interests of both the Ethiopians and the Byzantines. Thus, although the Yemenite ruling elite soon acquired independence, it remained nominally a vassal province of the Abyssinian kingdom. In 570 AD, close to the time of Muḥammad's birth, the Christian Abraha launched a military campaign with a view towards subduing the Hejaz, a campaign that seems to have been dictated by a broader Byzantine policy to secure the trade routes from India to the Syrian territories in the north. The decimation of the Ḥimyarites was only the first step in the process. The subjugation of the Arabian trading tribes in the Hejaz, especially at Mecca, was supposed to be the second.

The latter scheme, however, reportedly fell apart when disease wrought havoc with Abraha's military campaign, and sent it back to the Yemen in ruins. This setback signaled the end of Abraha's rule, and with it the hegemony of the Abyssinian kingdom over the Yemen. In 575 AD, the Sasanids conquered the country and restored to the throne the descendants of Dhū Yazan. Their rule, however, did not last for long: by the end of the century or the very beginning of the seventh, the Yemen was ruled exclusively by Sasanid governors who initiated a policy of rebuilding the country and restoring the economic networks that linked its cities.

The Sasanid occupation of the Yemen was an extension of their imperial policies, begun three centuries earlier in the lands that bordered on theirs and on the Byzantine vassal state of the Ghassānids. In southern and western Iraq, they set up an autonomous state headed by the Lakhmid kings to rule Ḥīra, a major city on the west side of the Euphrates. Opposite this, and competing bitterly with the Sasanids, stood the Roman and, later, Byzantine Empires which relied on the Ghassānids to do their bidding against their arch-enemy and to protect their interests in this region. The Ghassānids set up their state at Busra Askisham in the Ḥūrān region, and Palmyra functioned, for all practical purposes, as their second capital.

It was not a coincidence that both the Ghassānids and the Lakhmids were chosen for their respective roles as vassal kingdoms. As southern tribal confederations, they had a long experience with citied life, high civilization and, like all urban populations, obedience to central authority. Both originally came from the eastern parts of the Yemen which, since the second or third century BC, if not earlier, had enjoyed a high level of culture, complex forms of political life and knowledge of agriculture, trade and commerce. Ḥīra, the Lakhmid capital, was a center of the fine arts, science (particularly medicine), architecture and literature. It had been the recipient of massive Arab migration since the first century AD, when the Azd, a constituent group of the Tanūkh confederation, settled its surrounding area. Ḥīra and its hinterland boasted a rich agriculturalist and commercial economy, exclusively controlled by the Lakhmid tribal confederation. It manufactured leather and steel armor, and produced all sorts of cotton, wool and linen textiles. The Lakhmids had adopted Christianity at an early date, perhaps as early as the fourth century AD, and although the majority of the inhabitants of Ḥīra and of the surrounding areas appear to have adopted the Nestorian version (especially ʿAbd Qays, Tamīm and Bakr b. Wāʾil), there were many who were Jacobites, as well as a considerable number of Magians, Zoroastrians, Jews and pagans.[2]

Like the Lakhmids, the Ghassānids were also southern tribes who migrated to the Syrian north during the early part of the sixth century AD, having succeeded other tribal confederations that had settled in the area after the collapse of the Nabatean kingdom. Granted the title of king by the

[2] D. T. Potts, *The Arabian Gulf in Antiquity*, 2 vols. (Oxford: Clarendon Press, 1990), I, 242. See also M. J. Kister, "Al-Ḥīra: Some Notes on its Relations with Arabia," *Arabica*, 15 (1968): 143–69.

Byzantine emperor Justinian, the Ghassānid chief Arethas (al-Ḥārith b. Jabala; r. 529–69 AD) and his successors continued to battle their imperial counterparts, the Lakhmids, until shortly before the Islamic conquests. And like their enemies in Ḥīra, they constructed a sophisticated agriculturalist economy and an active trade network, and engaged in the manufacture of a variety of products. Culturally and religiously, they were (as might be expected) influenced by the Roman–Byzantine heritage, but the discovery of Sasanid architectural forms in local archaeological excavations hints at influence on the part of the empire to the east.

Between the Byzantine and Sasanid empires, in the north, west and center of the Peninsula, lay a vast area inhabited by Arabian Bedouin whose lifestyle greatly depended on what Hodgson called "camel-nomadism."[3] This area was arid, affording little rain and, consequently, sparse vegetation. The steppes were dotted with oases where the agriculturalists could produce wheat, grapes, dates and other foodstuffs sufficient to sustain settlement and sedentary existence and to provide services for the passing caravans. The domestication and exploitation of the camel, which the Bedouin mastered like no one else, became a well-established feature of Arabian life no later than the first century AD. But camel-nomadism could not have existed, and certainly could not have flourished, without an agrarian economy which was, in a sense, its infrastructural support. The Bedouin tribes, as part of their normal activities, engaged in an extensive system of trade and commerce, a system that prevailed in the lands between the lower eastern Mediterranean and the Arabian Sea and between this latter and north-eastern Arabia. They provided passing caravans with camels, afforded them protective escorts, and themselves engaged in trade on a significant scale. And when none of these services were in demand, they simply raided the caravans, thereby making their services as protectors all the more valuable. The agriculturalists in turn depended to some extent on the resources afforded by camel-nomadism and by the commercial and trading activities based on the camel industry. The Bedouin and the agriculturalists, therefore, complemented each other, and the two forms of material existence constituted a sort of an economic ecology in the greater part of the Arabian Peninsula.[4]

[3] Marshall Hodgson, *The Venture of Islam: Conscience and History in a World Civilization*, 3 vols. (Chicago: University of Chicago Press, 1974), I, 147.

[4] Fred Donner, "The Role of Nomads in the Near East in Late Antiquity (400–800 C.E.)," in F. M. Clover and R. S. Humphreys, eds., *Tradition and Innovation in Late Antiquity* (Madison: University of Wisconsin Press, 1989), 73–88.

To be sure, the Bedouin played an important role in the life of the three polities that surrounded them. In the south, the large tribe of Kinda functioned as a vassal to the Ḥimyarites and later to the Sasanids. Its Bedouin members controlled the trade routes from the Yemen through Ḥaḍramawt and its ports, just as they controlled the routes that connected the Yemen and Ḥaḍramawt with the Najd territory.[5] The Lakhmids, fighting on behalf of their Sasanid overlords, had lost Bahrain to the Kinda between 450 and 530 AD. By the beginning of the seventh century AD, the Yemen and Ḥaḍramawt were predominantly Arabic speaking. In the north-east, the Arab migrations had already begun to displace Aramaic-speaking populations as early as the first century AD. East Arabian and North-East Arabian dialects gradually became dominant. Likewise, the entire area that lay between northern Arabia and Palmyra, including Edessa, was considerably, if not mostly, Arabic speaking on the eve of Islam's emergence. The spread of Arabic and the displacement of Aramaic was in good part due to the energetic work of the Bedouin Arabs as traders, caravanists and soldiers. In other words, the economic life of the two northern empires, the Byzantine and the Sasanid, was dependent on the Bedouin, who alone were able to cross the otherwise impenetrable terrains of the mostly arid Peninsula.[6]

The Bedouin Arabs were certainly in close contact with each other throughout the territory that they inhabited and roamed, from Syria to Iraq, and from Najd to the Hejaz, Ḥaḍramawt and the Yemen. Concomitant with the trade routes there also existed large fairs and markets which provided excellent opportunities for the recital of poetry and for orations and tales, in addition to the exchange of goods. Conducting their own markets in Ḥīra and its environs, the Lakhmids gave economic privileges to the Tamīm, whose noblemen were granted the right to supervise and control the markets. As part of this control, the tribes collected taxes, usually on the exchange and sale of goods. Tamīm's market, al-Mushaqqar, was held in what is now Hufūf, but their economic alliances extended far beyond the limits of Ḥīra, reaching as far as northern Najd and Mecca. These wide-ranging connections gave them unparalleled influence over Peninsular caravan traffic.[7]

5 M. B. Piotrovsky, "Late Ancient and Early Medieval Yemen: Settlement, Traditions and Innovations," in G. R. D. King and Avril Cameron, eds., *The Byzantine and Early Islamic Near East*, vol. II (Princeton: The Darwin Press, 1994), 213–20, at 217.

6 Potts, *Arabian Gulf*, I, 227; R. Dussaud, *La Pénétration des arabes en Syrie avant l'Islam* (Paris: Paul Geuthner, 1955).

7 Potts, *Arabian Gulf*, I, 251.

In addition to the market in Dūmat al-Jandal in the northern Nufūd oasis, which may have been the oldest market of all,[8] there was another international market on the coast of Oman frequented by merchants from India and China, sailing through the Arabian Sea (Indian and Chinese merchant activity is also documented in excavations in Dibba, an island in the Persian Gulf, and in Chinese sources as well).[9] In eastern Ḥaḍramawt, Kinda controlled one of the largest markets of Arabia, known as the Tomb of the Prophet Hūd. They also controlled al-Rabiyya and al-Shiḥr, two famous markets, and imposed their own taxes there.[10] In Yathrib alone four markets were in operation before Islam appeared, two of which were owned and controlled by the Jews of the city (for other markets, see map 1).[11]

The markets of Arabia had a religious function as well. It appears that the location of the market was determined by the presence of a deity or an idol in the market itself or its vicinity. In fact, it may well have been that these markets began as religious festivals, acquiring a commercial dimension with the passage of time. The markets of Dūmat al-Jandal and ʿUkāẓ are cases in point.[12]

The nexus of this network of trade, markets and worship was Mecca, surely the most significant commercial center of western and central Arabia. Strategically located at the juncture of two intersecting trade routes, it was in contact with the Syrian and Iraqian north, with the Yemenite south, central and eastern Najd, and, through the Red Sea coastal area, with Abyssinia and eastern Africa. The city's involvement in trade had certainly started before the first century AD, when the Romans, through their vassals the Nabateans, were most active on the south–north trade

[8] ʿAbd al-Raḥmān al-Sudairī, *The Desert Frontier of Arabia: al-Jawf through the Ages* (London: Stacey International, 1995), 40–41.

[9] Potts, *Arabian Gulf*, II, 332, 339–40. On the basis of archaeological and other evidence, Potts casts doubt on earlier findings that there was no direct sailing between China and the Arabian Gulf. Recent excavations have also revealed contacts between the Gulf of Oman and Bactria and Margiana in Central Baluchistan. See also E. C. L. During Caspers, "Further Evidence for 'Central Asian' Materials from the Arabian Gulf," *Journal of the Economic and Social History of the Orient*, 37 (1994): 33–53. For trading with the Chinese during the fifth century, from both Aden and the mouth of the Euphrates, see J. Levenson, *European Expansion and the Counter-Example of Asia, 1300–1600* (Englewood Cliffs, N.J.: Prentice Hall, 1967), 11, on the authority of Joseph Needham, *Science and Civilization in China*, vol. I (Cambridge: Cambridge University Press, 1954), 179–80.

[10] Piotrovsky, "Late Ancient Yemen," 217.

[11] M. Lecker, "On the Markets of Medina (Yathrib) in Pre-Islamic and Early Islamic Times," in M. Lecker, *Jews and Arabs in Pre- and Early Islamic Arabia* (Aldershot: Variorum, 1998), article IX, 63 ff.

[12] Jawād ʿAlī, *al-Mufaṣṣal fī Tārīkh al-ʿArab Qabl al-Islām*, 10 vols. (Beirut: Dār al-ʿIlm lil-Malāyīn, 1970–76), VII, 371–73, 382–84; al-Sudairī, *Desert Frontier*, 41.

route. Archaeological excavations show that imperial forces had vested interests in the Hejaz, which they attempted to penetrate militarily more than once, but without success. Julius Galus' failed campaign was only the most notorious. The Hejaz nonetheless appears to have been a cultural satellite of the Nabatean Arabs, as evidenced by the fact that the people of the region adopted Nabatean Arabic for writing and worshiped major Nabatean deities, such as Hubal, Manāt and al-Lāt, all of whom came to play a significant role in the religious life of Mecca and Yathrib, a role that Muḥammad continued to battle until the end of his days. But the Hejaz was also a commercial satellite of the Nabateans and focus of their trade, and various pecuniary contracts related, among other things, to the sale of wheat, raisins and barley – contracts whose forms were to survive into Islam.[13]

The Quraysh, the tribal confederation at Mecca, under the leadership of a certain enterprising Quṣayy, managed to construct an active network of regional trade that connected the Peninsula with a larger international system. The Quraysh struck treaties with several other tribal confederations, including the Hudhayl and Thaqīf in the Yamāma (especially the Thaqīf of the neighboring town of Ṭā'if), the ʿAbd Qays in eastern Najd, the Lakhmids of Ḥīra, the Ghassānids of Syria and the Ḥimyarites and their successors in the Yemen. The strategic role of Mecca permitted the Quraysh to levy taxes on passing caravans, especially those that did not benefit from previously concluded treaties of cooperation. The commodities that wended their way through Mecca included, among other things, wheat, barley, oils, wine, gold, silver, ivory, precious stones, sandalwood, incense, spices, silk and cotton textiles and leather. Basic local production of light weaponry (mainly swords) and pottery must have contributed modestly to the otherwise intense commercial activity.

Mecca gained a prominent position in the Peninsula for engaging in other, non-commercial activity, although the latter could not always be separated from the business of trading. In addition to literary contests and prestigious poetic fairs, Mecca had for long boasted the Kaʿba as a place of worship, and by the sixth century AD it seems to have become the most important destination for pilgrimage in the Peninsula, surpassing in prestige all the other *kaʿbas* found throughout the territory. To secure

[13] See, e.g., Muwaffaq al-Dīn Ibn Qudāma, *Mughnī*, 14 vols. (Beirut: Dār al-Kutub al-ʿIlmiyya, 1973), IV, 312. See also, more generally, C. Edens and Garth Bawden, "History of Taymā' and Hejazi Trade during the First Millennium BC," *Journal of the Economic and Social History of the Orient*, 32 (1989): 48–97.

traffic to Mecca from all quarters of the Peninsula, the Quraysh established a calendar that was widely accepted by the other tribes. Four months of the year were designated as *ḥarām*, which meant that during one-third of every year no violence was permitted. And this seems to have been normative, with violations being rare indeed. Maintaining order in this fashion enabled the Quraysh to gain economic power and a social and religious status seldom equaled in Arabia.

A commercial, religious and literary center, Mecca was connected not only with every major tribe and locale in the Peninsula, but also with the Near East at large. Its commercial relations with the Lakhmids, Tamīm and ʿAbd Qays placed it in indirect contact with the culture of Sasan, and even of the Orient, India and Central Asia; its relations with the Ghassānids and their predecessors brought to Mecca elements of Roman and Byzantine cultures; its close contact with Abyssinia exposed it to East Africa; and the Yemen mediated its familiarity with aspects of Indian culture. As a result of this hybridity, Meccan society was unusual in Arabia, featuring in its ranks non-tribal members and foreigners who would otherwise have had no place in a strictly tribal social structure. Foreign merchants, African slaves, singing female slaves, wayfarers, the poor and downtrodden found their way to the city. A Byzantine merchant bearing the common name Anastasius (Arabicized as Nisṭās) is said to have journeyed to Mecca and taken up permanent residence there. He became the client (*mawlā*) of Ṣafwān b. Umayya, a status of artificial kinship created to accommodate an outsider within a given group. Another Byzantine citizen by the name of John was adopted as a client by Ṣuhayb al-Rūmī who, as his names indicates, was himself a Byzantine; he in turn was a *mawlā* of ʿAbd Allāh b. Jadʿān b. Kaʿb.[14] Mecca also hosted Egyptian Copts, Persians and Abyssinians. It was familiar with foreign cuisines, and ʿAbd Allāh b. Jadʿān himself – who appears to have been a prominent merchant – is credited with introducing culinary curiosities from the lands of Sasan. Furthermore, the Meccans themselves did not restrict their residence to the city: as merchants, they traveled far and wide and owned farms and houses in places as remote as Homs in Syria and the cities of the Yemen.

All this goes to show that the Peninsular Arabs were not mere nomads subsisting on a primitive desert economy. While there were tribes, such as certain clans of the Kinda, who did lead a nomadic lifestyle, the majority of

[14] See Sayyid Sālim, *Tārīkh al-ʿArab fī ʿAṣr al-Jāhiliyya* (Alexandria: Muʾassasat Shabāb al-Jāmiʿa, 1990), 360, on the authorities of Iṣbahānī and Ibn Hishām.

Bedouins, as we have seen, engaged in pastoral, agricultural and trading activities.[15] Evidence shows that most of Arabia was not entirely nomadic, and that there was no necessary relationship between tribal nomadism and a "primitive" lifestyle. Although Arabian society was almost exclusively tribal, it was at the same time largely sedentary. Eastern Arabia had several major oases: of these al-Aḥsāʾ was the largest; with its cultivated palm trees and gardens, it was sufficiently fertile to support settled life from Hellenistic times down to the early Islamic period. Similarly, in the areas of Hufūf, al-Qaṭīf and al-Mubarraz, and very likely in al-Qasīm and the valleys of Ṣudayr and al-ʿAriḍ, a sedentary lifestyle appears to have continued uninterrupted since ancient times.[16] There is also evidence to show that Bahrain and the Omani coast at Suḥār supported sedentary populations for centuries before Islam.[17] The mills of Oman make an appearance in written communications between the Prophet and Jaifar, the king of Julanda.[18] Archaeological evidence from al-Kharj and al-Aflāj in the south of Najd suggests a sophisticated irrigation system that was fully operational by the beginning of the seventh century AD. Archaeologists have shown that al-Maʿbiyyāt, Madāʾin Ṣāliḥ and al-Khurayba in the Hejaz had been centers of settlement since the second century AD. Furthermore, it is now established that inhabitants of the town of al-Rabadha, on the commercial and, later, pilgrimage route of Darb Zubayda, engaged in versatile economic activity, including camel husbandry, agriculture, and the manufacture of metal, glass and soapstone objects.[19] G. King suggests that the presence in this locale of glass-smelting and alkaline blue glaze wasters reflects the production there of this common ware, along with copper and bronze items and certain forms of ceramics.[20] From this evidence, King concludes:

If a small town like al-Rabadha displays the continuous settlement that is indicated by the Saudi excavations, then there is a good reason to consider whether such village settlement was not more widespread in pre-Islamic and early Islamic times in western Arabia. The evidence of al-Rabadha demonstrates that in this region, past land use was not solely nomadic, and the level of village life demonstrated by

[15] Donner, "Role of Nomads in the Near East."

[16] G. R. D. King, "Settlement in Western and Central Arabia and the Gulf in the Sixth–Eighth Centuries AD," in G. R. D. King and A. Cameron, eds., *The Byzantine and Early Islamic Near East*, vol. II (Princeton: The Darwin Press, 1994), 181–212, at 184.

[17] Ibid., 210–11.

[18] Potts, *Arabian Gulf*, II, 342.

[19] On Darb Zubayda, see the remarkable study of Saad al-Rashid, *Darb Zubayda: The Pilgrim Road from Kufa to Mecca* (Riyadh: Riyadh University Libraries, 1980).

[20] King, "Settlement," 197–98.

the excavation gives new impression of the nature of society, the land and small-scale village manufacture in pre-Islamic and early Islamic times in this particular district.[21]

In many parts of Arabia, towns and villages sprang up around wells and oases. The fertile, rain-watered highlands from central Hejaz to the Yemen, for instance, were inhabited by sedentary populations. It is noteworthy that the Bedouin also formed part of these settlements, merging as it were with populations inside or around towns. Bedouin nobility took up permanent residence in some of these towns which over time fell under their domination. Indeed, even in large cities they often constituted an important part of the population. An example in point is Qaryat al-Faww, located on the trade route to the Yemen. Excavations have revealed that the city, with its market complex and dwelling quarters, was dominated by the tribes of Kinda, Qaḥṭān and Madhhij.[22] Just as the Ghassānid tribes merged with the local populations of Palmyra and Busra, and the Lakhmids with those of Ḥīra, so did many of their Najdite, Hejazite and Yemenite brothers come to settle in the towns and cities of the Peninsula and, with the passage of time, blend into their populations.

The picture that emerges is one of a dual culture in which sedentary populations coexisted and interacted with nomads and pastoralists, and where no clear lines could be drawn between the two. The Bedouin Arabs might settle on the fringes of a town, only to move away later, but they might just as easily penetrate the town and establish permanent roots in it. They might maintain their social structure of families and clans, or become fragmented and, like other urban families, continue to bear names after their fathers and grandfathers, or after a profession that a family member practiced. Therefore, when the sources speak of a clan in an urban setting, we cannot necessarily assume it to be a nomadic group, though it might have at one point originated as such.

It also emerges that Peninsular society led a dynamic existence, with direct and indirect ties to an international market of material goods and cultural and institutional products. Although the Peninsula's geographical conditions did not allow the full absorption of southern and northern empire institutions, it nonetheless received a level of culture and sorts of material products that played a part in Arabian sedentary life. The more archaeological excavations are undertaken, the more this picture is

[21] Ibid., 200.

[22] Piotrovsky, "Late Ancient Yemen," 216–17.

confirmed. The image of Arabia as an impoverished desert, empty save for primitive tribesmen roaming around and raiding each other, should be abandoned.[23]

Arabian society was in possession of two sets of laws, one serving sedentary, agriculturalist and commercial needs, the other supporting nomadic tribal conditions, and heavily dependent on customary laws. This dichotomy clearly was not collateral with social structure, but rather with the type of activity engaged in by a particular group. In criminal matters, for instance, both the Bedouin nomads and the sedentary populations followed, more or less, the same set of customary Bedouin laws. The murder of a man, Bedouin or not, required either commensurate revenge or payment of blood-money, an ancient Near Eastern law that was as much present in the pre-Islamic Peninsula (as documented in the Quran) as in ancient Mesopotamia.[24] In commercial dealings, on the other hand, even the nomads entered into pecuniary and mercantile transactions and contracts that had commonly been practiced in the Near East for centuries, probably as long ago as Babylonian and Assyrian times. In the ancient Thamūdite and Liḥyānite inscriptions (dating several centuries before Islam in north-west Arabia), many texts deal with property rights, both movable and immovable (wells, land), as well as with penal cases and pecuniary transactions.[25] As early as the first century BC, the Yemen had already produced a sophisticated system of law. The Qaṭabānian kingdom was in possession of a trade code, including a Law Merchant, which, among other things, applied to foreign merchants in their dwelling places outside the city gates. Piotrovsky reports that such places accommodated merchants and pilgrims to holy places and have been in existence near ancient, medieval and even modern towns.[26]

The close contacts that the Arabs of the Peninsula maintained between and among themselves, coupled with their extensive relations with their neighbors to the south, north-west and north-east, exposed them to the general legal culture of the Near East. In other words, all the knowledge available to us, whether literary, archaeological or epigraphic, indicates that the Arabs of the Peninsula, Iraq and Syria lived in a well-knit system of kin and material relationships. By all indications, Muḥammad the Prophet and the influential men who surrounded him and who continued their

[23] For a detailed account of economic and material life in pre-Islamic Arabia, see ʿAlī, *Mufaṣṣal*, VII.
[24] Russ VerSteeg, *Early Mesopotamian Law* (Durham, N.C.: Carolina Academic Press, 2000), 107 ff.
[25] ʿAlī, *Mufaṣṣal*, V, 475.
[26] Piotrovsky, "Late Ancient Yemen," 214. See also ʿAlī, *Mufaṣṣal*, V, 476.

bid to establish a Muslim state, were thoroughly familiar with the cultures of Ḥīra and, especially, Syrian Busra, which they visited regularly in their role as prominent merchants. Muḥammad's own sophisticated knowledge of legal practices comes across clearly in the Quran and the so-called Constitution of Medina, two documents whose authenticity cannot be doubted.

2. THE EMERGENCE OF A QURANIC LEGAL IDENTITY

As a product of a mercantile tribal society, Muḥammad was familiar with all the religions and cultures of the Peninsula and of its neighbors, particularly Judaism and Christianity, religions that had many adherents among the major Arab tribes. Medina, to which he was forced to migrate with some followers, had been inhabited by several Jewish tribes. But Muḥammad also knew Yemenite Judaism and was familiar with certain Arab clans that had adopted this religion in western Arabia. Christianity and Christian missionaries, especially of the Nestorian version, likewise had been well established throughout Arabia since the fifth century AD. The Yemen had a large Christian population, but so did eastern Arabia and, as we have seen, southern Iraq and Syria.

Before migrating to Medina, Muḥammad's mission was religious and ethical, calling for humility, generosity and belief in a God who has neither a partner nor a father nor a son, and who is dissociated from the worldly deities worshiped by the Arabian tribes. In Mecca, and probably immediately after arrival in Medina, his message was articulated in terms of continuity with Judaism and Christianity: Islam represented little more than a pure form of these two religions, the Original Faith that, in its Judaic and Christian forms, had been corrupted by later followers of the two religions. Already in Mecca, Muḥammad conceived of himself as a Ḥanīf, probably under the influence of a certain Zayd b. ʿAmr. Fundamentally monotheistic, Ḥanīfiyya appears to have been a specifically Meccan religious development that was formed around the figure of Abraham and the worship of the Kaʿba, which he was believed to have constructed.[27]

Prior to his arrival in Medina, Muḥammad did not, in all probability, have in mind the establishment of a new polity, much less a new law or

[27] Uri Rubin, "*Ḥanīfiyya* and Kaʿba: An Inquiry into the Arabian Pre-Islamic Background of *Dīn Ibrāhīm*," *Jerusalem Studies in Arabic and Islam*, 13 (1990): 85–112.

legal system. Up to that point, and for a short time thereafter, he was largely concerned with faith, morality and the purity of mundane existence. But a new reality forced itself upon him. In Medina, he came face to face with Jews who, like the Meccan tribes, opposed him or at least were dubious about his message. In their view, this message presented a novel form of monotheism, independent and distinct from Judaism and Christianity. Deeply disappointed by their position, Muḥammad began to veer away from certain rituals that the new religion had thus far shared with Judaism: Jerusalem was replaced by the Kaʿba as the sacred shrine of nascent Islam, and emerged as the true site of Abraham the Ḥanīf, who worshiped God directly, and who needed no intercession or intermediate deities. More fundamentally, the Jews presented Muḥammad with an epistemic threat, for their doubts about his message were backed by the fact that they were considered the custodians and interpreters of monotheism and monotheistic scripture. Part of the solution to this threat came at an early stage, when Muḥammad, exploiting a conflict that erupted between the Jewish tribe of Banū Qunayqāʿ and some Medinan Arabs, acted against the former. Having besieged the tribe, he forced them to leave the town with their property, thereby reducing the threat and strengthening his position in Medina.

At the end of the fifth year of the Hijra (early 626 AD), Quranic revelation began to reflect a new development in Muḥammad's career, whereby, apparently for the first time, he started thinking of the new Islamic community, the Umma, as capable of possessing a Law that parallels, but is distinct from, other monotheistic laws. At about this time, Sūra 5 of the Quran was revealed, ushering in a list of commands, admonitions and explicit prohibitions concerning a great variety of issues, from eating swine meat to theft. Throughout, we find references to the Jews and Christians and their respective scriptures. In 5:43 God asks, with seeming astonishment, why the Jews resort to Muḥammad as an arbiter "when they have the Torah which contains the judgment of God." "We have revealed the Torah in which there is guidance and light, [and by which] the prophets who surrendered [to God] judged the Jews, and the Rabbis and Priests judged by such of Allah's Scriptures as they were bidden to observe" (5:43). In the next two verses, the Quran turns to the Christians, saying in effect that God sent Christ to confirm the Prophethood of Moses and the Gospel to reassert the "guidance and advice" revealed in the Torah. "So let the People of the Gospel judge by that which God had revealed therein, for he who judges not by that which God revealed is a sinner" (5:47).

If the Jews and Christians were favored with legally binding revelations, so too are the Muslims, the Quran declares. Sūra 5:48, which marks a turning-point, states:

We have revealed unto you the Book [i.e., the Quran] with the Truth, confirming whatever Scripture was before it . . . so judge between them by what God had revealed, and do not follow their desires away from the Truth . . . *for We have made for each of you* [i.e., Muslims, Christians and Jews] *a law and a normative way to follow*. If God had willed, He would have made all of you one community. (italics mine)

But God obviously chose not to do so, creating instead three communities with three separate and different sets of law, so that each community could follow *its own* law. The Quran repeatedly stresses that the believers must judge by what was revealed to them,[28] for "who is better than God in judgment" (5:49–50). It is worth noting here that the "normative way" in verse 5:48 is represented by the term "*minhāj*," a cognate of the Hebraic word "*minhāg*" (the Law). The creation of an Islamic legal parallel here speaks for itself.

These verses mark the beginning of substantive legislation in the Quran, i.e., legislation above and beyond matters of ritual, such as prayer and pilgrimage. In other words, the bulk of the substantive legislation seems to have been revealed after the year 5/626, when a distinct body of law exclusive to the Umma, the Muslim community, was first conceived. The traditional count of all the legal verses comes to about five hundred – a number that at first glance seems exiguous, considering the overall size of the Quran. However, as Goitein has perceptively remarked, these verses represent a larger weight than the number may indicate. It is common knowledge that the Quran repeats itself both literally and thematically, but this tendency of repetition is absent in the legal subject matter. The proportion of the legal verses, therefore, is larger than that suggested by an absolute number. And if we consider the fact that the average length of the legal verses is twice or even thrice that of the non-legal verses, it is not difficult to argue, following Goitein, that the Quran contains no less legal material than does the Torah, which is commonly known as "the Law."[29]

This course of Quranic legal development was to be expected. Historically, there can be no doubt that Judaism and Christianity constituted the religious and historical background of Islam. Arab

[28] Quran 2:213; 3:23; 4:58, 105; 5:44–45, 47; 7:87; 10:109; 24:48. Quran 5:44, for instance, states: "He who does not judge by what God has revealed is a disbeliever."
[29] S. D. Goitein, "The Birth-Hour of Muslim Law," *Muslim World*, 50, 1 (1960): 23–29, at 24.

monotheism, including the Ḥanīfiyya, arose on the basis of, and in conjunction with, these two religions. Theologically, Quranic Islam arrived, first, as a corrective and, second, as the final form of Judaism and Christianity, the form they should have taken, but did not. This much is undeniable. These connections account for the Quran's strong tendency to emulate and counter-balance the two other monotheistic religions, especially Judaism. But to argue for historical and theological influences without acknowledging the "*minhāg*ic" influences – which had been incubating among Meccan and Medinan Arabs for generations – would be a serious misreading of history.

It should come as no surprise that Quranic revelation from the last few years of Muḥammad's life shows a conscious tendency toward legislation, a means to assert the independence and uniqueness of the new religion. The legal subject matter grew increasingly larger, while, at the same time, the Umma was slowly differentiating itself from other monotheistic and pagan communities. The Bedouins' gaming, the Arabian markets' practices of risk-cum-gambling ventures, the Christians' and Bedouins' indulgence in wine-drinking, and a multitude of other practices shunned by the new puritan and deeply moral religion, were subjected to limitations or outright prohibition. Legislation was also intended to strengthen the Umma in other ways. The ancient tax of the *zakāt*[30] was rehabilitated in order to provide for the weak and dispossessed, and to assist in the common cause of the new religion. Similarly, a ban on feuding was imposed, and criminal penalties were made commensurate with the injury caused. The fixing of penalties and the establishment of a centrally distributed alms-tax permitted the creation of a true community, an Umma, whose members regarded themselves as individuals independent of tribal affiliation. In other words, these legislations were designed to transpose the individual from the tribal to the Islamic domain, where he or she would have a status in a community of equal members.[31]

The limitations placed on tribal affiliation are also evidenced in the Quranic legislation on inheritance, according to which the family, including the deceased's male agnates, are the sole heirs. And while the male retained much of the powerful status that he had enjoyed in pre-Islamic

30 The *zakāt* is attested as early as during fourth-century Yemen and South Arabia, where the ancient deities exacted a tithe on commerce, to be expended on public works. See A. F. L. Beeston, "The Religions of Pre-Islamic Yemen," in *L'Arabie du sud*, vol. I (Paris: Editions G.-P. Maisonneuve et Larose, 1984), 259–69, at 264.

31 Hodgson, *Venture*, I, 181. Hodgson's comments on marriage and inheritance in the Quranic "reform" should be read with caution.

Arabia, Islam granted wives and daughters substantial rights. Meccan practice, nearly identical to Mesopotamian law prevalent since Assyrian times,[32] required the bride's family (normally her father) to give her the dowry that the husband had paid to them. This practice of enhancing the financial security of women was adopted by the Quran, and further augmented by allotting a daughter a share of inheritance equal to one-half of the share of her brother. This allotment appears to have been unprecedented in Arabia. Rights of dowry and inheritance were wedded to another principle that was to become central in later Islamic law, namely, the financial independence of wives: all property acquired by the woman during marriage, or property that she brought into the marriage (including her dowry), remained exclusively hers, and the husband could not claim as much as a hundredth part of it.[33]

Another novel rule was the introduction of the principle of *ʿidda*, a waiting period imposed on divorced women. Whereas before Islam divorce was complete and final upon its declaration by the husband, the Quran now prescribed the postponement of the irrevocable dissolution of the marriage until three menstrual cycles had been completed or, if the woman were pregnant, until the birth of the child. During this period, which allowed for reconciliation between the spouses, the husband was obliged to provide both domicile and financial support for the wife. Furthermore, a divorced woman with a child was to suckle it for a period of two years, and the father was required to provide for mother and child during this same period. If she chose to do so, she could remarry her husband only after she had been married to (and divorced by) another,[34] the intention being, then and now, to force men to think hard before they rushed into divorcing their wives.

Marriage was regulated by restricting spousal eligibility to a limited circle of relations. A man might marry any woman provided that she was not his mother, daughter, sister, aunt, niece, foster-mother, foster-sister, mother-in-law, step-daughter or daughter-in-law. Nor was he permitted to be married to two sisters at the same time. Marriage to women of the Scriptures was permitted, irrespective of whether or not they converted to Islam. A marriage that had not been consummated, furthermore, might be

[32] See M. Stol, "Women in Mesopotamia," *Journal of the Economic and Social History of the Orient*, 38, 2 (1995): 123–44, at 126. For other striking parallels between Peninsular and Mesopotamian laws, see VerSteeg, *Early Mesopotamian Law, passim.*

[33] Quran, 4:19 ff.

[34] Ibid., 2:237; 65:1–6; 2:233; 2:230.

legally dissolved without a waiting period. But if the marriage was consummated, the husband owed the wife half of the dowry.[35]

The Quran provided more or less detailed coverage in other areas of family law, as well as in ritual, commercial and pecuniary areas. Yet, although these rules surely did not constitute a system, their fairly wide coverage, and their appearance within a short span of time, pointed clearly toward the elaboration of a basic legal structure. The articulation of a Quranic law exclusive to the Umma escaped neither the Muslims themselves nor their neighbors, who were fully aware of the legal thrust of Muḥammad's mission. Writing in the 660s AD, the near contemporary Armenian Bishop Sebeos duly recognized the fact that Muḥammad upheld a law particular to the new religion, and distinct from other laws.[36]

This new conception of Quranic law does not mean that there occurred a clean break with the legal traditions and customary laws of Arabia. Despite his critical attitude toward the local social and moral environment, Muḥammad was very much part of this environment which was deeply rooted in the traditions of Arabia. Furthermore, as a prominent arbitrating judge (*ḥakam*), he could not have abandoned entirely, or even largely, the legal principles and rules by which he performed this prestigious (but now prohibited) function. Yet, while maintaining continuity with past traditions and laws, Quranic Islam exhibited a tendency to articulate a distinct law for the Umma, a tendency that marked the beginning of a new process whereby all events befalling the nascent Muslim community henceforth were to be adjudicated according to God's law, whose agent was none other than the Prophet. This is clearly attested in both the Quran and the Constitution of Medina.[37]

While new problems encountered by the Prophet and the emerging Umma were to be judged in accordance with the new principles and worldview of Islam, the old institutions and established rules and customs remained largely unchallenged. Indeed, as we shall see later, much of Arabian law continued to occupy a place in Sharīʿa – the later, more mature system of Islamic law. A few examples may serve to illustrate the point. First, a number of ritual practices, such as prayer and fasting, were

[35] Ibid., 4:24 ff.; 2:236; 5:5.

[36] P. Crone and M. Cook, *Hagarism: The Making of the Muslim World* (Cambridge: Cambridge University Press, 1977), 7. For other non-Muslim sources speaking to this effect, see Robert G. Hoyland, *Seeing Islam as Others Saw it: A Survey and Evaluation of Christian, Jewish and Zoroastrian Writings on Early Islam* (Princeton: The Darwin Press, 1997), 414.

[37] On the Constitution of Medina, see R. B. Serjeant, "The Constitution of Medina," *Islamic Quarterly*, 8 (1964): 3–16, at 3.

distinctly pre-Islamic Arabian practices that survived in the legal and religious system of the new faith.[38] Second, the pre-Islamic customary laws of barter and exchange of agricultural products – e.g., bartering unripe dates still on the palm tree against their equal value in picked dried dates (a practice common to oasis-based agriculturalists) – were to persist in Sharīʿa. So were a variety of contracts, mainly pecuniary and commercial. The ancient Near Eastern contracts of sale, dating back to the second millennium BC, and involving immediate delivery with a later payment, or immediate payment for a later delivery, were prevalent in the pre-Islamic Hejaz and wholly incorporated (under *ʿarāyā* and *salam*) into Islamic law.[39] Third, several elements of customary penal laws were retained, such as *qasāma* (compurgation), according to which, if the body of a murdered person is found on lands occupied by a tribe, or in a residential quarter in a city, town or village, fifty of the inhabitants must each take an oath to the effect that they had neither caused the person's death nor had any knowledge of who did. If less than fifty persons were available, those present had to swear more than once until fifty oaths had been obtained. By doing so, they freed themselves of criminal liability, but nonetheless remained bound to pay blood-money to the agnates of the person slain. The adoption of these ancient laws by the mature Sharīʿa was justified by the jurists on the grounds that the Prophet did not repeal them and, in fact, sanctioned them implicitly or in his actual practice.[40]

3. CONCLUSIONS AND METHODOLOGICAL REMARKS

Mounting archaeological, epigraphic and other evidence suggests that the Arabian Peninsula in general, and the Hejaz – the cradle of Islam – in particular, were part and parcel of the general culture that pervaded the entire Near East since the time of Hammurabi. Through intensive contacts with the Lakhmids and the Ghassānids and with their Arab predecessors who had dominated the Fertile Crescent for a century or more before the rise of Islam, the Arabs of the Peninsula maintained forms of culture that were their own, but which represented a regional variation on the cultures of the north. The Bedouin themselves participated in these cultural forms,

38 See S. D. Goitein, *Studies in Islamic History and Institutions* (Leiden: E. J. Brill, 1966), 73–89, 92–94.

39 VerSteeg, *Early Mesopotamian Law*, 178; Joseph Schacht, *An Introduction to Islamic Law* (Oxford: Clarendon, 1964), 218.

40 Muḥammad Ibn Ḥazm, *Muʿjam al-Fiqh*, 2 vols. (Damascus: Maṭbaʿat Jāmiʿat Dimashq, 1966), II, 838–39.

but the sedentary and agricultural settlements of the Hejaz were even more dynamic participants in the commercial and religious activities of the Near East. Through trade, missionary activities and connections with northern tribes (and hence constant shifting of demographic boundaries), the inhabitants of the Hejaz knew Syria and Mesopotamia quite as well as the inhabitants of the latter knew the Hejaz. When the new Muslim state began its expansion to the north, north-west and north-east, it did not enter these territories empty-handed, desperately in search of new cultural forms or an identity. Rather, the conquering Arabs, headed by a sophisticated leadership hailing from commercial and sedentary Medina and Mecca, were very much products of the same culture that dominated what was to become their subject territories.

All this must have a profound effect on how modern scholars conceive of the formation of Islamic law, and what elements went into its making. To view the new Muslims as desert dwellers who, before embarking on their conquests, lived an impoverished life of nomadism and tribalism can only lead to a theory in which all Muslim cultural forms, including legal institutions, were borrowings from the high imperial cultures of the north, especially that of Byzantium. Such a view would comport with the now widespread perception of Muslims as backward, always in need of assimilating "western" culture and values so as to keep pace with modernity and progress.[41] The preceding discussion has shown, however, that such a view of the sixth- and seventh-century Near East, including Arabia, is untenable. The Arabian Peninsula was as much a part of the Near East as were, among others, Palestine, Syria and Egypt.

But we would run an even greater risk if we were to characterize the culture of the Near East as Hellenic, attributing to it features that ultimately were imported from Greece and Rome. For one could still agree that the pre-Islamic Peninsular Arabs participated in the general culture of the Near East, yet still insist that that culture, in any of its varieties, was essentially Greek and Roman, the very same traditions that formed the cultural foundations of Byzantium. The risk stems from the erroneous assumption that because Byzantium, and before it Rome and Greece, adopted these cultural forms, they must then be originally Roman and/or Greek. Take, for example, the case of Beirut's law school, thought to be an eminently Roman institution. In a recent study, Warwick Ball aptly avers:

[41] For an analysis of this theme within the context of writing the origins of Islamic law, see Hallaq, "Quest for Origins"; see also the introduction in Hallaq, ed., *The Formation of Islamic Law.*

At the beginning of the third century the [Phoenician, but Roman] Emperor Septimius Severus founded Beirut's most famous institution. This was the Law School, the first such institution in the Roman world, and it was enthusiastically supported by the [originally Near Eastern] Severan emperors. The Beirut Law School was to have a profound effect on Roman civilization. It represents the birth of Roman – hence European – jurisprudence, of which Justinian's monumental *Digest* was the first great achievement. It attracted many prominent legal minds, mostly drawn from the Phoenician population of the Levant itself. The most famous was Papinian, a native of Emesa, and his contemporary Ulpian, a native of Tyre. Both were patronised by the Severan dynasty . . . and both were acknowledged in Justinian's *Digest* as forming the basis of Roman Law . . . Beirut and its justly famous law school, and with it its profound legacy, is regarded as a "western" and Roman enclave in the Near East. But it was founded and promoted by emperors whose origins and destinies were intimately bound to Phoenician culture. Above all, it must be emphasised that . . . the environment of Beirut and its law school is the Near East, not Italy. Many of the great scholars who dominated it were natives of the Near East, however Romanised, notably Papinian and Ulpian. It drew upon literary traditions that stretched back to Sanchuniathon of Beirut in the seventh century BC and legal traditions that stretched back even further to the Judaic traditions of the early first millennium and the Mesopotamian law codes of the early second millennium. Ultimately, therefore, should we be viewing Beirut in the context of Rome or of Babylon?[42]

The example of Beirut's law school is merely a small part of the much larger story of Rome's dependence on the Semitic Orient. It is increasingly becoming clear to modern scholarship that the Near East not only had a long history of urbanism and urban structures that pre-dated both the Greeks and the Romans, but also that what came to be known as the Roman heritage of the Near East was in many respects a heritage heavily indebted to the indigenous Semitic cultures of the ancient Near East, not, in fact, to Greece or Rome.[43]

Thus, whatever cultural and legal institutions existed in the Byzantine–Roman Near East cannot be taken, prima facie, to have emanated from Rome and Byzantium. Methodologically, therefore, any claim of cultural transmission must pass the test of "genealogy," namely, that

[42] Warwick Ball, *Rome in the East: The Transformation of an Empire* (London and New York: Routledge, 2000), 173–74.

[43] See ibid., *passim*, as well as Maurice Sartre's *L'Orient romain* (Paris: Seuil, 1991), which in some respects anticipates Ball's work. Also see Wael Hallaq, "Use and Abuse of Evidence: The Question of Roman and Provincial Influences on Early Islamic Law," *Journal of the American Oriental Society*, 110 (1989): 79–91, reproduced in W. Hallaq, *Law and Legal Theory in Classical and Medieval Islam* (Aldershot: Variorum, 1994), article IX, 1–36, at 30–31, and sources cited therein (n. 17).

whenever a claim is made to the effect that one civilization had absorbed a cultural form from another, it is indispensable for the validity of the claim to show that that form originated in the latter civilization and that it is not a regurgitated or rehabilitated form, ultimately taken either from a third civilization or from an earlier incarnation of the very culture that is said to have engaged in borrowing.

Even if we assume that the Peninsular Arabs came to the Fertile Crescent devoid of any "high culture," as some modern scholars assert, whatever these new Muslims happened to incorporate into their new empire and legal system was fundamentally Near Eastern and Semitic, however thin or thick were the Byzantine and Roman veneers. But we need not go this far: this chapter has showed that these Arabs were, demographically, religiously and commercially (and, we may add, politically and militarily) an integral part of the larger Near East and its culture. They hardly could have found the Fertile Crescent to be as new or different as, more recently, the French found Algeria or the British India. The Fertile Crescent was no more than a cultural neighbor whose home and conduct – nay, problems – they knew and understood; and when they took over that dwelling-place, they moved with much of their belongings, and managed to live in it comfortably and even renovate and expand it dramatically.

CHAPTER 2

The emergence of an Islamic legal ethic

1. THE ARAB CONQUESTS

In 11/632 the Prophet died, leaving unsettled the question of succession. The dispute over governance was resolved in favor of Abū Bakr, a distinguished Meccan of senior age who had adopted Islam when Muḥammad was still preaching his new religion in the city. Abū Bakr's short tenure as caliph, however, allowed him to accomplish little more than to quell the so-called apostasy rebellions that erupted among the Arab tribes upon the death of the Prophet. By the time of his death in 13/634, order was restored, the tribes having been largely subdued. With this reassertion of Islamic dominance over the entire Arabian Peninsula, the nascent state emerged all the more powerful, with a reinforced assurance of its military strength and religious conviction.

The consolidation of the military and political standing of the young state permitted ʿUmar b. al-Khaṭṭāb (ʿUmar I), the second caliph, to undertake intensive military campaigns directed mainly at the Syrian and Iraqian north, ruled, respectively, by the vassal kingdoms of Byzantium and Sasanid Persia. During the two decades of this aggressive and dynamic caliph's rule, much was achieved, in terms of both military expansion and administrative organization. From a historical perspective, his reign was arguably the most momentous of all, for it predetermined the success of the Islamic state enterprise that laid the foundations for the civilization that was to come.

The earliest military campaigns and conquests, although not systematic, were geared toward major centers. The Muslim army consisted primarily of tribal nomads and semi-nomads who, rather than take up residence in the newly won cities of the Fertile Crescent, Egypt and Iran, for the most part inhabited garrison towns, the *amṣār*, as a separate class of conquerors. In her description of the early military encampment of Fusṭāṭ, located at the head of the Nile Delta, Janet Abu-Lughod characterized the pattern of settlement in all major garrison towns:

During the seven months that the Arab invaders under [the military commander] ʿAmr besieged the Byzantine fortress at Babylon, they pitched their tents on the high dusty plain above riverine Babylon. Once capitulation was achieved, the troops were arranged somewhat more formally. Northeast of the fortress (renamed Qaṣr al-Shamʿ by the Arabs) at the firm bank of the Nile, ʿAmr erected the first mosque in Africa. With the mosque at its core, flanked by the commercial markets which usually accompanied the central mosque in Islamic cities, a quasi-permanent army camp was established. It formed an elongated semicircle stretching as far north as the mouth of the Red Sea Canal and as far south as the inland lake, the Birkat al-Ḥabash.

This was hardly a unique Arab settlement. Indeed, throughout the conquered territories, Arabs set up similar encampments ... Always located at the edge of the desert, each had a similar plan of widely scattered nuclei. The *raison d'être* of this physical design can only be understood in terms of the social characteristics of the founders. The Arab army consisted of diverse and often incompatible tribes and ethnic groups, was accompanied by a straggling retinue of women, children, and slaves, and was composed of men whose past nomadic life made close quarters repellent ...

At first, segregation was rigid, with each ethnic group or tribe assigned its own isolated quarter. However, during the sixty years following the conquest, as the temporary camp was transformed into a permanent commercial as well as military settlement, there was both a retrenchment toward the central nucleus at the Mosque of ʿAmr and its radiating markets, and a filling in of the spaces purposely left open by the original plan. The ultimate result was a fairly compact town of a permanent nature, having little relation except in name to the army camp which had been its progenitor.[1]

Under capable military commanders, recruited mostly from Mecca, Medina and the powerful Yemeni/Ḥaḍramawti tribes, the troops subsisted on booty allotted to them in the form of pensions – an important motivation, although certainly not the sole one. Kūfa and Baṣra in southern Iraq and Fusṭāṭ in Egypt constituted the chief settlements at the early stage of conquests. Damascus in Syria was exceptional: here the new arrivals chose to dwell in an already established city – one that was familiar to the Muslim Arabs from before the rise of the new religion.

The Arab conquests were conducted with a clear sense of mission, and were by no means limited to material and territorial gain. The Islamic "cause," in other words, was as much of a driving force as any purely

[1] Janet L. Abu-Lughod, *Cairo: 1001 Years of the City Victorious* (Princeton: Princeton University Press, 1971), 13.

military objective. The new Muslims – at least the leading class – saw themselves as promulgators of a religion whose linchpin and cornerstone was the command of God, a command embedded in, and given expression by, the revealed Book. It did not escape the Muslim political leaders of Medina, the capital, or their military representatives in the garrison towns that their warriors needed to learn the principles of the new order, its new ethic and worldview. Tribal Bedouins to the core, the soldiers found alien the military organization to which they were subjected, and which must have constricted their freedom. Even more alien to them must have been the new ideas of Islam, its mode of operation and its generally non-tribal conception, if not organization. ʿUmar I quickly realized the potentially explosive situation, for he could not count for long upon appeasing the largely Bedouin contingents in his armies through allocations of booty. In each garrison town and in every locale where there happened to be a Muslim population, a mosque was erected.[2] This place of worship was to serve several functions for the emerging Muslim community, but at the outset it was limited mainly to bringing together the Muslims residing in the garrison town for the Friday prayer and sermon – both intended, among other things, to imbue the Bedouins with religious values. The sermon, which played an important role in the propagation of the new Islamic ethic, included extensive passages from the Quran and other messages that were relevant, in the emerging religious ethos, to the living experience of the Muslim community in the garrisons.

To each of these garrison towns ʿUmar I appointed a military commander-cum-administrator who also functioned as propagator of the new religious ideas that were gradually but steadily taking shape. His primary duties were to lead the Friday prayer, distribute booty pensions and command military campaigns. His duties also involved the resolution and arbitration of conflicts that arose between and among the tribesmen inhabiting the garrison town. ʿUmar I's aim, consistent with that of the Prophet before him, was to promote Islamic and, particularly, Quranic values as the basis of communal life, for not only were these values the distinctive features of the new enterprise, they were also essential to its continued success. To this end, he deployed to the garrison towns Quran teachers who enhanced the religious values propagated by the commanders and their assistants.[3] It cannot be

[2] Hoyland, *Seeing Islam*, 561 ff., 567–73, 639.

[3] Abū Isḥāq al-Shīrāzī, *Ṭabaqāt al-Fuqahā*ʾ, ed. Iḥsān ʿAbbās (Beirut: Dār al-Rāʾid al-ʿArabī, 1970), 44, 51; Muḥammad Ibn Ḥibbān, *Kitāb al-Thiqāt* (Hyderabad: ʿAbd al-Khāliq al-Afghānī, 1968), 149, 157.

overemphasized that the Quran represented the rallying doctrine that shaped the identity of the conquerors, thereby distinguishing and separating them from the surrounding communities.

The new religious ethic needed to be promoted in Arabia itself as much as elsewhere. The greater majority of tribes inhabiting Mecca, Medina, Ṭāʾif and the various agricultural oases, not to mention the nomads of the desert, were still little accustomed to the new political order and even less so to its unworldly and uniquely monotheistic ideas and principles. In the spirit of the Quran, and in accordance with what he deemed to have been the intended mission of the Prophet (to which he himself had contributed significantly), ʿUmar I promulgated a number of ordinances and regulations pertaining to state administration, family, crime and ritual. He regulated, among other things, punishment for adultery and theft, declared temporary marriage (*mutʿa*) illegal, and granted rights to concubines who bore the children of their masters. Similarly, he upheld Abū Bakr's promulgations, such as enforcing the prohibition on alcohol and fixing the penalty for its consumption at forty lashes.[4] He is also reported to have insisted forcefully on adherence to the Quran in matters of ritual and worship – a policy that culminated in a set of practices and beliefs that were instrumental in shaping the new Muslim identity, and that later became integral to the law.

At this early period, the Quran's injunctions, combined with the public policies of the new order, represented the sole modification to the customary laws prevailing among the Peninsular Arabs, laws that contained indigenous tribal elements and, to a considerable extent, legal provisions that had been applied in the urban cultures of the Near East – including the cities of the Hejaz – for over a millennium. These customs and laws were still the only "system" of law known to the conquerors, while the Quranic injunctions contained and symbolized the mission in whose name these conquerors were fighting. When Abū Bakr deployed his armies to conquer Syria, he commanded his generals "to kill neither old man nor child," to establish a covenant with the conquered peoples who did not resist, and "to give them assurances and to let them live according to their laws." On the other hand, he advised: "those who do not receive you, you are to fight, conducting yourselves carefully in accordance with the ordinances and upright laws transmitted to you from God, at the hands of our Prophet."[5]

[4] ʿAbd al-Ghanī b. ʿAbd al-Wāḥid al-Jammāʿīlī, *al-ʿUmda fī al-Aḥkām*, ed. Muṣṭafā ʿAṭāʾ (Beirut: Dār al-Kutub al-ʿIlmiyya, 1986), 463.

[5] Cited from a near contemporary Monophysite source. See S. P. Brock, "Syriac Views of Emergent

While Abū Bakr and ʿUmar I's enforcement of Quranic laws points to the centrality of the Quran in the emerging state and society, it is also clear that the new order had to navigate an uncharted path for which the Quran provided little guidance. A large portion of pre-Islamic Arabian laws and customs remained applicable, and indeed survived into the legal culture that was being constructed. But the new Quranic laws created their own juristic problems that rendered many of the old customary laws irrelevant. For instance, the Quran prohibited the consumption of alcohol, but did not specify a penalty. ʿUmar I soon allocated the punishment of eighty lashes for this infraction, apparently on the ground that inebriation was analogous to falsely accusing a person of committing adultery (*qadhf*), for which offense the Quran fixed the penalty at eighty lashes. The connection between fornication and inebriation is at best tenuous, but the analogy shows us how, from the beginning, the Quran provided the framework for legal thinking, bringing its contents to bear upon as many situations as nominally could be justified. Generally speaking, any matter that could be conceived as falling within its juristic purview, even by tortuous reasoning, was dealt with in Quranic terms or an extension thereof. And it was within this larger framework of the permeating Quranic effect that pre-Islamic customary laws underwent modification or significant change.

The importance of the Quran as the principal guide of Muslim life required the fixing of a vulgate. During Muḥammad's life and immediately thereafter, the text existed as fragments, written down on parchment (sometimes even on shoulder-blades and stones) by a number of Companions, possibly as early as the Meccan period. Some parts of it had also been committed to memory by certain of the Prophet's supporters and relatives. Abū Bakr attempted to create an official collection of the text, but the project seems to have failed. Several versions were still circulating in the conquered territories during ʿUmar I's reign, and various controversies appear to have arisen over the correct reading of given passages. ʿUthmān, the third caliph (23/644–35/655), commissioned Zayd b. Thābit, said to have been the Prophet's scribe, to undertake the task of compiling a standard text, which he seems to have accomplished successfully. Several copies of this text were made and later distributed to the garrison towns, all other previous collections having reportedly been destroyed. The creation of a vulgate must have had a primary legal significance, for it defined the

Islam," in G .H. A. Juynboll, ed., *Studies on the First Century of Islamic Society* (Carbondale: Southern Illinois University Press, 1982), 9–21, at 12, n.200. For more on how Abū Bakr's policy contributed to legal construction, see Schacht, *Origins*, 204–05.

content of the Quran and thus gave the legally minded a *textus receptus* on which to draw.

2. THE PROTO-*QĀḌĪS*

The early activity of the Islamic magistrate, the *qāḍī*, may be considered the best yardstick by which we can measure the evolution of an Islamic legal ethic. The question at hand, therefore, is the nature of the early *qāḍī*'s duties and their Islamic content. The sources report that the Prophet himself deployed *qāḍīs* to the lands that came under Medinese dominion, particularly the Yemen. ʿAlī, who was to become the fourth caliph after ʿAbū Bakr, ʿUmar I and ʿUthmān, is said to have been, together with Muʿādh b. Jabal and Abū Mūsā al-Ashʿarī, one such *qāḍī*.[6] The same sources, however, are not clear as to whether these were appointed as *qāḍīs* per se or as governors. In due course, it will become obvious that their functions involved far more provincial administration as military commanders than anything having to do with law, *stricto sensu*, except for the most basic of matters legal. It is perhaps indicative of the nature of these commanders' involvement in law that when a paternity dispute was brought before the young ʿAlī, he solved it by drawing lots. Upon hearing of ʿAlī's methods, the Prophet reportedly laughed so hard that "his molars came into view."[7] Whether authentic or not, this anecdote – one of many – reveals the primitive nature of the legal reasoning employed by these proto-*qāḍīs*, as compared to the manner in which a later *qāḍī* would have dealt with the case. Yet, we cannot conclude from such anecdotes that ʿAlī's solution necessarily reflected the overall juristic competence of Muslim leadership, for if this were the case, the Prophet would not have been so amused.

The proto-*qāḍīs* whom ʿUmar I is reported to have sent to the garrison towns do not seem to have fared much better. Kaʿb b. Suwar al-Azdī is said to have been appointed by this caliph as *qāḍī* of the military camp of Baṣra in 14/635, and to have remained in office until he was killed in 23/644. The sources report that a dispute over property was brought before Kaʿb: one man had purchased land from another on the understanding that it was cultivable, but the buyer later discovered that the land was barren and rocky. Kaʿb asked the buyer if he would have attempted to nullify the sale had he found gold in the land. Upon hearing a negative answer, Kaʿb ruled

[6] Muḥammad b. Khalaf Wakīʿ, *Akhbār al-Quḍāt*, 3 vols. (Beirut: ʿĀlam al-Kutub, n.d.), I, 84 f., 100.
[7] Ibid., I, 91–95.

that he was not entitled to restitution.[8] As late as 65/684, if not after that, such arbitrary rulings were common. When a charge of fraud was brought before Hishām b. Hubayra – where a group of men was accused of the fraudulent commingling of barley with wheat and selling it as pure wheat – he found the defendants guilty and ordered that their heads and half their beards be shaved as punishment.[9] Now these solutions, dictated by practical considerations and ad hoc common sense, ran counter to the standard principles that evolved later on: in the case of Kaʿb, the buyer would have had the option to void the sale if the object bought was defective, and, in the case of Hishām, payment of damages equal to the reduced value of the wheat would have been due. Kaʿb and Hishām certainly did not have at their disposal the technical legal knowledge necessary to deal with such cases, irrespective of whether or not this knowledge existed in their time. It is significant, however, that these men were appointed to deal with disputes arising in the midst of a population of conquerors.

As for the conquered communities outside what came to be the garrison town of Baṣra – and elsewhere in Iraq – it is likely that they still applied the ancient Mesopotamian law of property rights and damages that allows for some form of restitution.[10] Indeed, it is even more likely that one form of damages or another had for long been known to the Peninsular Arabs who inhabited the trading towns of the Hejaz, and possibly elsewhere. Thus, the fact that Kaʿb, Hishām and ʿAlī resorted to primitive adjudication among the tribal soldiers is no indication in itself that technical legal knowledge was unavailable. The absence of legal acumen among them must therefore be explained by the specific nature of their appointments, and the contexts in which they operated.

The early appointments to *qaḍāʾ* (judgeship) recorded in the sources must be viewed as quasi-legal in nature. Many of the *qāḍī*s appointed were persons whose involvement in the law did not go beyond the experience of having been arbitrators (*ḥukkām*; sing. *ḥakam*). The latter were men deemed to be in possession of experience, wisdom and charisma (as well as, in pre-Islamic times, supernatural powers), to whom tribesmen resorted to adjudicate their disputes. Although their verdicts were not binding in

8 Ibid., I, 279.

9 Ibid., I, 300. Such a punishment, however, was not unknown in the pre-Islamic Near East.

10 Another element of Mesopotamian – in this case Babylonian – law that survived in Islamic law is contractual offer and acceptance. See Joseph Schacht, "From Babylonian to Islamic Law," in *Yearbook of Islamic and Middle Eastern Law* (London and Boston: Kluwer Law International, 1995), 29–33.

the strict legal sense, disputants normally conformed to their findings. Many of the so-called *qāḍīs* were recruited from the ranks of these pre-Islamic arbitrators, although other appointees did not have the benefit of such experience. The sources report that some of the earliest *qāḍīs* were illiterate, as in the case of ʿĀbis b. Saʿīd al-Murādī who was appointed *qāḍī* of the important garrison town of Fusṭāṭ by the caliph Muʿāwiya (41/661–60/80).[11] Yet, his illiteracy did not mean that ʿĀbis lacked the experience and acumen to deal with legal and quasi-legal problems arising mostly from a tribal social context.

It is of fundamental importance to realize that early judicial appointments were neither general in jurisdiction nor intended to regulate and supervise the affairs of the conquered provinces. Rather, they were confined to the garrison towns where the conquering Arab armies resided with their families and other members of their tribes.[12] The policy of the central power at Medina was clear on this matter from the outset: the conquered communities were to regulate their own affairs exactly as they had been doing prior to the advent of Islam. Abū Bakr's letter to his generals is typical, and represents the standard Muslim policy adopted during the entire period of the conquests. The invading Arabs were to "establish a covenant with every city and people who receive[d]" them, and to give these people "assurances and to let them live according to their laws."[13] Thus, the so-called *qāḍīs* appointed to the provinces during the first decades of Islam, and for a while thereafter, were in fact state officials whose jurisdiction did not extend beyond the population of the conquering tribes.

This explains why most early appointments were not related exclusively to *qaḍāʾ*, however general and vague the meaning of this term may have been. With the exception of Syria – the center of Umayyad rule – most appointees had other weighty responsibilities, having to do with policing and financial administration. The illiterate *qāḍī* ʿĀbis b. Saʿīd al-Murādī was charged in Fusṭāṭ with the task of adjudicating conflicts – in keeping, it would seem, with the original meaning of the term "*qaḍāʾ*" – and of heading the police section (*shurṭa*).[14] Egypt appears to have had a high number of such appointments, although this practice existed elsewhere.

[11] Wakīʿ, *Akhbār*, III, 223; Muḥammad b. Yūsuf al-Kindī, *Akhbār Quḍāt Miṣr*, ed. R. Guest (Cairo: Muʾassasat Qurṭuba, n.d.), 311–13.
[12] Abū Zurʿa al-Dimashqī, *Tārīkh*, ed. Shukr Allāh al-Qawjānī, 2 vols. (n.p., 1970), I, 202.
[13] Brock, "Syriac Views," nn. 204–05.
[14] Wakīʿ, *Akhbār*, III, 223.

According to one count, six out of fifteen *qāḍī*s appointed to Fusṭāṭ in this early period were also charged with supervising the *shurṭa.*[15]

Many *qāḍī*s, especially after 50/670, were also charged with the collection of taxes, except, again, in Syria, where the caliphs themselves appear to have taken charge of this function.But as secretaries of public finance (*bayt al-māl*), proto-*qāḍī*s were appointed fairly early, as evidenced by the case of Ibn Ḥujayra, who combined this office with *qaḍā'*.[16] The secretariat of finance mainly involved administering the collection and distribution of booty, in the form of pensions, to the conquering tribes of the garrison towns.[17] This function appears to have overlapped with that of the *ʿarīf*, who also distributed stipends to the warrior-tribesmen and managed the payment of blood-money. In some cases, he was also charged with overseeing the property of orphans and of supervising conduct in the markets, as was the case with the renowned *qāḍī* Shurayḥ.[18]

The *qāḍī*-cum-administrator was usually subservient to the chief commander (*amīr*) of the garrison town, who appointed, supervised and dismissed him. The proto-*qāḍī* was seen as the commander's assistant, his *wazīr*, as well as his deputy whenever he quitted the garrison. For example, when Muʿāwiya left for the Battle of Ṣiffīn in 38/658, the proto-*qāḍī* Faḍāla b. ʿUbayd al-Anṣārī acted as governor of Syria during his absence.[19] However, in some cases, the appointment to *qaḍā'* was conferred upon the same person designated chief commander, as evidenced in the case of ʿUbayd Allāh b. Bakara, who was given the title of "*amīr* and *qāḍī*" over Baṣra.[20] During Muʿāwiya's reign, Faḍāla too was charged with military duties, including raiding, as well as *qaḍā'*. This tradition of dual appointment continued as late as the middle Umayyad period. Around 100/718, for instance, ʿAbd al-Raḥmān al-ʿUdharī combined the *qaḍā'* of Damascus with the military post of commander.[21]

The fact that some *qāḍī*s who performed financial, military and policing tasks were illiterate strongly suggests that *qaḍā'* was limited in nature – limited, that is, in terms of both geography and jurisdiction.

15 Irit Bligh-Abramsky, "The Judiciary (Qāḍīs) as a Governmental-Administrative Tool in Early Islam," *Journal of the Economic and Social History of the Orient*, 35 (1992): 40–71, at 46.

16 Kindī, *Akhbār*, 317; Wakīʿ, *Akhbār*, III, 225.

17 For other appointments which combined *qaḍā'*, financial and policing responsibilities, see Wakīʿ, *Akhbār*, I, 118; III, 225, 226, 227, 322; Kindī, *Akhbār*, 322, 324, 327, 332.

18 Wakiʿ, *Akhbār*, II, 196, 212; Kindī, *Akhbār*, 325.

19 Dimashqī, *Tārīkh*, I, 198–99; Shīrāzī, *Ṭabaqāt*, 43; Emile Tyan, *Histoire de l'organisation judiciare en pays d'Islam*, 2 vols., 2nd ed. (Leiden: E. J. Brill, 1960), I, 132 ff.

20 Wakīʿ, *Akhbār*, I, 302.

21 Bligh-Abramsky, "Judiciary," 44–45.

Geographically, it was restricted to the garrison towns and their inhabitants, and jurisdictionally, to disputes and conflicts that arose among tribal groups whose main occupation was soldiering. During the first decades of Islam, when military activities were at their peak, it cannot be expected that the Arab soldiers would experience the entire gamut of social and economic life that fully developed urban populations knew and lived. But since these soldiers inhabited the garrison towns together with their families and fellow tribesmen, the problems that they encountered would most often have related to family status, inheritance and crime – all of which areas were fairly well regulated either by Quranic legislation or tribal customary law.[22] It was only with the passage of time, when this occupying population settled in these towns, that their life acquired its own complexity, and was expanded into a full-fledged society whose daily, mundane problems spanned the entire range of law. This was to become the state of affairs nearly a century after Muḥammad's death, as reflected in the changing character of the *qāḍī*'s office.

The *qāḍī*'s function as a magistrate, initially limited, underwent gradual expansion. Criminal jurisdiction seems to have been assigned to this office as a distinct category sometime in the 40s/660s, that is, during Muʿāwiya's reign. Sulaym b. ʿItr[23] is reported to have been the first *qāḍī*, at least in Fusṭāṭ, to be charged, among other things, with the specific responsibility of adjudicating criminal cases among the conquering tribes inhabiting this garrison town.[24] Sulaym reportedly conveyed to the secretary of the military register (*ṣāḥib dīwān al-jund*) the amount of compensation to which an injured party was entitled, whereupon the secretary disbursed – over a three-year period – the compensation to this party out of the pension of the convicted assailant.[25]

The *qāḍī*'s office and the tasks that it involved expanded primarily in a religious direction, however. Despite the lack of formal legal education (which Islamic culture had not yet developed), and the patent illiteracy of some of them, *qāḍī*s were expected, if not required, at least to have a degree of religious knowledge. At the time this meant possessing a reasonable knowledge of the legal stipulations of the Quran plus knowledge of the rudimentary socio-religious values the new religion had developed. When Marwān b. Ḥasan was appointed governor of Egypt in 65/684, he called on

22 Wakīʿ, *Akhbār*, III, 224–25.
23 An alternative rendering of this name, provided by Wakīʿ, is Sulaymān b. ʿAnz.
24 Kindī, *Akhbār*, 309.
25 Ibid.

ʿĀbis b. Saʿīd, then the *qāḍī* of Fusṭāṭ, with the intention of checking his credentials. Having heard that ʿĀbis was illiterate, Marwān was concerned about his competence. It is reported that the first question he asked him was whether he knew the Quran, especially its laws of inheritance.[26]

A significant function of the early *qāḍīs* was story-telling. It appears that many officials were appointed with the double function of *qāḍī* and story-teller (*qāṣṣ*; pl. *quṣṣāṣ*). This function usually entailed recounting stories of a generally edifying nature, related to the Quranic narratives of ancient peoples and their fates, biblical characters and, more importantly, the exemplary life of the Prophet. The first official appointment was made by Muʿāwiya in, or sometime immediately after, 41/661,[27] with the specific duty of "cursing the enemies of Islam" after the morning prayer and of explaining the Quran to worshipers after the Friday prayer. This last performance may have ranged from popular ceremonies to a more serious discussion of the Prophet's biography and interpretation of the Divine Text. The latter activities, it should be noted, may well have marked the beginning of scholarly circles in Islam, an intellectual institution that was to develop during the next four centuries into a full-fledged system of legal education, among other things.

Story-telling was not limited to official appointment, however, since many *quṣṣāṣ* were already active on a private level before Muʿāwiya incorporated some of them into government ranks. In fact, they may have been associated with the so-called *akhbārīs* who, since pre-Islamic days, had been collecting reports of ancient events, genealogies and poetry. The story-tellers appear to have played a role in the then emerging religious life of Iraq, Medina and other cities, but there is little to suggest that they were appointed, at that time and in this capacity, to government posts.[28] Be that as it may, their appearance is a strong indication of the rapid evolution of the religious orientation that emphasized the Quranic and Prophetic narratives. The fact that many proto-*qāḍīs* were also appointed as story-tellers is significant because this government policy provides evidence of

[26] Wakīʿ, *Akhbār,* III, 223. This report must be authentic, since the sources make no mention whatsoever of Prophetic Sunna or consensus, the knowledge of which became – a century or two later – as essential to the *qāḍī* as the Quran. The veracity of this report is also corroborated by the fact that ʿĀbis' appointment was renewed even though he answered the question in the negative, saying that whatever he did not know he would enquire about in learned circles. Ignorance of the Quran would automatically disqualify any later would-be *qāḍī*, and such a state of affairs would not have a chance of coming down in the form of a report.

[27] Dimashqī, *Tārīkh,* I, 200.

[28] Muḥammad Ibn Ḥibbān, *Kitāb Mashāhīr ʿUlamāʾ al-Amṣār,* ed. M. Fleischhammer (Cairo: Maṭbaʿat Lajnat al-Taʾlīf wal-Tarjama wal-Nashr, 1379/1959), 73, 75, 79 and *passim.*

the development of the religious character of the *qāḍī*'s office. Although some story-tellers were regarded as little better than charlatans, most of the early *qāḍī*s who functioned in a dual capacity as *quṣṣāṣ* appear to have been men of piety and faith. The *qāḍī* and story-teller Sulaym b. ʿItr, for example, is characterized in the sources as a pious man who reportedly spent his nights reading the Quran.[29]

But knowledge of the Quran and various religious narratives should not be taken to mean that the proto-*qāḍī*s always applied Quranic law, even if there was a growing tendency to do so from the very beginning. The application of Islamic content to the daily life of the community came after the articulation of a certain ethic, depending on the particular sphere of life or the case at hand. In matters of inheritance, for instance, where the Quran offered clear and detailed provisions, the proto-*qāḍī*s seem to have applied these provisions as early as the caliphates of Abū Bakr and ʿUmar I; indeed, we earlier saw examples of governmental insistence on faithful adherence to the Quranic stipulations on inheritance. On the other hand, many areas of life were either lightly touched by Quranic legislation or not at all. Even such Quranic prohibitions as those pertaining to wine-drinking were not immediately enforced, and remained largely inoperative at least for several decades after the death of the Prophet. In fact, the early Kūfan legists permitted its consumption. Furthermore, it is telling that Shurayḥ, portrayed in the Muslim tradition as an archetypal *qāḍī* of legendary proportions, is commonly reported to have indulged in drinking doubly distilled, strong intoxicants.[30] Telling, because if a *qāḍī* such as Shurayḥ was publicly involved in practices so flagrantly contradictory to the Quranic letter and spirit, then one can safely assume that, apart from certain highly regulated areas in the Quran (marriage, divorce, inheritance, etc.), there was little concern at the time for an Islamic system of legal morality. (This is to assume that law and morality in developed Islamic law were not only intertwined, but often interchangeable.)

3. THE RELIGIOUS IMPULSE

Shurayḥ's habitual consumption of alcohol (*ṭilāʾ*) is reported in the sources without censure. No doubt, the practice must have been viewed by later

[29] Wakīʿ, *Akhbār*, III, 221. For a detailed discussion of story-tellers, see K. ʿAthamina, "al-Qasas: Its Emergence, Religious Origin and its Socio-Political Impact on Early Muslim Society," *Studia Islamica*, 76 (1992): 53–74.

[30] Wakīʿ, *Akhbār*, II, 212, 226.

believers as abhorrent, but it was understood – even tolerated – in the case of this early figure who had converted to a religion that had barely emerged. In the nearly 200-page biography dedicated to Shurayḥ by Wakīʿ,[31] no condemnation or criticism of his practice is recorded. Nor is there any reproach directed at the influential and highly learned lady who, in the 60s/680s, used to offer wine to men on their way to pilgrimage.[32] It is a reflection of the growth of religious sentiment that in less than two decades after Shurayḥ's career had ended, censure of wine-drinking – as well as other practices condemned by the Quran – began to surface. In 89/707, ʿImrān b. ʿAbd Allāh al-Ḥasanī, *qāḍī* of Fusṭāṭ since 86/705, convicted in his court a scribe of ʿAbd Allāh b. ʿAbd al-Malik, then Egypt's governor. The charge was wine-drinking, and the evidence was witness testimony. The governor accepted the verdict, but refused to allow ʿImrān to implement any penalty. The latter resigned his post in protest, after failing to persuade the governor to change his mind.[33] The change from an environment in which a *qāḍī* himself would indulge in drinking alcohol publicly to one in which another would resign a fairly lucrative post in protest against official interference with his attempts to punish the same behavior is indeed remarkable.

ʿImrān's confrontation with the governor took place in a social and ethical environment that was significantly different from the one that had existed half a century before. By the year 60/680, most of the Prophet's generation, even young contemporaries, were dead.[34] Many of these must have believed in the message brought to them by Muḥammad, but they – especially those who had only briefly been his supporters – could hardly have internalized the spirit of the new, as yet largely undeveloped, religion. After all, the great majority were tribal Bedouins whose way of life did not conform readily to the principles and imperatives of the Quranic worldview; indeed, for many, the material gain brought about by the conquests was the main attraction of the new order. Nonetheless, they did fight in the name of Islam, and they must have accepted, in one form or another, its basic ideas.

[31] Ibid., II, 189–381. For a detailed discussion of Shurayḥ's career, see Khaleelul Iqbal Mohammed, "Development of an Archetype: Studies in the Shurayḥ Traditions" (Ph.D. dissertation, McGill University, 2001).

[32] Dimashqī, *Tārīkh*, I, 333.

[33] Kindī, *Akhbār*, 328.

[34] Only a few Companions remained alive after this time. ʿAbd Allāh b. ʿĀmir was one of the last to die, in 89/707. See Ibn Ḥibbān, *Mashāhīr*, 17.

The subsequent generation – those who were born and raised during the early military and ideological expansion of Islam – grew up under the influence of Quranic teachings and various kinds of religious preaching and instruction. Unlike their parents, who had become Muslims at a later stage in their lives, often under coercion (by virtue of the apostasy wars), they, together with the children of non-Arab converts, imbibed from infancy the rudimentary religious morality and values. By the time they reached majority, they were frequent mosque-goers (i.e., regular consumers of religious preaching and religious acculturation), and were involved in various activities relating to the conquests and building of a religious empire. It was therefore the learned elite of this generation – which flourished roughly between 60/680 and 90/708 – who embarked upon promoting a religious ethos that permeated – indeed, impregnated – so much of Muslim life and society.

It was this ethos that ʿImrān, the *qāḍī* we just encountered, was attempting to reinforce. Many *qāḍī*s like him began to show interest in religious narrative, including stories and biographical anecdotes about the Prophet. The story-tellers were among those who promoted this narrative, which was to become paradigmatic. By the 60s/680s, some *qāḍī*s had started propounding Prophetic material, the precise nature of which is still unclear to us. Ṭalḥa b. ʿAbd Allāh b. ʿAwf, the *qāḍī* of Medina between 60/679 and 72/691, is said to have narrated Prophetic reports that the famous Ibn Shihāb al-Dīn al-Zuhrī (d. 124/741) memorized and later transmitted.[35] Our sources suggest that he was one of the first *qāḍī*s to be associated with this activity, although he may have engaged in it only after his tenure as a judge.[36] Among the other *qāḍī*s who reportedly narrated Prophetic material were Nawfal b. Musāḥiq[37] and ʿUmar b. Khalda al-Zuraqī, who succeeded Ṭalḥa to the office between 76/695 and 82/701.[38]

That the initial interest in Prophetic narrative began nearly half a century after the Prophet's death is a problem worth explaining, especially in light of the fundamental importance of the authority of *ḥadīth* (the textual narrative of what the Prophet had said, done or tacitly approved) to later law and legal theory. The new preoccupation with Prophetic material reflected a dramatic change of attitude in a considerable body of writings

35 Ibid., 122; Wakīʿ, *Akhbār*, I, 120.

36 Ibn Ḥibbān lists his death as having occurred in 97/715: *Thiqāt*, 122.

37 Ibid., 272.

38 Wakīʿ, *Akhbār* I, 125, 130.

found in papyri, inscriptions and elsewhere.[39] One such change may be found in Umayyad numismatics.[40] Upon the accession of Marwān in 64/683, the coins begin, for the first time, to exhibit the formula "The Messenger of God" (*Rasūl Allāh*), a formula that was to remain a standard feature of Arab numismatics.[41] The earliest inscription bearing this formula appears to be that engraved on the southern, south-western and eastern outer faces of the Dome of the Rock, dated 72/691.[42] All other evidence from early sources appears to support the view that legal authority during the better part of the first Islamic century was in no way exclusively Prophetic. It must be remembered that by the time Muḥammad died, his authority as a Prophet was anchored in the Quranic event and in the fact that he was God's spokesman – the one through whom this event materialized. To his followers, he was and remained nothing more than a human being, devoid of any divine attributes (unlike Christ, for instance). But by the time of his death, when his mission had already met with great success, he was the most important living figure the Arabs knew. Nonetheless, these Arabs also knew of the central role that ʿUmar I, Abū Bakr and a number of others had played in helping the Prophet, even in contributing to the success, if not survival, of the new religion. Like him, they were charismatic men who commanded the respect of the faithful (and in the case of ʿUmar I, the ability to instill fear in his adversaries). Inasmuch as Muḥammad's authority derived from the fact that he upheld the Quranic Truth and never swerved from it, these men – some of whom later became caliphs – derived their own authority as privileged Companions and caliphs from the same fact – namely, upholding the Quranic Truth. This is not to say that caliphal authority was necessarily or entirely derivative of that of the Prophet; in fact, it ran parallel to it. Muḥammad was the messenger through whom the Quranic Truth was revealed – the caliphs were the defenders of this Truth and the ones who were to implement its decrees.

The caliphs – until at least the middle of the second/eighth century – tended to see themselves as God's *direct* agents in the mission to implement His statutes, commands and laws. The titles they bore speak for themselves: "God's Deputy on Earth" and "The Commander of the

39 See Hoyland, *Seeing Islam*, 545 ff., 687 ff.

40 Patricia Crone and M. Hinds, *God's Caliph: Religious Authority in the First Centuries of Islam* (Cambridge: Cambridge University Press, 1986), 24–25.

41 The coins themselves are dated 66/685 and 67/686. See Hoyland, *Seeing Islam*, 694, no. 21; for the Umayyad–Sasanid coin of Baṣra's governor Khālid b. ʿAbd Allāh, minted in 71/690–91. see ibid., 695, no. 26.

42 Ibid., 696–97.

Faithful." They held their own courts and personally acted as *qāḍīs*.[43] In fact, throughout the entirety of the first Islamic century, they adjudicated – in practical terms – the majority of issues that required authority-statement solutions, without invoking Prophetic authority. As late as the 90s/710s, and for some decades thereafter, most *qāḍīs* appear to have relied on three sources of authority in framing their rulings: the Quran, the *sunan* (including caliphal law) and what we will call here discretionary opinion (*ra'y*). Abū Bakr b. Ḥazm al-Anṣārī, *qāḍī* of Medina after 94/712, drew explicitly on these three sources in nearly all of his decisions reported in biographical works.[44] The same is true of Iyās b. Muʿāwiya, Baṣra's *qāḍī* around the same time, whose rulings are also described in detail by Wakīʿ.[45] The *qāḍīs*' practice of writing letters seeking caliphal opinion on difficult cases confronting them in their courts was evidently a common one. So were caliphal letters to the *qāḍīs*, most of which appear to have been solicited, although some were written on the sole initiative of the caliph himself or – presumably – in his name, by his immediate advisors. Iyās, for instance, used to grant neighbors – merely by virtue of being neighbors – the right of preemption (*shufʿa*), a practice that did not seem to accord, for some reason, with caliphal public policy.[46] On hearing of Iyās' practice, ʿUmar II (99/717–101/720) wrote a letter ordering him to confine preemption rights to domiciles having a shared right of access (e.g., two houses sharing one gate) and to properties owned as partnerships of commixion.[47] The same caliph wrote to another *qāḍī* in Egypt imposing a similar, but even more restrictive decree, saying: "We used to hear (*kunnā nasmaʿ*) that preemption rights can be enjoyed by the partner only, not by the neighbor."[48] It seems reasonable to infer that many *qāḍīs* were in the habit of bestowing rights of preemption on the neighbor, and this caliph deemed it necessary to intervene.

43 Crone and Hinds, *God's caliph*, 43.

44 Wakīʿ, *Akhbār*, I, 135 ff.

45 Ibid., I, 312–74.

46 Preemption is the right to buy an adjoining property by virtue of the fact that the neighbor has priority, over any third party, to ownership of that property. For a description of preemption law in later doctrine, see Ibn Naqīb al-Miṣrī, *ʿUmdat al-Sālik*, trans. N. H. M. Keller, *The Reliance of the Traveller* (Evanston: Sunna Books, 1993), 432–34; Schacht, *Introduction*, 142. It is likely that the caliphal restriction of this right was due to the fact that such laws as applied by Iyās b. Muʿāwiya would ultimately have led to Muslims being deprived of the right to purchase houses in the predominantly non-Muslim cities and towns that had been conquered.

47 Wakīʿ, *Akhbār*, I, 332. Partnership of commixion refers to a property owned by two or more persons without clear definition of their individual shares in it, such as a residential property inherited by two or more persons.

48 Kindī, *Akhbār*, 334–35.

Caliphal legislation and legislative intervention, however, did not always derive authority from the office itself, as has been argued by some scholars.[49] The incipit of 'Umar II's statement ("We used to hear") clearly refers to past authority, in this case unidentified. Much of caliphal legal authority rested on precedent, mainly generally accepted custom and the practice of earlier caliphs, of the Prophet's close Companions and, naturally, of the Prophet himself. In fact, any good model was to be emulated. 'Umar I reportedly advised Shurayḥ to see that his rulings conformed with Quranic stipulations, the decisions (*qaḍā'*, but not yet the Sunna) of the Messenger of God and those of the "just leaders."[50] There is no reason to believe that the caliphs themselves did not abide by the same sources for legal guidance. When 'Iyāḍ al-Azdī, Egypt's *qāḍī* in 98/716, asked 'Umar II about a case apparently involving criminal liability pertaining to a boy who had violated a girl with his finger, the caliph answered: "Nothing has come down to me in this regard from past authorities." He delegated to the *qāḍī* full authority to deal with the case "in accordance with your discretionary opinion (*ra'y*)."[51] Had the caliphs been legislators in their own right, they would have had their own codes of law, and 'Umar II would not have hesitated to rule in this matter. The caliphs and their office, in other words, were not independent agents of legislation, but integrally dependent on prior exemplary conduct and precedent, only one source of which happened to be the decisions of previous caliphs. (It must be emphasized here that not all caliphs enjoyed equal religious authority. Abū Bakr, 'Umar I, 'Uthmān and 'Umar II seem to have enjoyed a higher level of legal authority than other caliphs.)

The *qāḍīs* operated within the same scheme of authoritative sources. In the late 60s/680s, some four decades after the death of 'Umar I, the Medinese *qāḍī* 'Abd Allāh b. Nawfal appears to have used this caliph's practice, among other things, as the basis for his rulings.[52] So did Abū Bakr b. Ḥazm al-Anṣārī, Iyās b. Mu'āwiya and others.[53] But all of these men resorted also to the Quran and to their own notions of reasoning and precedent. 'Umar II reportedly declared on one occasion that *qāḍīs* must be cognizant of the rulings and *sunan* that came before them.[54] In short, the sources of authority that governed the emerging Islamic law were

[49] Crone and Hinds, *God's Caliph*.

[50] Wakī', *Akhbār*, II, 189.

[51] Kindī, *Akhbār*, 334. The judge ruled for the girl, granting her fifty *dīnārs* in damages.

[52] Wakī', *Akhbār*, I, 113.

[53] Ibid., I, 139, 325, 326, 330, 332 and *passim*.

[54] Ibid., I, 77.

three: the Quran, the *sunan* and discretionary opinion. It is to the latter two that we shall now turn.

Sunna (pl. *sunan*) is an ancient Arab concept, meaning an exemplary mode of conduct, and the verb *sanna* has the connotation of "setting or fashioning a mode of conduct as an example that others would follow." As early as the fifth century AD, the Arabs of the north saw Ishmael, for instance, as a sort of saint who provided them with a model and a way of life.[55] In pre-Islamic Arabia, any person renowned for his rectitude, charisma and distinguished stature was, within his family and clan, deemed to provide a *sunna*, a normative practice to be emulated. The poet al-Mutallamis, for instance, aspired to leave "a *sunna* that will be imitated."[56] Some caliphal practices came to constitute *sunan* since they were viewed as commendable. When ʿIyāḍ b. Ghunm conquered Rahā during ʿUmar I's reign, he was invited to dinner in the city's church by its patriarch, an invitation he immediately refused. His reason for refusal was ʿUmar I's conduct when he visited Jerusalem following the city's conquest: the caliph had turned down a similar invitation from that city's patriarch.[57] For ʿIyāḍ, ʿUmar I's refusal constituted a *sunna*. The concept of *sunna* thus existed before Islam and was clearly associated with the conduct of individuals, and not only with the collective behavior of nations, as is abundantly attested in the Quran.

When the caliphs and proto-*qāḍī*s referred to *sunan*, they were speaking of actions and norms that were regarded as ethically binding but which may have referred to various types of conduct. Such *sunan* may have indicated a specific way of dealing with a case, of the kind that ʿUmar II failed to discover when answering his *qāḍī*'s question about the girl's rape, or ʿUmar I's refusal of the patriarch's invitation. But they could also have constituted, collectively, a general manner of good conduct, such as when it was said (and quite often it was) that "so-and-so governed (or, for a *qāḍī*, 'adjudicated a case') with justice and followed the good *sunna*." The earlier Prophets, as well as Muḥammad, represented a prime source of *sunan*. In a general sense, therefore, *sunan* were not legally binding narratives, but subjective notions of justice that were put to various uses and discursive strategies.

55 Irfan Shahid, *Byzantium and the Arabs in the Fifth Century* (Washington, D.C.: Dumbarton Oaks Research Library and Collection, 1989), 180.

56 M. M. Bravmann, *The Spiritual Background of Early Islam* (Leiden: E. J. Brill, 1972), 139 ff. See also Zafar Ishaq Ansari, "Islamic Juristic Terminology before Šāfiʿī: A Semantic Analysis with Special Reference to Kūfa," *Arabica*, 19 (1972): 255–300, at 259 ff.

57 Abū Muḥammad Aḥmad Ibn Aʿtham, *al-Futūḥ*, 8 vols. (Beirut: Dār al-Kutub al-ʿIlmiyya, 1986), I, 252.

During the first decades of Islam, it became customary to refer to the Prophet's biography and the events in which he was involved as his *sīra*. But while this term indicates a manner of proceeding or a course of action concerning a particular matter, *sunna* describes the manner and course of action as something established, and thus worthy of being imitated.[58] Yet, the Prophet's *sīra*, from the earliest period, constituted a normative, exemplary model, overlapping with notions of his Sunna. At the time of his election as caliph, for instance, ʿUthmān promised to follow "the *sīra* of the Prophet." This phrase in ʿUthmān's oath refers to the personal and specific practice of the Prophet, a practice that is exemplary and thus worth following. It was the violation of this practice that allegedly led to ʿUthmān's assassination. ʿUthmān, an early poem pronounced, violated the established *sunna* (*sunnat man maḍā*), especially the Prophet's *sīra* which he had promised to uphold.[59]

In a meticulous study of the earliest Islamic discourse, Bravmann has convincingly argued that the concepts of *sīra* and *sunna* were largely interchangeable, both possessing the notions of exemplary conduct, with the difference that *sunna* has the added element of an established conduct, rooted in past practice. He has also shown that these concepts refer to personal, individual practices, and not to long-standing, collective customs and practices of uncertain origins.

> *Sunna* (pl. *sunan*) in the early Arab and Islamic conception basically refers to usages and procedures established by certain individuals and not to the anonymous practice of the community. Indeed, "the practice of the community" . . . , which of course exists, is in the Arab conception based on the practices and usages created and established by certain individuals, who acted in such and such a specific way, and hereby – intentionally – instituted a specific practice.[60]

By the caliphate of ʿUthmān (23/644–35/656), the Prophet's *sīra* and Sunna no doubt carried significant weight as exemplary conduct. In fact, evidence suggests that the Sunna of the Prophet emerged immediately after his death, which was to be expected given that many far less significant figures had been seen by the Arabs as having laid down *sunan*. It would be difficult to argue that Muḥammad, the most influential person in the nascent Muslim community, was not regarded as a source of normative practice. In fact, the Quran itself explicitly and repeatedly enjoins believers to obey the Prophet and to emulate his actions. The implications of Quran

[58] Bravmann, *Spiritual Background*, 138–39, 169.
[59] Ibid., 126–29, 160.
[60] Ibid., 167; also at 130, 154–55.

4:80 – "He who obeys the Messenger obeys God"– need hardly be explained. So too Quran 59:7: "Whatsoever the Messenger ordains, you should accept, and whatsoever he forbids, you should abstain from." Many similar verses bid Muslims to obey the Prophet and not to dissent from his ranks.[61] Moreover, Quran 33:21 explicitly states that "in the Messenger of God you [i.e., believers] have a good example." All this indicates that to obey the Prophet was, by definition, to obey God. In establishing his *modus operandi* as exemplary, the Prophet could hardly have received better support than that given to him by the society in which he lived and by the Deity that he was sent to serve.

One of the first attestations of "the Sunna of the Prophet" appears toward the end of ʿUmar I's reign, probably around 20/640. In an address to his army, the Muslim commander Yazīd b. Abī Sufyān declared that he had just received orders from that caliph to head for the Palestinian town of Qīsāriyya in order to take it "and to call the people of that area to the Book of God and the Sunna of his Messenger."[62] Probably in the same year, but certainly before the death of ʿUmar I in 23/644, "the Sunna of the Prophet" and that of Abū Bakr were invoked.[63] Similarly, in 23/644, ʿUthmān and ʿAlī, the two candidates for the caliphate, were asked whether they were prepared to "work according to the Sunna of the Prophet and the *sīra*s of the two preceding caliphs," Abū Bakr and ʿUmar I.[64] During his caliphate, ʿUmar I apparently referred to the decisions of the Prophet in a matter related to meting out punishment for adulterers, and in another in which the Prophet enjoined him to allot distant relatives the shares of inheritance to which they are entitled.[65] Subsequently, the number of references to "the Sunna of the Prophet" increased, frequently with specific mention of concrete things said or done by the Prophet, but at times with no other substantive content than the general meaning of "right and just practice." This is also the connotation attached to many early references to the *sunan* of Abū Bakr, ʿUmar I, ʿUthmān and others. By such references it was meant that these men set a model of good behavior in the most

[61] See, e.g., Quran 3:32, 132; 4:59 (twice), 64, 69, 80; 5:92; 24:54, 56; 33:21; 59:7.

[62] Ibn Aʿtham, *Futūḥ*, I, 244.

[63] Ibid., I, 248.

[64] Ansari, "Islamic Juristic Terminology," 263.

[65] G. H. A. Juynboll, *Muslim Tradition: Studies in Chronology, Provenance and Authorship of Early Ḥadīth* (Cambridge: Cambridge University Press, 1983), 26–27. For other instances in which ʿUmar I refers to the "Sunna of the Prophet," see Ansari, "Islamic Juristic Terminology," 263; Bravmann, *Spiritual Background*, 168–74.

general meaning of the term, not that they necessarily or always laid down specific rulings or ways of dealing with particular issues.

The vitally important issues raised in the Quran represent a portrait of concrete Prophetic Sunna. It would be inconceivable that all these issues, many of which we enumerated in chapter 1, should have been confined to the Quran alone. Matters pertaining to alms-tax, marriage, divorce, inheritance, property and criminal law, among many others, are treated by the Quran in detail and are represented in concrete Sunna.

That the Prophet was associated with a *sunna* very soon after, if not upon, his death cannot be doubted. What is in question therefore is whether or not his Sunna came to constitute an exclusive or even an exceptional source in terms of model behavior. And the answer is that it did not until much later, perhaps as late as the beginning of the third/ninth century. However, the process that ultimately led to the emergence of Prophetic Sunna as an exclusive substitute for *sunan* was a long one, and passed through a number of stages before its final culmination as the second formal source of the law after the Quran. During the first few decades after Muḥammad's death, his Sunna was one among many, however increasingly important it was coming to be. In the hundreds of biographical notices given to the early *qāḍī*s by Muslim historians, it is striking that Prophetic Sunna surfaces relatively infrequently – certainly no more frequently than the *sunan* of Abū Bakr and ʿUmar I.

The second stage of development appears to have begun sometime in the 60s/680s, when a number of *qāḍī*s, among others, began to transmit Prophetic material, technically referred to by the later sources as *ḥadīth*. This activity of transmission is significant because it marks the beginning of a trend in which special attention was paid to the Sunna of the Prophet. It is also significant because it was the only *sunna* to have been sifted out of other *sunan*, and to have been increasingly given an independent status. No religious scholar or *qāḍī* is reported to have studied, collected or narrated the *sunan* of Abū Bakr, for instance; nor that of the more distinguished ʿUmar I. The fact that the Prophet's Sunna acquired an independent and special status is emblematic of the rise of the Prophet's model as embodying legal, not only religious, authority.[66] In fact, the appearance of "The

[66] For distinctions between religious and legal forms of authority, see Wael Hallaq, *Authority, Continuity and Change in Islamic Law* (Cambridge: Cambridge University Press, 2001), ix, 166–235.

Messenger of God" on Umayyad coins of this period points to the rise of other forms of Prophetic authority as well.

Even non-Muslim sources of the period attest to this development. Writing in 687 (68 H), the western Mesopotamian John bar Penkaye speaks of the current problems and issues distracting the Muslims of his day. In the course of his narrative, he depicts the Prophet as a guide and instructor whose tradition the Arabs upheld "to such an extent that they inflicted the death penalty on anyone who was seen to act brazenly against his laws (*nāmōsawh*)."[67] This narrative surely cannot be taken at face value, for it presents the Prophet as a full-fledged legislator, no matter what law was being applied. What John may have been trying to convey was the image that his Muslim sources were seeking to construct of the Prophet. The fact remains, however, that, by at least the sixties of the first century, a Prophetic super-model had begun to emerge.[68]

The isolation of Prophetic Sunna from other *sunan* constituted an unprecedented and a fundamental transformation. It was both the result of a marked growth in the Prophet's authority and the cause of further epistemic and pedagogical developments. Epistemic, because the need to know what the Prophet said or did became increasingly crucial for determining what the law was. In addition to the fact that Prophetic Sunna – like other *sunan* – was already central to the Muslims' perception of model behavior and good conduct, it was gradually realized that this Sunna had an added advantage in that it constituted part of Quranic hermeneutics; to know how the Quran was relevant to a particular case, and how it was to be interpreted, Prophetic verbal and practical discourse, often emulated by the Companions, was needed. And pedagogical, because, in order to maintain a record of what the Prophet said or did, approved or disapproved, certain sources had to be mined, and this information, once collected, needed in turn to be imparted to others as part of the age-old oral tradition of the Arabs, now imbued with a religious element.

Along with the Prophet's Companions, the story-tellers contributed to the crystallization of the first stage of Prophetic dicta. Both of these groups constituted the sources from which the Prophetic biography, in both its real and legendary forms, was derived. At this early stage, however, all Prophetic information was practice-based, oral, fluid and mixed with non-Prophetic material. The story-tellers appear to have spoken of the fates of the Israelites and the Egyptian Pharaohs as much as they spoke of the

[67] Hoyland, *Seeing Islam*, 196–97, 414.

[68] For several non-Muslim sources describing Muḥammad as a law-giver, see ibid., 414.

Prophet himself, for these former were of primary interest to the story-tellers' audience, who saw themselves as victorious chastisers of other nations that have swerved from the Path of God. The story-tellers, in other words, had several and varied interests in propounding Prophetic material, probably little of which, by the seventh decade of the Hijra (680s AD), was of a strictly legal nature.[69]

On the other hand, the men and women who had been close to the Prophet, especially those who had interacted with him on a daily basis, could speak in real and credible terms of details of the Prophet's life. They knew him intimately, and they knew the Quran equally well. These persons, and to a lesser extent the story-tellers, kept the memory of the Prophet alive, and it was these people and the information they stored in their minds and imaginations that became important for another group of Muslims: the legists. This is not to say, however, that the story-tellers and legists were separate groups, since some of the former also belonged to the latter.

It is important to realize that the Muslim leadership, including the caliphs, was acting within a social fabric inherited from tribal Arab society in which forging social consensus before reaching decisions or taking actions was a normative practice. This is one of the most significant facts about the early Muslim state and society. In the spirit of this social consensus, people sought to conform to the group, and to avoid swerving from its will or normative ways, as embodied in a cumulative history of action and specific manners of conduct. What their fathers had done or said was as important as, if not more important than, what their living peers might say or do. When an important decision was to be taken, a precedent, a *sunna*, was nearly always sought. This explains why ʿUmar II, when asked about the aforementioned case in which a girl was raped, answered that nothing "had come down" to him "from past authorities." The caliph, with all his authority and might, *first looked for precedent.* What he was looking for was nothing short of a relevant *sunna* that represented the established way of dealing with the case at hand. It should not then be surprising that the Prophet's own practice was largely rooted in certain practices, mostly those deemed to have fallen within the province of *sunan.*[70]

[69] On the relationship between story-telling and Sunna/*ḥadīth*, see Gregor Schoeler, *Charakter und Authentie der muslimischen Überlieferung über das Leben Mohammeds* (Berlin: W. de Gruyter, 1996), 108, 116 and *passim* (see index, under *quṣṣāṣ*).

[70] A well-studied example is that of "surplus of property." The Prophet is said to have spent the surplus of his personal revenue on the acquisition of equipment for war-like projects, whereas the pre-Islamic Arabs used to spend theirs on charitable and social purposes. ʿUmar I adopted this practice as a Prophetic Sunna. See Bravmann, *Spiritual Background*, 129, 175–77, 229 ff.

Like ʿUmar II, all of the early caliphs, *qāḍīs* and pious men were in search of such *sunan*. The Quran, or at least its major legal provisions, reigned supreme in the hierarchy of authoritative legal sources, a status that it had achieved prior to the Prophet's death. But when the Quran lacked relevant provisions, the natural thing to do was to look for leading models of behavior or a collective conduct dictated by a perception of a good course of action. It was expected therefore that the Prophet's *sīra* should have been the focus of such a search, for he was the most central figure of the Muslim community, the Umma. It was this constant pursuit of a model combined with available Prophetic dicta (accumulated during the first few decades after Muḥammad's death) that explain the emergence by the 60s/680s of a specialized interest in his Sunna.

This is not to say, however, that the Prophetic Sunna replaced, except in a slow and gradual fashion, other sources of authority, or that it was committed to writing at an early date. By this time, Prophetic Sunna was, among the available *sunan*, no more than a *primus inter pares*, used by *qāḍīs* along with the *sunan* of Abū Bakr, ʿUmar I, ʿUthmān, ʿAlī and other Companions. In fact, even during much later periods, reference to non-Prophetic *sunan* was not uncommon. The *sunna* of ʿUmar II, for instance, remained a constant point of reference for more than a century after his death.[71] Furthermore, as we have seen, caliphs and *qāḍīs* alike made reference to *sunan* in a general sense, this being an invocation of fair, just and good conduct, even of the common customary laws of pre-Islamic Arabia. Some of the *sunan*, we may recall, were lacking in concrete subject matter.

Apart from this repertoire of *sunan* and the superior Quran, the *qāḍīs* and caliphs also relied heavily on discretionary opinion, which was, during the entire first Islamic century and part of the next, a major source of legal reasoning and thus of judicial rulings. In section 1 above, we detailed a number of examples illustrative of the operation of this sort of thinking. Another example of discretionary opinion was the positing of a minimal rule of evidence, such as the acceptance of the testimony of one man and two women in cases of divorce. This rule of procedure was applied by Iyās b. Muʿāwiya, for instance. However, the latter's contemporary, the *qāḍī* ʿAdī b. Arṭaʾa, refused to allow women's testimony in divorce, and, when

[71] ʿUmar II's "model behavior" was the basis for the later designation "Renewer of the Second Century," a title bestowed on the most prominent scholars of Islam. ʿUmar II was the only caliph (and in a sense non-scholar) to receive this title. See Ella Landau-Tasseron, "The Cyclical Reform: A Study of the *Mujaddid* Tradition," *Studia Islamica*, 70 (1989): 79–117; Wakīʿ, *Akhbār*, III, 8, 33.

he heard that Iyās had done so, he wrote to ʿUmar II asking for an authoritative ruling on this procedural matter. ʿUmar II pronounced Iyās mistaken, upholding ʿAdī's practice.[72] Iyās is also reported to have disallowed the marriage of young women with undersized heads; for this, he thought, was an indication that such women had not reached full mental capacity.[73] In the case of a man who caused another man's slave to lose his arm, Iyās ruled that the ownership of the slave be transferred to the defendant, although the latter had to pay the equivalent of slave's value to the original owner, presumably the plaintiff.[74]

Discretionary opinion, however, included other elements, not all of which were based on personal reasoning, as illustrated by the cases adjudicated by Iyās. Around 65/684, Shurayḥ was asked by another *qāḍī*, Hishām b. Hubayra, about the value of criminal damages for causing the loss of any of the hand's five fingers, and in particular whether or not they are of equal value. Shurayḥ answered: "I have not heard from any one of the people of *raʾy* that any of the fingers is better than the other."[75] Here, "the people of *raʾy*" are persons whose judgment and wisdom is to be trusted and, more importantly, emulated. In Shurayḥ's usage, *raʾy*, or discretionary opinion, comes very close to the notion of *sunna* – from which, in this case, *raʾy* cannot in fact be separated.

From the very beginning, *raʾy* stood as the technical and terminological counterpart of *ʿilm*, which referred to matters whose settlement could be based on established norms that one could invoke from the past. *Raʾy*, on the other hand, required the application of new norms or procedures, with or without reference to past experience or model behavior. While both might apply to social, personal, legal and quasi-legal matters, they stood distinct from each other. With regard to a military issue, the commander ʿAmr b. al-ʿĀṣṣ was prepared – around the year 20/640 – to act on the basis of norms derived analogically from situations in the past, but refused to make use of his own *raʾy* on that very question. In another situation, ʿUmar I called upon his advisors to give him their counsel on the basis of both their *ʿilm* and *raʾy*.[76] In both cases, *ʿilm* reflected knowledge of past experience – what we might call an authority-statement. At this juncture, it is instructive to note that with the gradual metamorphosis of the content

[72] Wakīʿ, *Akhbār*, I, 330.
[73] Ibid., I, 356.
[74] Ibid., I, 335.
[75] Ibid., I, 299.
[76] Bravmann, *Spiritual Background*, 178, 184.

of past, secular experience into a Prophetic and religious narrative, authority-statements became gradually less secular, acquiring an increasingly religious meaning. This metamorphosis is evidenced in the absorption of pre-Islamic customary and other practices into caliphal and Prophetic *sunan*; the latter would emerge more than two centuries later as the exclusive body of authority-statements.

Yet, inasmuch as *ra'y* was at times dependent on *'ilm*, so was *ijtihād*, a concept akin to *ra'y*. *Ijtihād*, from the very beginning, signified an intellectual quality supplementing *'ilm*, namely, the knowledge of traditional practice and the ability to deduce from it, through *ra'y*, a solution.[77] It is no coincidence therefore that the combination *ijtihād al-ra'y* was of frequent use, signaling the exertion of *ra'y* on the basis of *'ilm*, knowledge of the authoritative past.

Technically, *'ilm*, *ra'y* and *ijtihād* were interconnected and at times overlapping. So were the concepts of *ra'y* and derivatives of *ijmā'*, consensus, a concept that was to acquire central importance in later legal thought. The notion of consensus met *ra'y* when the latter emanated from a group or from a collective tribal agreement. Consensual opinion of a group (*ijtama'a ra'yuhum 'alā* . . .) not only provided an authoritative basis for action but also for the creation of *sunan*. A new *sunna* might thus be introduced by a caliph on the basis of a unanimous resolution of a (usually influential) group of people. Other forms of consensus might reflect the common, unanimous practice of a community, originally of a tribe and later of a garrison town or a city.

4. CONCLUSIONS

Whatever "law" existed during the first few decades after the Prophet's death, it was restricted in application to the garrison towns of the Arab conquerors and to the sedentary towns and agricultural oases of the Hejaz, the only territories that came under the direct control of the early caliphs. The tribal nomads of the Peninsula, on the other hand, were not subjected to such control, while the conquered populations were deliberately left to govern themselves by their own denominational laws and canons. (This picture was to persist throughout later centuries, when the Bedouin populations of the Near Eastern deserts and the Atlas mountains of North Africa, among others, remained largely outside the purview of Islamic

[77] Ibid., 186–88.

law; so did the Christian and Jewish minorities, the unconverted remnants of the conquered populations.)

The new leadership of the Islamic state realized the importance of the policy of religious indoctrination, which they viewed as essential to achieving unity among the unruly tribal Arabs engaged in the conquests. Booty alone could not appease them for long, and the need was felt – especially during the caliphate of ʿUmar I – for implanting a religious (Islamic) ethic that had earlier been the driving force among the Prophet's supporters. Rallying around the cause of Islam meant the propagation of the Quranic ethic, at that time the only ideological tool of the new military and religious state. To this end, the early caliphs built mosques in each garrison town, and deployed Quranic teachers who enhanced the military commanders' religious program already in place. Private and public preachers whose function overlapped with that of the story-tellers and the commanders, were as much part of this religious deployment as the *qāḍī*s were. The religious activities of the commanders, the Quranic teachers, story-tellers, preachers and *qāḍī*s all combined to propagate an Islamic religious ethic and instill it in the hearts and minds of the new Muslims. In all of this, the Quran was again the most fundamental and pervasive element, whose spirit – if not yet letter – was totally, or near totally, controlling. In this sense, Islamic law as Quranic law existed from the very beginning of Islam, during the Prophet's lifetime and after his death.[78]

The first *qāḍī*s were appointed exclusively to the garrison towns where they acted as arbitrators, judges and administrators. Their role was in part a continuation of the pre-Islamic tribal practice of arbitration, since many of them had earlier functioned in that capacity, and the Arab tribes that fell under their jurisdiction were accustomed to this type of conflict resolution. These proto-*qāḍī*s applied Quranic law in conjunction with an amalgam of other laws derived from model behavior (*sunan*), customary Arabian practices, caliphal decrees and their own discretionary opinion. But these were not distinct categories, for Arabian customs were often based on what was perceived as *sunan*, and these latter at times represented the practices of the caliphs, of the Prophet himself and of his influential Companions. At

[78] This assertion is made having duly taken note of such writings as those of Schacht, *Origins*; P. Crone, "Two Legal Problems Bearing on the Early History of the Qurʾān," *Jerusalem Studies in Arabic and Islam*, 18 (1994): 1–37; J. Burton, *The Collection of the Qurʾān* (Cambridge: Cambridge University Press, 1971); J. Wansbrough, *Qurʾānic Studies* (Oxford: Oxford University Press, 1977); J. Wansbrough, *The Sectarian Milieu* (Oxford: Oxford University Press, 1978). Cf., in this regard, J. Brockopp, *Early Mālikī Law: Ibn ʿAbd al-Ḥakam and his Major Compendium of Jurisprudence* (Leiden: Brill, 2000), 123, n. 22.

other times, these customs were the normative ways of Arabian life, dictated by social consensus and/or the exemplary behavior of charismatic leadership. Even discretionary opinion (*ra'y*) was often based on *sunan*, given expression by the conduct or opinion of *ahl al-ra'y* who (to put it tautologically) at times fashioned the *sunan*.

During the half century following Muḥammad's death, Prophetic Sunna (based in part on his *sīra*) was only one of several types of *sunan* that constituted an authoritative legal source for *qāḍī*s, although it certainly gained increasing importance during this period. Thus, far from possessing the status of the exclusive sunnaic source of legal behavior that it would later acquire, there is no indication that it was distinguished from the other *sunan* during this period, although in stature it may have been more prestigious. This situation was to change soon, however. Beginning in the 60s/680s, many *qāḍī*s and learned men began to recount Prophetic biography as a separate oral genre, distinguished from the *sunan* of Abū Bakr, ʿUmar I and others. The beginnings of specialization in what gradually came to be an independent field of knowledge marked the rudimentary beginnings of a fundamental transformation that culminated in Prophetic Sunna as the exclusive source of *sunan*-based law, steadily pushing aside the other *sunan* and finally replacing them almost completely some two centuries later. Meanwhile, between the early 60s/680s and the late 80s/700s, there was a noticeable shift toward the adoption of Prophetic Sunna, although other sources, including caliphal authority, non-Prophetic *sunan*, and discretionary opinion continued to share the landscape of the world of the *qāḍī*s' and legally minded scholars.

CHAPTER 3

The early judges, legal specialists and the search for religious authority

I. THE EARLY JUDGES

In the previous chapter, we saw that the proto-*qāḍī*'s office was not limited to resolving legal disputes and that it involved other activities related to tribal arbitration, financial administration, story-telling and policing. These were normative functions in *qāḍīs*' appointments down to the 80s/700s and even 90s/710s.[1] Whatever change this office subsequently underwent was by no means sudden. From the ninth decade of the Hijra, the *qāḍī*'s office increasingly was limited to conflict resolution and legal administration. From this point on, some *qāḍīs* were appointed *qua qāḍīs*, with no explicit stipulation of other duties that they should undertake. In fact, the distinctness of these duties and functions was made obvious by the nature of appointments. Thus, when ʿAbd al-Raḥmān al-Jayshānī was dismissed from his function as judge of Egypt sometime during the 130s/750s, he was immediately reappointed there as a tax-collector.[2] The expansion and growing complexity of state functions appear to have required a narrowing down of the duties assigned to officials. However, these appointments seem to have been relatively few in number and for a few decades thereafter many judges continued to combine this office with other functions.[3]

The centralization of Umayyad legal administration appears to have begun during the last years of the first century H, a policy that marked a change in the nature of judicial appointments. Sulaymān b. ʿAbd al-Malik (r. 96/714–99/717) seems to have been the first caliph to appoint judges directly from Damascus, thereby initiating the policy of removing from local governors the authority to make such appointments.[4] ʿIyāḍ b. ʿUbayd

[1] Kindī, *Akhbār*, 322, 324, 325, 327, 332, 348 and *passim*.

[2] Wakīʿ, *Akhbār*, III, 232.

[3] Kindī, *Akhbār*, 322, 324 and *passim*.

[4] Bligh-Abramsky, "Judiciary," 57–58, assigns the first caliphal appointment to the time of al-Manṣūr (r. 136/754–58/75). See next note.

Allāh al-Azdī appears to have been the first to receive such an appointment in 98/716, and a year or so later his post was renewed by Sulaymān's successor, the caliph ʿUmar II.[5] Thereafter, and until the fall of the Umayyad dynasty, most judges were appointed directly by the caliphs.[6] This change in policy partly reflected the coming to maturity of centralization policies and partly a change in the scope of the judges' functions, especially the gradual removal from their purview of non-judicial, administrative tasks. It also reflected the growing awareness of a separate province of law distinct from other administrative functions – a province that was gradually acquiring an independent status. Although the appointments that marked an independent judiciary did not become the norm until the middle of the second/eighth century, the beginnings of this process must be located during the 90s/710s.

By this time, law had begun to acquire its own independent character – separate from tribal arbitration[7] and financial and police administration – and its application was to spread to other towns as well as to non-Muslims. After the third quarter of the first century H, judges began to be appointed to such towns as Alexandria in Egypt and Ḥimṣ in Syria, and to large cities in the former Sasanid world, primarily Khurāsān. This legal expansion mirrored a collateral demographic movement that saw the Arabs relocate from the chief garrison towns to the smaller cities and towns previously inhabited exclusively by non-Muslims (and frequently by non-Arabs). The penetration of this Muslim population into the conquered cities brought the new masters into direct contact with Christians (who were mostly Arabs), Jews and people of other faiths. Inevitably, legal disputes arose in the midst of these mixed communities, and many of these (including all those involving Muslims) were brought before Muslim judges. It is reported of the Egyptian judge Khayr b. Nuʿaym, for instance, that once he finished presiding over cases brought to him by Muslims, he would move his court session out to the gate of the mosque in order to adjudicate disputes between Christians (whom we may assume to have been Copts).[8]

[5] Kindī, *Akhbār*, 333, 335–36. Bligh-Abramsky (see citation in previous note) apparently overlooked this account of Kindī, and instead adopted his later account (p. 368) which makes ʿAbd Allāh b. Lahīʿa the first judge to be appointed by a caliph, in 155/771.

[6] Kindī, *Akhbār*, 340.

[7] During his tenure between 115/733 and 120/737, the Egyptian judge Tawba b. Nimr apparently refused to interfere in tribal disputes. It is reported that he sent all such disputes back to the chiefs of the tribes for arbitration: Kindī, *Akhbār*, 345–46. This certainly was part of the proto-*qāḍī*'s jurisdiction, as it represented a continuity of the practices of *ḥakam*, the pre-Islamic arbiter.

[8] Kindī, *Akhbār*, 351. Khayr b. Nuʿaym held the judgeship between 120/737 and 127/744.

The gradual specialization of the function of *qaḍāʾ* and the growing complexity of this function led to developments within the *qāḍī*'s court (*majlis*). At this juncture, it is important to note in passing that the *majlis al-qaḍāʾ* – the equivalent of a law court in the West – revolved around the figure of the judge, so that the court structure was an extension of his functions and judicial personality. In the West (both continental and common law systems), the court, comparatively speaking, has tended to be less dependent on the judge. Physically, the courtroom or courthouse in the West is a structure specifically designated for holding the public sessions of a court, with its various offices. The court, in other words, is the combined phenomenon of magistrate and building occupied and appropriated according to the law for the holding of trials.[9] The Muslim *qāḍī*, by contrast, had no specific place in which to conduct his sessions, a situation that was to persist in Islam for nearly a millennium.[10] Hence, the *majlis al-qaḍāʾ*[11] was frequently held in the mosque, but also at the *qāḍī*'s private residence, in the marketplace and even in public streets.[12]

One of the earliest developments in the *qāḍī*'s court was the keeping of minutes and the registration of legal transactions. The rudimentary beginnings of this practice appear to have been around the 50s/670s, reportedly because the judges' rulings were either forgotten or misconstrued by the parties to litigation. But it is also likely that such practices were already normative in the courts of the communities conquered by Muslims, and that these practices were quickly adopted by the first Muslim judges. For instance, sometime before 60/679, Sulaym b. ʿItr is said to have been the first judge (at least in Egypt) to keep a record of his rulings, or a part thereof. He is supposed to have begun the practice after resolving a dispute among heirs to an estate over the wording of his ruling in their case. When the parties to the dispute reappeared in his *majlis* seeking to establish the precise nature of the decision he had rendered earlier, he wrote down a summary of the ruling and had the military commander attest to it.[13] It is unlikely, however, that Sulaym or any other contemporary judge made the recording of court minutes a regular or systematic practice. Nor were the records themselves particularly detailed or complete. Sometime after

[9] *Black's Law Dictionary*, 5th ed. (St Paul: West Publishing Co. 1979), 320.

[10] Wael Hallaq, "The *Qāḍī*'s *Dīwān* (*sijill*) before the Ottomans," *Bulletin of the School of Oriental and African Studies*, 61, 3 (1998): 415–36, at 418.

[11] Literally, *majlis* means a place where one sits. *Majlis al-qaḍāʾ* means the place where the activity of *qaḍāʾ*, whose agent is the judge, transpires. By extension, it is the place where the judge sits.

[12] Wakīʿ, *Akhbār*, I, 339, 341; II, 316.

[13] Kindī, *Akhbār*, 309–10.

86/705, ʿAbd al-Raḥmān b. Khadīj began the practice of recording orphans' pensions in "a book he had,"[14] which suggests that such matters were not registered prior to that time. Expectedly, Ibn Khadīj's practice does not seem to have been thorough enough, for we know that Khayr b. Nuʿaym improved on it some five decades later.[15] To be sure, the judge's register, properly known as a *dīwān*, continued to develop until the end of the second/eighth century, when it seems to have taken a final shape. But the intermittent beginnings of this process can be traced to the third quarter of the first century (ca. 670–95 AD), and acquired a sort of normative status during the fourth, when *qāḍā*ʾ began to be defined as a specifically legal institution.

The second significant development was the evolution of a court staff, the members of which aided the judge in one way or another. By the end of the first century, it appears that the court sheriff (*jilwāz*), whose function was to keep order in the courtroom, had already become an established functionary.[16] It is highly likely that this function originated concomitantly with the proto-*qāḍī*s, who were often appointed as chiefs of police and thus possessed the power to retain policing personnel to serve them in maintaining order. And if this is the case, we can assume that the *jilwāz*'s function dates back to the middle of the first century (ca. 670 AD), if not earlier.

Likewise, toward the end of the first century – and probably shortly before – the function of the court scribe emerged, as was to be expected; the need to keep written records of court business and legal transactions made such a post imperative. And although, as we have seen, some early judges had themselves begun taking notes of decisions, it was not a task that they retained, especially as the business of the court grew in complexity. Most judges therefore had one scribe (*kātib*), but some had more, depending on how busy the court was. Our sources report that the Egyptian judge Yaḥyā b. Maymūn had three scribes and possibly more.[17]

The court scribes also issued documents on behalf of the judge to litigants, usually attesting to a right or a transaction (e.g. a verdict in favor of X, or the purchase of a house by Y). It appears that the scribes themselves used their position as a springboard to higher jobs (and continued to do so for centuries to come), especially *qāḍā*ʾ; Thus, the

14 Ibid., 325.
15 Ibid., 355.
16 Wakīʿ, *Akhbār*, II, 417.
17 Kindī, *Akhbār*, 340.

young Saʿīd b. Jubayr, a scribe serving the Kūfan *qāḍī* ʿAbd Allāh b. ʿUtba around 95/713, later became a judge himself.[18] Being a scribe appears to have been, from the very beginning, part of the apprenticeship required for *qāḍāʾ*.

The practice of witnesses giving testimony, among other things, to adjudication procedure and documentary evidence was an ancient institution,[19] and it was natural that witnesses became a feature of the court. Each judge appointed a number of these for such purposes, delegating to them as well the task of signing court minutes at the end of each litigation. Known as court witnesses (later called *shuhūd ḥāl*), they were distinct from witnesses procured by the plaintiff or defendant to attest in favor of a fact or a claim. These latter, generally known as *shuhūd ʿayān*, had been used in conflict resolution since Prophetic times. Nonetheless, even as late as the third decade of the second century (ca. 740 AD), the procedural law concerning this type of witness had not yet been fully developed. For example, in court cases of a similar nature tried at about this time, most judges appear to have accepted a claim on the basis of a single witness, while only some insisted upon two. Yet it was the latter that became the normative procedure in later Islamic law.[20]

If witnesses and scribes became part of the courtroom apparatus, then it is not surprising that written communication between judges (known in later times as *kitāb al-qāḍī ilā al-qāḍī*) became, by 100/718, a fairly established practice.[21] This communication – duly attested to, and conveyed, by court witnesses – took place when a judge in a particular locale wrote to a judge in another jurisdiction concerning a person's right that he, the first judge, was able to establish against another person. The idea was that the receiving judge would apply the effects of the communication in his jurisdiction. Although we cannot confirm the exact procedures followed in the early phases of this practice, it is unlikely that they conformed to the strict requirements of attestation that later became the norm. Legal institutions of this sort were still evolving, as evidenced by the fact that the rules of procedure in this area were not yet settled. However, by the 140s/760s, it appears that some judges began to insist that all written instruments between and among *qāḍī*s be attested by witnesses. The Kūfan judge Ibn

[18] Shams al-Dīn Aḥmad Ibn Khallikān, *Wafayāt al-Aʿyān*, 4 vols. (Beirut: Dār Iḥyāʾ al-Turāth al-ʿArabī, 1417/1997), I, 367.

[19] Attested in Quran 2:282.

[20] Kindī, *Akhbār*, 346; Wakīʿ, *Akhbār*, I, 145–46, 287.

[21] Wakīʿ, *Akhbār*, II, 11, 12; see also Wael B. Hallaq, "*Qāḍī*s Communicating: Legal Change and the Law of Documentary Evidence," *al-Qanṭara*, 20, 2 (1999), 437–66.

Abī Laylā is said to have been one of the earliest judges to follow such procedures, a practice that the Baṣran judge Sawwār b. ʿAbd Allāh adopted soon thereafter.[22]

The increasing specialization of the judge's office manifested itself in the growing dependence of the *qāḍī* upon legal specialists who made it their concern to study the law and all emerging disciplines with which it was associated. The first signs of the tenet that the judge should consult legal experts (a tenet that was to become the basis of practice throughout much of Islamic legal history) seems to have emerged during the last decade of the first century (ca. 715 AD).[23] This assertion is based upon two considerations. First, by this time (as we shall see momentarily), a class of legal experts was already on the rise. Second, there existed even then a distinction, albeit vague, between the judges and the legal specialists who would later be called *muftī*s (jurisconsults). The legal specialists were, by definition, knowledgeable in the law as a substantive and technical discipline, which was not necessarily the case with the judges. For while some judges were known for their expertise in the law – since they themselves came from the circles of legal specialists – many others were not. For example, the Egyptian judge Ghawth b. Sulaymān is said to have been a shrewd and seasoned *qāḍī* (i.e., he understood people and was highly skilled as a conflict mediator) but to have lacked a mastery of law as a technical discipline.[24] It was thus natural and far from uncommon for a provincial governor or a caliph to enquire, prior to making a judicial appointment, whether a candidate was a legal specialist or not.[25] In a nutshell, the judge's knowledge of the law as a technical legal discipline was not yet taken for granted.

Indeed, by the end of the first century it was no longer possible to employ illiterate judges, for the growing complexity of social and economic life made it necessary to appoint men who could resolve intricate disputes successfully and who could apply the law as elaborated by the legal specialists. Furthermore, with the gradual rise of the class of legally minded scholars, a more educated group of men was available to fill a variety of state functions, including *qaḍā*ʾ. But this did not mean that they always had to be legal experts. (Even in much later times, when law became a professional discipline, *qāḍī*s *qua qāḍī*s were, as a rule, never associated with the

22 Wakīʿ, *Akhbār*, II, 67.
23 Ibid., II, 415, 423.
24 Kindī, *Akhbār*, 357–58.
25 See, e.g., ibid., 364.

best legal minds or even first-rate expertise in law and jurisprudence.)[26] We have seen that they were, and long continued to be, state functionaries whose involvement with the law remained provisional, occupied as they were with other non-legal functions.

2. THE LEGAL SPECIALISTS EMERGE

The locus of legal expertise, therefore, was not the *qāḍīs*, but rather a group of private individuals whose motivation to engage in the study of law was largely a matter of piety. While it is true that a number of these did serve as *qāḍīs*, their study of the law was not necessarily associated with this office or with benefits or patronage accruing therefrom. Nor was it – in this early period – associated with a search for career opportunities in government, accumulation of wealth, or any form of worldly power. Rather, they were driven above all by a profoundly religious commitment which demanded of them, among other things, the articulation of a law that would deal with all the problems of society.

The rudiments of legal scholarship appear to have developed within the generation that flourished between 80 and 120 H (roughly between 700 and 740 AD). This is not to say of course that Islamic law as a nascent religious system began to surface only at that point. We have seen that the Quran – as a spiritual and legal guide – was of central importance from the very beginning and that caliphal law also acquired a religious sanctity by virtue of the fact that the caliphs were God's and Muḥammad's deputies on Earth. Added to this was the steady infusion into *sunan* of a pronounced religious element. Yet, what was different about this period was the emergence of a new activity, namely, personal study of religious narratives and the evolution of specialized circles of learning, properly known as the *ḥalaqa* (lit. circle; pl. *ḥalaqāt*).

Private study was not dissociated from the activity that took place in the *ḥalaqa*, for one appears to have complemented the other. Private study prepared one for the often intense debates that went on in the *ḥalaqa*, and this latter activity must have challenged the minds of the learned and encouraged their individual pursuit of knowledge. The *ḥalaqa* was usually held in the mosque, which had served as a place of public discussion and instruction since the first two or three decades of Islam. It may well have developed out of the activity of story-tellers, especially those who focused

26 Hallaq, *Authority*, 167–74.

their attention on Quranic exegesis, Prophetic *sīra* and proper conduct or religious service. Some *ḥalaqa*s were exclusively concerned with Quranic interpretation, while others were occupied with Prophetic narrative (emerging later as Prophetic Sunna). But some *ḥalaqa*s were of an exclusively legal nature. During the opening decade of the second century H, Abū ʿAbd Allāh Muslim b. Yasār, one of the most distinguished legal specialists of Baṣra, regularly held a legal *ḥalaqa* in that city's grand mosque.[27] In Kūfa, ʿĀmir al-Shaʿbī (d. 110/728), also a distinguished legist, is reported to have had an enormous *ḥalaqa*.[28] So did Ḥammād b. Abī Sulaymān (d. 120/737), another distinguished Kūfan authority.[29] We are told that as many as forty students and learned men regularly attended the circle of the Medinese legist Rabīʿa b. Abī ʿAbd al-Raḥmān (otherwise known as Rabīʿat al-Raʾy; d. 136/753).[30] In Medina too ʿAṭāʾ b. Abī Rabāḥ, Nāfiʿ (d. 118/736) and ʿAmr b. Dīnār had their own circles of study in which there participated a number of legists who came to prominence during the next generation.[31] Equally important were small mosque gatherings of scholars who would exchange religious ideas related to the Quran and matters legal. We know, for example, of the famous discussions that took place among Qatāda b. Diʿāma al-Sadūsī (d. 117/735), Saʿīd b. al-Musayyab (d. 94/712 or 105/723) and al-Ḥasan al-Baṣrī (d. 110/728).[32] Sometime around 120/737, another small group of prominent specialists is reported to have held legal discussions that frequently lasted until the early hours of the morning.[33] Similarly, the leading legal specialists of Medina – including Saʿīd b. al-Musayyab, al-Qāsim b. Muḥammad, Khārija, Sulaymān b. Yasār and ʿUrwa – are said to have met regularly to discuss the legal issues of the day, issues that also faced the Medinese judges in their courts.[34]

During the period in question, the eminent legal specialists conducted their activities in the major centers of the new empire, namely, Medina, Mecca, Kūfa, Baṣra, Damascus, Fusṭāṭ, Yemen and, marginally, Khurāsān. A statistical survey of an important early biographical work dedicated to jurists reveals that these centers of legal scholarship generated eighty-four

[27] Shīrāzī, *Ṭabaqāt*, 88.

[28] Wakīʿ, *Akhbār*, II, 421.

[29] I. Goldziher, *The Ẓāhirīs: Their Doctrine and their History*, trans. Wolfgang Behn (Leiden: E. J. Brill, 1971), 13, on the authority of Dhahabī's *Ṭabaqāt al-Ḥuffāẓ*.

[30] Shīrāzī, *Ṭabaqāt*, 65; Ibn Khallikān, *Wafayāt*, I, 330.

[31] Harald Motzki, "Der Fiqh des–Zuhrī: die Quellenproblematik," *Der Islam*, 68, 1 (1991): 1–44, at 14, and sources cited therein.

[32] Ibn Ḥibbān, *Thiqāt*, 222.

[33] Wakīʿ, *Akhbār*, III, 79.

[34] Dutton, *Origins*, 13.

towering figures who are considered the elite of the legally minded in the Islamic tradition. Their distribution between the above centers was as follows: twenty-two from Medina (26.2 percent); twenty from Kūfa (23.8 percent); seventeen from Baṣra (20.2 percent); nine from Syria (10.7 percent); seven from Mecca (8.3 percent); five from Yemen (6 percent); three from Egypt (3.5 percent); and one from Khurāsān (1.2 percent).[35] The Hejaz and Iraq, therefore, could claim the lion's share of this pool of talent, generating close to 70 percent of the entire body of legal scholarship, and close to 80 percent, if we include the Yemen. Syria generally occupied a secondary position, while Fusṭāṭ and Khurāsān were of marginal importance. It would not be inaccurate, therefore, to assert that the early rise of legal scholarship took place where the Arabs, together with their Arabicized clients, constituted a significant proportion of the population.[36]

Among Medina's chief legal specialists were Qāsim b. Muḥammad, Sulaymān b. Yasār (both d. ca. 110/728), Saʿīd b. al-Musayyab, ʿAbd al-Malik b. Marwān, Qabīṣa b. Dhuʾayb, ʿUrwa b. al-Zubayr (d. 94/712), Abū Bakr b. ʿAbd al-Raḥmān (d. 94/712), ʿAbd Allāh b. ʿUtba (98/716), Khārija b. Zayd (d. 99/717) and Rabīʿat al-Raʾy.[37] In Mecca, they were ʿAṭāʾ b. Abī Rabāḥ (d. 105/723), Mujāhid b. Jabr (d. between 100/718 and 104/722), ʿAmr b. Dīnār (d. 126/743) and ʿIkrima (d. 115/733).[38] In Kūfa, they were Saʿīd b. Jubayr (d. 95/713), ʿĀmir al-Shaʿbī, Ibrāhīm al-Nakhaʿī (d. 96/714) and Ḥammād b. Abī Sulaymān (d. 120/737).[39] In Baṣra, they were Muḥammad b. Sīrīn (d. 110/728), Abū ʿAbd Allāh Muslim b. Yasār, Qatāda b. Diʿāma and Abū Ayyūb al-Sakhtiyānī (d. 131/748).[40] In Syria and Yemen, they were Makḥūl (d. 113/731 or 118/736) and Ṭāwūs (d. 106/724), respectively.[41]

These men are acknowledged in the sources as having excelled in law, but not yet in jurisprudence as a theoretical study – a discipline that was to develop much later. Some of them possessed a special mastery of Quranic law, especially inheritance, while others were known for their outstanding competence in ritual law. ʿAṭāʾ b. Abī Rabāḥ, of Mecca, for instance, seems to have had remarkable expertise in the latter, and was able to issue

35 Shīrāzī, *Ṭabaqāt*, 54–94.
36 For more on this, see H. Motzki, "The Role of Non-Arab Converts in the Development of Early Islamic Law," *Islamic Law and Society*, 6, 3 (1999): 293–317.
37 Ibn Ḥibbān, *Thiqāt*, 59, 65, 80, 90, 146; Shīrāzī, *Ṭabaqāt*, 58, 59, 60, 62, 65.
38 Shīrāzī, *Ṭabaqāt*, 69–71; Ibn Ḥibbān, *Thiqāt*, 189–90.
39 Shīrāzī, *Ṭabaqāt*, 81–84.
40 Ibid., 88–89.
41 Ibid., 73, 75; Dimashqī, *Tārīkh*, I, 245.

trustworthy opinions (*fatwās*) on such matters.[42] The Medinan Khārija b. Zayd, on the other hand, achieved a reputation for his expertise in the law of inheritance, as well as for his notarial skills. He is described as having developed proficient knowledge in "writing documents for people," and his legal opinions are reported to have been most reliable.[43] Others, first and foremost Shaʿbī of Kūfa, developed what seems to have been exceptional knowledge of legal precedent. Shaʿbī is reported to have gained unmatched knowledge of *sunan māḍiya*, the model and authoritative conduct of leading men of the past.[44] These *sunan*, as we have seen, constituted one of the chief sources of the law, and continued to do so for more than a century after Shaʿbī's death.

By virtue of their pedagogical activities, these men of learning initiated what was to become a fundamental feature of Islamic law, namely, that legal knowledge as an *epistemic* quality was to be the final arbiter in law making. The learned were thought to know best what the law was, for soon this emerging doctrine had its own justification. Working with the law, even with quasi-legal matters, began to emerge for the first time as a textual activity, not merely as a matter of practice. This textual activity belonged to the generation described above, whose scholarly endeavor was concentrated in the last two decades of the first century and the first two of the second (700–35 AD). It is this gradual textualization of law, legal knowledge and legal practice that should be seen as the first major development in the production of permanent forms that were to survive into, and contribute to, the further formation of later Islamic law.

As noted, the activity of collecting the Quran had a primary legal significance, for it defined the subject matter of the text and thus gave the legal specialists a *textus receptus* upon which to draw. Of immediate concern to these men were certain passages that bore on the same issues but that seemed mutually contradictory. Their attempts to harmonize such Quranic texts marked the rudimentary beginnings of the theory of abrogation (*naskh*), a theory that later stood at the center of legal hermeneutics. The primary concern was with neither theology nor dogma, but rather with

42 Ibn Ḥibbān, *Thiqāt*, 189–90; Shīrāzī, *Ṭabaqāt*, 69.

43 Shīrāzī, *Ṭabaqāt*, 60. On others writing documents at this time, see Ibn Ḥibbān, *Thiqāt*, 122, 199, 241; Ibn Ḥibbān, *Mashāhīr*, 113, 124, 133, 135, 136, 141, and *passim*. Also Hoyland, *Seeing Islam*, 687–703. In a terse but revealing statement, Dimashqī, *Tārīkh*, I, 243, reports, on the authority of Yazīd b. ʿAbd Rabbih, that the latter had read in an army stipend ledger (*dīwān al-ʿaṭāʾ*) that a certain Ibn Miʿdān and someone known as Ibn ʿAdī both died in 104/722. This statement attests to the survival of *dīwāns* for more than a century after they had come into existence.

44 Shīrāzī, *Ṭabaqāt*, 81; Ibn Khallikān, *Wafayāt*, II, 6–8.

the actions through which Muslims could realize obedience to their God, in adherence to the Quranic command. Thus it was felt necessary to determine the Quranic stand on particular issues. When more than one Quranic decree was pertinent to a single matter, such a determination was no easy task. To solve such difficulties, it was essential to determine the chronological order in which different verses had been revealed. Generally speaking, the provisions of later verses were thought to supersede those of earlier, contradictory ones.

Although the Prophet's Companions and their younger contemporaries were reportedly involved in initiating such discussions, Muslim sources make relatively few references to their contributions to this textual activity. It was the generation that flourished roughly between 80 and 120 (ca. 700–35 AD) that was most closely associated with discussions on abrogation and with controversies about the status of particular verses. Nakhaʿī, Muslim b. Yasār (d. 101/719), Mujāhid b. Jabr (d. between 100/718 and 104/722) and al-Ḥasan al-Baṣrī (d. 110/728) were among the most prominent in this debate.[45] Qatāda b. Diʿāma al-Sadūsī and Shihāb al-Zuhrī (d. 124/742) are also associated with writings that attest to the beginning of a theory of abrogation, a theory that by then had already been articulated in a rudimentary literary form.[46] It is likely that this theory developed in a context where the provisions of some verses contradicted the actual practice of the community, thus giving rise to the need for interpreting away, or canceling out, the legal effect of those verses deemed inconsistent with other verses more in line with prevailing customs. However the case may be, the very nature of this theory suggests that whatever contradiction or problem needed to be resolved, this was to be done within the purview of Quranic authority. It was generally accepted as an overriding principle that nothing can repeal the word of God except another word from the same source.

The authority of the Quran extended itself to nearly all areas of Muslim life, including the administrative regulations of the caliphs. Whenever the Divine Text was held to express a rule or a law on any particular matter, the caliphs generally followed that rule without qualifications and enacted further regulations in compliance with the spirit, if not always the letter,

45 David S. Powers, "The Exegetical Genre *Nāsikh al-Qurʾān wa-Mansūkhuh*," in Andrew Rippin, ed., *Approaches to the History of the Interpretation of the Qurʾān* (Oxford: Clarendon Press, 1988), 117–38, at 119.

46 Andrew Rippin, "al-Zuhrī, *Naskh al-Qurʾān* and the Early *Tafsīr* Texts," *Bulletin of the School of Oriental and African Studies*, 47 (1984): 22–43, at 22 ff.; Ibn Ḥibbān, *Thiqāt*, 222.

of the Quran. We have seen that the caliphs not only promulgated laws and regulations enforceable in both the capital and the provinces, but also presented themselves as a (mediating) source of law for the proto-*qāḍīs* as well as for the judges of the turn of the century. Seeking the caliph's opinion on difficult cases was and continued to be a frequent practice of judges at least to the middle of the Umayyad period (with a marked decrease thereafter). This practice, however, was in no way insulated from the rising tide of legal thinking and the articulation of juristic doctrine that was developing within the circles of legal specialists whom, in turn, the caliphs themselves consulted. Caliphal law, like Companions' and Successors' law, was subjected to their scrutiny, for it now had to conform to the evolving systematization of legal doctrine and thought. Seen as deriving from the authority of the Companions (including the first four caliphs[47]) and that of the Successors (living during the reigns of the middle and late Umayyad caliphs), this law was integrated – but also modified – by the specialists. We may therefore assert that the juristic activities of this first generation of legal specialists marks a process whereby caliphal legislation and caliphal legal authority began, as part of the *sunan*, to lose ground in favor of the evolving culture of the *fuqahā'*, the individual Muslim jurists. It should not come as a surprise then that one of the most distinguished later works cites Yazīd b. ʿAbd al-Malik (r. 101/718–105/723) as the last caliph whose practices and decrees constituted authority-statements.[48] From that point onward, caliphal law ceased to constitute *sunna*, although caliphal legal involvement (aided by the jurists themselves) did continue for about a century or more thereafter.[49]

Generally speaking, wherever the Quran was silent or bore only indirectly on certain matters, it was left to precedent, the *sunan* and considered opinion (*ra'y*) to adjudicate. Thus, even in the absence of its articulation by Muslim men of learning, we may infer that the hierarchy of legal sources was as follows: the Quran, *sunan* – including caliphal law and the Prophet's model – and *ra'y*. It has to be kept in mind, however, that these sources were not mutually exclusive; rather, they encroached on each other heavily. Caliphal law, for instance, was often a derivative of *sunan*, whether caliphal, Prophetic or otherwise; at times it was Quranic in letter or in spirit; at others, it was pure *ra'y*, namely, the opinion of a particular caliph or of his predecessors, or of another Companion or jurist.

[47] With the exception of Abū Bakr. See n. 61 below.
[48] This work is Mālik's *Muwaṭṭa'*, written in Medina around 150/767. See Dutton, *Origins*, 121.
[49] See chapter 8 below.

3. THE RISE OF PROPHETIC *ḤADĪTH*

By around 120/737, it was clear that Prophetic authority was on the rise, and growing at a steady pace as a distinct type of *sunan*. Muḥammad's authority, perceived to be expressed *inter alia* in his *sīra*, had no doubt been a part of these sanctified *sunan*. But what enhanced the value of the Prophetic biography as a superior model was the Quranic insistence on this model as a unique, nearly divine, example. Yet, the delay in perceiving the Prophetic model in these terms can be attributed in part to the gradual assimilation of Quranic and other religious values in the new Muslim society. The Quran's meanings were obviously not fixed, but grew with the religious growth of the Muslim community. Indeed, the gradual rooting of the Quranic imperative in the Muslim psyche may be illustrated by the example of the proto-*qāḍīs*' attitudes towards the consumption of wine.[50] The slow enforcement of its prohibition typically reflected the gradual but steady infiltration of religio-ethical values into the minds and hearts of Muslims. Another illustrative example is the rise of ascetic piety, which had been nearly absent among the Peninsular Arabs and which had become a permanent social ethic during the second/eighth century and thereafter. There is little doubt, furthermore, that the textualization of Islam toward the end of the first/seventh century significantly contributed to a widespread and thorough assimilation of Quranic values, for it was during this period that the Quran was subjected to an unprecedented hermeneutic in which close attention was paid to its legal minutiae. With the full legal implications of the Quran articulated, Prophetic biography acquired a special status, above and beyond any other. Indeed, as we will see, the process of "constructing" Prophetic authority involved the assimilation into *ḥadīth* of materials that had been the preserve of non-Prophetic *sunan*.

The *sunan* constituted in themselves a source of the law even as the search for Prophetic Sunna got underway. Yet, by the end of the first century (ca. 715 AD), Prophetic Sunna had emerged as the queen of all *sunan*, though not of the legal sources on the whole. Hence the recently emerging preference for Prophetic Sunna did not amount to the proposition that law was exclusively or largely based on it, for the available Prophetic *ḥadīth* were as yet insufficient to constitute the basis of a substantial doctrine of positive law. Furthermore, the mere fact that men

[50] See chapter 2, section 3 above.

of learning should have coveted the Prophet's Sunna did not necessarily make it, historically or logically, an automatic source of the law. True, the Prophet's standing progressively gained prestige from the beginning, but his Sunna had largely been intermeshed with the other *sunan.* Nor were these *sunan* seen as a distinct source of law or genre, since they were regarded as a natural extension of the Prophet's legacy. The *sunan* of the Companions and the caliphs – which formed the basis of legal practice in the garrison towns and provinces – were thought to reflect first-hand knowledge of what the Prophet said or did, or of what he would have done in a particular case needing a solution. The Companions and early caliphs were thus seen as invested with the highest knowledge of the Prophet and his ways, and their *sunan* therefore represented – in one important and fundamental sense – a rich guide to legal conduct. (This also explains why – during the second/eighth century – their narratives were projected back onto the Prophet, as part of what some modern scholars have unjustifiably characterized as a process of *ḥadīth* forgery.)

The relationship between Prophetic Sunna and *sunan* may be illustrated by the following anecdote. When Ṣāliḥ b. Kaysān and Shihāb al-Din Zuhrī collaborated in an effort to collect the *sunan,* they reportedly disagreed as to whether or not the Companions' *sunan* should be part of their project. Zuhrī, who deemed the incorporation of these *sunan* necessary, finally prevailed, and a collection of both types of *sunan* – Prophetic and Companion – was made.[51] Yet, the very fact that such a disagreement broke out suggests – especially in light of the centrality of the Companions' *sunan* during the first century – that these *sunan* were entering into a phase in which they were increasingly contested, thereby losing prestige in favor of Prophetic Sunna. It also suggests that this latter, already a component of *sunan,* had just set out on the path that eventually would lead it to a privileged position. For while, qualitatively, the Prophetic materials represented a superior authority to many specialists, quantitatively such materials were still relatively small. In one of the most comprehensive registers of Zuhrī's transmitted doctrines, the majority of references go back to the Companions, not to the Prophet.[52]

This quantitative disadvantage, however, is only one indication of the fact that by the end of the first century (ca. 715 AD) Prophetic Sunna was

[51] M. J. Kister, "… *lā taqraʾū l-qurʾāna ʿalā l-muṣḥafiyyīn wa-lā taḥmilū l-ʿilma ʿani l-ṣaḥafiyyīn* …: Some Notes on the Transmission of *Ḥadīth,*" *Jerusalem Studies in Arabic and Islam,* 22 (1998): 127–62, at 136.

[52] See Motzki, "Fiqh des–Zuhrī," 12.

still far from being regarded as an exclusive source of law. At this stage, it was even sometimes used without referring to any specific content, in a manner similar to that in which other *sunan* had often been used. For instance, in Ḥasan al-Baṣrī's famous tract (properly known as *al-Risāla* and composed around 85/704), the Quran is the only yardstick of truth, for "any opinion that is not based on the Quran is erroneous."[53] Yet, Baṣrī does refer to the Sunna of the Prophet and gives it special importance without, however, adducing any *ḥadīth*.[54] In such references, the Prophet's conduct had the status of an exemplary model, one to be followed as the best example of the forebears' ways.

In this context, it is important to note that *ḥadīth* was not yet synonymous with the verbal expression of Prophetic Sunna. Some *ḥadīth*s were seen to contradict the widespread knowledge of established Sunna or *sunan* (especially when these constituted the basis of legal practice in the garrison towns and Medina), a fact to be expected in a milieu in which Prophetic biography eventually became the concern of a multitude of story-tellers, traditionists, judges, jurists and others. In an environment where fabrications of Prophetic materials were known to be widespread, it was inevitable that some circulated reports came to contradict local knowledge of the Sunna/*sunan*, knowledge that was transmitted mostly through practice and not orally.

Yet, many of the references to Prophetic Sunna did have specific content, at least insofar as law was concerned. Although these formed a relatively small portion of legal doctrine, their importance is attested by the reported activity of the caliph ʿUmar II, who is credited with one of the earliest attempts to collect Prophetic *ḥadīth*.[55] As part of this effort, he commissioned a number of scholars and probably governors to "look for what there is of the *ḥadīth* of the Apostle and of his Sunna."[56] The caliph, a highly learned man, reportedly worked on the project, also collecting *ḥadīth*. But the larger task of coordinating this material was assigned to Zuhrī. Upon completion, copies of the compilation were made and sent to each province or city for the benefit of judges and administrators.[57] None of these documents seems to have survived intact, nor is there any trace of

[53] Schacht, *Origins*, 141.

[54] Ibid., 74.

[55] On Muslim narratives claiming an early recording of *ḥadīth*, see Kister, "*lā taqraʾū l-qurʾāna . . .*," 127–38.

[56] Nabia Abbott, *Studies in Arabic Literary Papyri*, vol. II: *Qurʾānic Commentary and Tradition* (Chicago: University of Chicago Press, 1967), 26.

[57] Ibid., 30–31; Kister, "*lā taqraʾū l-qurʾāna . . .*," 156.

their later transmission. But it seems beyond doubt that Zuhrī, ʿUmar II's chief scholar, wrote down[58] a vast quantity of *ḥadīths* and that he was engaged in transmitting and teaching these materials.[59]

The memorizing and writing down of *ḥadīth* thus emerged as a significant activity within and without the sphere of law. Nearly all the 418 Companions[60] and their children (mainly sons) participated at least to some extent in transmitting Prophetic *ḥadīth*. A large number of these persons transmitted no more than a pair of *ḥadīths*, or perhaps only a few. Of the remainder, several are credited with a large number of transmissions, notably ʿAbd Allāh b. ʿUmar, Anas b. Mālik, Ibn ʿAbbās, Abū Hurayra, Ibn Masʿūd, ʿUmar b. al-Khaṭṭāb (ʿUmar I), ʿAlī and ʿUthmān.[61] Furthermore, the dispersal of the Companions – 188 of whom are reported to have migrated from Medina and Mecca to Iraq, Syria, Egypt and Khurāsān – had an effect on the interest in *ḥadīth*, which seems roughly to have corresponded with the geographical distribution of the legal specialists. A statistical survey of an early source – which affords us a list of traditionists who flourished roughly between 80 and 120 (ca. 700–35 AD) – reveals the following: Kūfa claimed 28 percent of *ḥadīth* transmitters; Baṣra 27 percent; Medina 24 percent; Syria 12 percent; Mecca 5 percent; Egypt 3 percent; and Khurāsān and other locales less than 1 percent. Note that the Hejaz (Medina and Mecca) claimed nearly a third of both legal specialists and traditionists; Kūfa and Baṣra shared about the same numbers but had a few more of the latter than of the former. So did Syria, which claimed about 20 percent more traditionists than it had legal specialists. (In absolute numbers, however, the traditionists were far more numerous than the legists). Yemen, on the other hand, had 6 percent of the total number of legal specialists but hardly figures in our sources as a hive of traditionist activity.[62]

58 The writing down of *ḥadīth* in the early period appears to have been a widespread practice. It was not uncommon for the scholars of a town to commit to writing the *ḥadīths* that they heard from a traditionist in transit. When the Yemenite scholar ʿUthmān b. Ḥāḍir arrived in Mecca, the local scholars are reported to have written down his *ḥadīth*. On the other hand, some scholars, such as ʿAbd Allāh b. Dhakwān (d. 130/747), did not possess a good memory and used writing to retain the *ḥadīth* they heard. Ibn Ḥibbān, *Mashāhīr*, 113, 124 (for Ibn Ḥāḍir), 133, 135 (for Ibn Dhakwān), 136, 141, 199 and *passim*; Wakīʿ, *Akhbār*, I, 328.

59 Motzki, "Fiqh des–Zuhrī"; Kister, "*lā taqraʾū l-qurʾāna* . . .," 158.

60 Listed by Ibn Ḥibbān, *Mashāhīr*.

61 It is interesting to note the nearly complete absence of Abū Bakr from the list of these Companions, a phenomenon that deserves further investigation.

62 This should be considered in conjunction with the fact that Ibn Ḥibbān is not consistent in identifying the geographical affiliations of traditionists.

In addition to the geographical configuration, these data also show that in relative and absolute numbers, the traditionists' activity was far more substantial and could be said to have involved a larger proportion of the population than that represented by the legal specialists. Furthermore, these data correct the view of some scholars[63] that the Hejaz lagged behind Kūfa and Baṣra as a locus of traditionist and legal activity.

Thus, Muslim men of religious learning were certainly engulfed by the evolving notions of a Prophetic Sunna that was becoming superior to its near relations, the *sunan*. The sacred nature of this Sunna – which reflected the dramatic rise in Prophetic authority – made it the focus of interest of many groups, including the story-tellers who contributed to it both legendary and factual elements. False attributions to the Prophet were made through both fabrications of subject matter and chains of transmission. In fact, the increasing importance and authority of *ḥadīth* as an embodiment of Prophetic Sunna made it attractive to the Umayyad – as well as the early ʿAbbāsid – caliphs as a tool for enhancing their legitimacy *vis-a-vis* their many opponents. As part of their efforts to enlist the support of the religious scholars[64] – including the legal specialists – they endeavored (as we will see in chapter 8) to gather around them traditionists and jurists who would be willing and ready to collect and promote any *ḥadīth* supportive of their rule, whether true or spurious. Although this policy did encourage the collection and writing of *ḥadīth*s, it also had the effect of contributing to the intensification of forgery. Even the names of transmitters were occasionally fabricated. The case of the traditionist Uways b. ʿĀmir must suffice to illustrate this point. One of the earliest and most knowledgeable authorities dealing with *ḥadīth* transmitters describes him as a Yemenite who lived in Kūfa. But the sources cannot agree on whether he died in Mecca or in Damascus. Some *ḥadīth* scholars, our authority declares, have even denied "his having ever existed in this world."[65] On the other hand, even some of the most distinguished scholars, whose historicity cannot be doubted, were responsible for injecting false materials into this Sunna, to be rejected later by the *ḥadīth* experts. Of these scholars no less than Qatāda b. Diʿāma, Ḥasan al-Baṣrī and Ḥabīb b. Thābit (d. 119/737) are cited in technical *ḥadīth* criticism as mendacious, having attributed to

[63] Schacht, *Origins*, 243 and *passim*.

[64] To be read with caution, on the relations between caliphs and religious scholars during this period, is K. ʿAthamina, "The ʿUlama in the Opposition: The ʿStick and the Carrot' Policy in Early Islam," *Islamic Quarterly*, 36, 3 (1992): 153–78, esp. at 154–61.

[65] Ibn Ḥibbān, *Thiqāt*, 15.

the Prophet a number of *ḥadīths* that were rejected as inauthentic.[66] It must be stressed, however, that notwithstanding these failings, the very same scholars are depicted in the sources as pious men whose contributions to religious learning were undeniable.

4. PROTO-TRADITIONALISM VS. RATIONALISM

It must first be stressed that the notion of rationalism or rationalistic jurisprudence is by no means a philosophical one. Rather, rationalism in Islamic jurisprudence merely signifies a perception of an attitude toward legal issues that is dictated by rational, pragmatic and practical considerations. Put differently, rationalism (always a description by the "Other") is substantive legal reasoning that, for the most part, does not directly ground itself in what came later to be recognized as the valid textual sources (namely, the Quran and Prophetic *ḥadīth*/Sunna). On the other hand, the traditionalists (*ahl al-ḥadīth*; often a self-description) were those who held that law must rest squarely on Prophetic *ḥadīth*, the Quran being taken for granted by both rationalists (*ahl al-ra'y*) and traditionalists. The traditionalists therefore must not be confused with the traditionists, whose main occupation was to collect, study and transmit *ḥadīth*. In other words, a traditionist might either be a rationalist or a traditionalist, depending on his point of view.

The methodological awareness of the traditionalists as defined in the previous paragraph was a development belonging to the second half of the second century H, and cannot be said to have crystallized any earlier. Only the vaguest beginnings of this trend can be detected in the first part of the century, a time when the proto-traditionalists were inclined to support some of their legal views by reference to Prophetic and Companion reports, unlike their counterparts, the so-called rationalists. Nevertheless, the proto-traditionalists had not yet come to the point at which they would insist upon exclusive reliance on Prophetic *ḥadīth*, or even on the reports of Companions and Successors.

The definition of rationalism makes it clear that this attribute and those who were given this label, i.e., the rationalists (*ahl al-ra'y*), were recognized in terms of their non-reliance upon *ḥadīth*. The definition is then a negative one: A rationalist is one who does not rely, or tends not to rely, on *ḥadīth*. Thus, there could not have been an identifiable group of

[66] Ibn Ḥibbān, *Mashāhīr*, 96, 145; Ibn Ḥibbān, *Thiqāt*, 33–34, 37, 39, 41, 43, 44, 49, 53, 90, 163, 222; Ibn Khallikān, *Wafayāt*, I, 219.

rationalists without *ḥadīth* having first evolved, for it was this evolution that gave rise to the binary opposites *ḥadīth/ra'y*. The faintest tendency to draw such an opposition appears to have surfaced at the turn of the first century H (ca. 715 AD) or shortly thereafter, at which time the pattern starts to become clear: The more *ḥadīth* spread, and the more important it became, the sharper the conflict between the traditionalists and the rationalists.

It must be remembered that before the rise of *ḥadīth* – which signaled an increase in the importance of Prophetic Sunna – rationalist reasoning (*ra'y*) was viewed in a positive light. The term *ra'y* was used to indicate sound and considered opinion, and we have therefore rendered it into English as "discretionary reasoning." To be erroneous, therefore, "opinion" had at that time to be qualified by a negative attribute, for its natural, default status was clearly positive.[67] The poet ʿAbd Allāh b. Shaddād al-Laythī (d. 83/702) regarded the approval accorded by the *ahl al-ra'y* (the people of good sense) to be a desideratum in acquiring a good reputation in society.[68] Even ʿUmar II, who was later associated with traditionalist tendencies,[69] is reported to have ordered one of his judges to solve certain problems through his *ra'y*.[70] And when the Baṣran judge Iyās b. Muʿāwiya was asked whether he was fond (*muʿjab*) of his own *ra'y*, he is said to have remarked: "Had I not been fond of my *ra'y*, I would not have decided cases in accordance with it."[71]

The fairly recent emergence of *ḥadīth* obviously could not have affected the established forms of legal reasoning. *Ra'y* continued to dominate throughout the early period and until the middle of the second/eighth century. According to one scholar's calculation, about two-thirds of Zuhrī's transmitted doctrine contained *ra'y* and only one-third consisted of reports from earlier authorities. Qatāda's *ra'y*, by the same estimate, amounted to 62 percent of his own transmitted doctrine. Even more significant is the fact that 84 percent of the remaining portion – i.e., 32 percent of his total doctrine – expresses the *ra'y* of earlier authorities.[72]

But the positive connotation of *ra'y* was to change with the passage of time. The challenge posed by the traditionalists had the effect of gradually

67 Ibn Aʿtham, *Futūḥ*, I, 172, 176, 178 and *passim*.
68 See Sayyid Aḥmad al-Hāshimī, *Jawāhir al-Adab fī Adabiyyāt wa-Inshā' Lughat al-ʿArab*, 2 vols. (Beirut: Mu'assasat al-Risāla, n.d.), I, 190; Ibn Aʿtham, *Futūḥ*, I, 176.
69 See Wael B. Hallaq, *A History of Islamic Legal Theories* (Cambridge: Cambridge University Press, 1997), 15.
70 Kindī, *Akhbār*, 334.
71 Wakīʿ, *Akhbār*, I, 346.
72 Motzki, "Fiqh des–Zuhrī," 6.

coloring this term in a negative hue, changing its meaning from "discretionary reasoning" into "arbitrary reasoning" or "fallible human thought," i.e., a way of thinking that failed to consider the authoritative texts, which were steadily acquiring a reputation as a more secure source of legal knowledge. A single Prophetic voice on which all Muslims could rely, the traditionalists claimed, was superior to the personal reasoning of individual judges whose fallibility could be demonstrated by the fact of their widely diverse opinions on any given issue. In short, the more the *ḥadīth*s circulated, the greater the traditionalists' power became, and, necessarily, the more negative the connotations associated with *raʾy*. Indeed, it can also be argued that the more powerful the traditionalists became, the more *ḥadīth*s went into circulation. In terms of causality, therefore, the complex relationship between *ḥadīth* production and the growth of the traditionalist movement was dialectical; namely, one element fed on the other.

The rise of *ḥadīth* was concomitant with an intense development in theological debate over issues of divine will, power and predestination.[73] Problems of law and theology were at several points necessarily interconnected, as the later intellectual tradition came to demonstrate. From the traditionalist viewpoint, the insistence on *raʾy* was no longer viewed as insistence on discretionary reasoning ultimately based on *ʿilm*, but rather as a deliberate refusal to acknowledge the divine imperative. In light of the tone of theological debates, "discretionary reasoning" was regarded as directly connoting "rational reasoning," this latter meaning a human, not divine, foundation of law. Hence, the appellation *ahl al-raʾy* now came to signify "rationalists" rather than "careful reasoners." (A critical source-analysis must therefore recognize that the later competing categories of traditionalists/rationalists are often projected backwards onto early sources and narratives, thereby producing an anachronistic account of the emergence of traditionist/traditionalist activity and, consequently, distorting the originally positive image of "discretionary opinion.")

5. CONCLUSIONS

By the second decade of the second century (730s AD), several developments came together to produce a distinctly new phase in the life of Islamic law. The Companions and those who felt strongly about the message of the

[73] See W. M. Watt, *The Formative Period of Islamic Thought* (Edinburgh: Edinburgh University Press, 1973), 82–118, and *passim.*

new religion had already embarked on defining Islam according to what they perceived to be the Quranic spirit, which had already claimed dogmatic supremacy from the very beginning. The generation that flourished between 80 and 120 (ca. 700–35 AH) made of piety a field of knowledge, for piety dictated behavior in keeping with the Quran and the good example of the predecessors (the all-important *sunan māḍiya*). Considered, discretionary opinion was part and parcel of this piety, since it often took into consideration the Quran and the exemplary models that were so highly recommended. At the very least, it could not have violated in any marked way the then widely accepted Quranic injunctions or the established ways of the predecessors. Any such violation would have been socially and politically – if not legally – unwarranted and would have met with opposition from the traditional, customary and venerated values of the Arabs. However, adherence to these legal sources was not even a conscious methodological act; considered opinion, the Quran and the *sunan* had so thoroughly permeated the ethos according to which judges operated and legally minded scholars lived that they had become paradigmatic.

As they had slowly developed into a body of knowledge, these religious values began to reign supreme, and those who made it their concern to study, articulate and impart this knowledge acquired both a special social status and a position of privileged epistemic authority. In other words, those men in possession of a greater store of knowledge grew more influential than others less learned, gaining in the process – by the sheer virtuousness of their knowledge – an authority that began to challenge the legal (but not political) authority of the caliphs (although this is not to say that caliphal authority was either integral or exclusive). Whether Arab or non-Arab, rich or poor, white or black, scholars emerged as distinguished leaders, men of integrity and rectitude by virtue of their knowledge, and their knowledge alone.

The emergence of legal specialists was one development that got underway once Muslims began engaging in religious discussions, story-telling and instruction in mosques. Another, concomitant, development was the gradual specialization of the *qāḍī*'s office, a specialization dictated by the fact that the Arab conquerors' expansion and settlement in the new territories brought with it an unprecedented volume of litigation, including legally complex cases usually associated with sedentary styles of life. Whereas prior to 80/699 it was mainly proto-*qāḍī*s who dominated the field of conflict resolution, after this period it was the *qāḍī*s who mainly staffed and operated the nascent judicial system. This operation was not isolated from the emerging circles of the legal specialists. Not only did some judges themselves belong to these circles, but the specialists also began to be seen as essential to the courtroom. Whence an early doctrine began to surface: a judge must consult the legal specialists, the *fuqahā'*, especially if he is not one of them.

A third development, which had started a couple of decades earlier, i.e., during the 60s/680s, was the rise of Prophetic authority as distinct from the authority of other *sunan*. With the increasing assimilation of the Quran and the articulation of the finer points in it, Muḥammad's authority as Prophet was increasingly augmented. The many Quranic injunctions to abide by the Prophet's example, coupled with the Arab emphasis on "the ways of the predecessors," generated the question: What would the Prophet have said or done were he to face a given issue? It should be abundantly clear that an answer to this question did not mean a change in positive law or replacement of the existing sources on which the judges drew. But it did mean that an evolving body of Prophetic narrative was beginning to surface independently of other narratives and practices. The Prophetic model may have, *in terms of authority*, challenged and competed with other *sunan* as well as with *ra'y*, but it was more often the case that the *sunan* and the *ra'y* constituted the subject matter from which the content of Prophetic narrative was derived. Prophetic *ḥadīth* was a logical substitution for these sources, since the latter – by virtue of the Companions' intimate knowledge of the Prophet – represented to Muslims an immediate extension of the former.

And here the embryo of yet another significant development began to form. The increasingly active groups of so-called traditionists – who transmitted, *inter alia*, Prophetic and Companions' materials – began to see *ra'y* as the shunning of religious values. By about 120 (ca. 740 AD), all that this meant was a mere traditionist disgruntlement with *ra'y*, but this was to develop during the next two centuries into one of the most intense intellectual and legal battles known to Islam and an issue that ultimately affected and determined the course of the religion's development. This was the traditionalist–rationalist conflict.

CHAPTER 4

The judiciary coming of age

1. DELEGATION AND THE CREATION OF JUDICIAL HIERARCHY

The period between the third and eighth decades of the second century (ca. 740–800 AD) witnessed the maturation of both the judiciary and legal doctrine, as all essential features of these two spheres acquired a final shape, only to be refined during the succeeding century or two. With the increasing specialization of the judge's office as a legal institution, and with the evolution of centralization policies of the government, came a gradual change in the source of judicial appointments. During this phase, especially with the rise of the ʿAbbāsids, investiture gradually shifted from the hands of the provincial governor to those of the caliph himself. This move toward judicial centralization, furthermore, seems to have been precipitated by the steady emergence of a professional legal elite whose interests were better served by direct caliphal supervision than by the perceived whims and arbitrariness of provincial military governors. As we shall see below in chapter 8, the perception of the caliphate as a religious and moral office – possessing the semblance of legality and capable of distributive justice – promised a better chance at equity and fairness than any military governor could have offered. It thus should not be surprising that, while promoting their own interests, the legists also pushed for caliphal supervision, as evidenced in juristic writings addressed to the caliphs.[1]

The shift to caliphal appointments, which started sporadically around 100/715 and became an established practice fifty years later, signaled an evolution in the concept of judicial delegation according to which judges were appointed as representatives of the power that invested them, although the ultimate source of authority remained the caliph himself. The signal development that sanctioned this concept was the appointment

[1] See Muḥammad Qasim Zaman, *Religion and Politics under the Early ʿAbbāsids* (Leiden: Brill, 1997), 85–88, and chapter 8, below.

by the ʿAbbāsid caliph Hārūn al-Rashīd of the distinguished Kūfan jurist and judge Abū Yūsuf (d. 182/798) as chief justice (*qāḍī al-quḍāt*) shortly after 170/786. But this newly created title was no innovation in terms of jurisdiction or competence, for it accorded no additional powers to the recipient beyond those the typical provincial judge had usually enjoyed. Rather, the title merely signified the final step in political centralization, for henceforth it was the chief justice who appointed the provincial judges, although the appointment itself formally came directly from the caliph's office and person. Thus, it became the practice that provincial judges received a letter of appointment (known as *kitāb*, and later *ʿahd*) directly from the caliph. Between roughly 140 and 270 (ca. 760 and 880 AD), it was sufficient for the appointee to receive and read the letter in order for the investiture to take effect, but immediately thereafter the letter had to be read in the grand mosque of the city in which the appointment was made, for the investiture to be valid.[2]

Just as the caliph delegated to the chief justice the authority to appoint provincial *qāḍīs*, these *qāḍīs* held the authority to appoint deputies or district judges who came to be known as *khalīfas* or *nāʾibs*. The judicial powers delegated at this level were frequently limited in jurisdiction. Some *nāʾibs* were given powers to hear certain types of disputes, while others had full jurisdiction but were limited in territorial terms. Thus, some judges were charged with administering criminal justice (*masāʾil al-dimāʾ*), while others were entrusted with settling estates. The chief justice in Baghdad, who also functioned as judge of that city, often appointed two deputies, one to the east side of the city and the other to the west side. Furthermore, he, like all other judges of large cities, appointed deputy judges who heard cases in the major villages surrounding the metropolis. In the ʿAbbāsid capital, some judges or deputy judges were appointed exclusively to hear disputes in the army,[3] a function that later acquired the title *qāḍī ʿaskar*.[4] At

2 Kindī, *Akhbār*, 492, 494, 495, 497.

3 Wakīʿ, *Akhbār*, III, 252, 269.

4 Tyan has rightly pointed out that the office of *qāḍī ʿaskar* did not appear in the early stages of Muslim history because the

> Arab-Muslim communities were nothing more than the body of the conquering forces, and the ordinary *qāḍī* appointed for these communities were precisely the same magistrate who was appointed by the conquerors. The *qāḍāʾ ʿaskar* took on the aspect of an autonomous institution only when a distinction was actually made between the civil communities established in the conquered territories and the armies which carried on the task of war and conquest.

Emile Tyan, "Judicial Organization," in M. Khadduri and H. Liebesny, eds., *Law in the Middle East* (Washington, D.C.: The Middle East Institute, 1955), 236–78, at 270.

times, however, it was the city *qāḍī* who would travel to the villages to hear disputes, as was the case with Khurāsān's judge ʿAbd Allāh b. Burayda.[5]

Dividing jurisdiction between or among *qāḍī*s was never a permanent arrangement. Thus, a city or a jurisdiction might have two judges at one point in time, but only a single judge at another. We are told that al-Hādī (r. 169/785–70/86) was the first caliph to divide the jurisdiction of the ʿAbbāsid capital into two, appointing Aḥmad b. ʿĪsā al-Burnī to the east side and Ismāʿīl b. Isḥāq to the west. But when Burnī was dispatched to adjudicate disputes in Nahrawān, Ismāʿīl was left in charge of the jurisdiction of the entire city until his death.[6] Later, however, Baghdad was again split into the two jurisdictions, each with a different judge, until 301/913, when the jurisdiction of the entire city was unified under Muḥammad b. Yūsuf.[7]

Nor was the appointment of judges from the capital city a permanent feature, although nominally the caliph as titular religious head was always presumed to be the highest authority sanctioning investiture. Egyptian judges, for instance, seem to have been regularly appointed by caliphal decree from Baghdad during the first century or more of ʿAbbāsid rule. However, under the Ikhshīdids, it was often – but by no means always – the case that the decision as to who was appointed was made by the local emirs. At times, the choice of candidate was made by the local religious elite and sanctioned, on behalf of the caliph, by the local military ruler. In 348/959, for instance, the religious leaders in Egypt convinced Kāfūr, the Ikhshīdid ruler, that Abū Ṭāhir Muḥammad b. Aḥmad should be appointed as judge, in which case Kāfūr issued a decree confirming their request.[8] It must be said, however, that appointments by what may be termed popular demand were rare, and that the great majority of judicial appointments were made by the caliph or the local governor, usually after consultation with the senior jurists frequenting the ruler's court.

The least permanent of all appointments, and the one that proved to be a fruitless experiment, was the appointment of two judges to the same position or jurisdiction, in what may be termed a shared appointment. In 137/754, during al-Manṣūr's reign, two judges were appointed to Baṣra, ʿUmar b. ʿĀmir al-Sulamī and the celebrated Sawwār b. ʿAbd Allāh. Soon, however, disagreements between the two over decisions and handling of

[5] Wakīʿ, *Akhbār*, III, 306.
[6] Ibid., III, 254, 281–82.
[7] Ibid., III, 282.
[8] Kindī, *Akhbār*, 493.

cases were so serious that Sawwār was finally dismissed, leaving Sulamī with exclusive jurisdiction.[9] Some two decades later, al-Mahdī (r. 158/775–169/785) appointed two judges to "sit" in the Grand Mosque of Baghdad, each presiding over his own court, and each with apparently unqualified jurisdiction.[10] We know that some competition ensued between the two, but nothing is said in the sources of how they fared in the long run. However, it is safe to say that such appointments, especially of two judges to the same court, never succeeded and we hear of no such cases during later periods. One of the distinguishing characteristics of the Islamic court in the long term remained its single-judge constitution.

The concept of delegation also meant that the judge was accountable to the power appointing him, the principal. The latter, conversely, was responsible for the former's conduct, and had the final say in his dismissal. Even if the caliph wished a deputy judge removed, the removal as a formal act had to emanate from the appointing agency, usually the chief judge of the city. Similarly, once a principal was dismissed, his deputies were automatically dismissed with him, for with the principal's dismissal their judicial power became null and void.

Delegation by way of appointing deputies always implied that the appointing authority had the power to substitute himself for the appointee. Thus, any litigant could address himself to the principal while circumventing the *nāʾib* or even the *qāḍī* or chief justice himself. This explains why in some cases litigants took their disputes to the caliph himself, bypassing the deputy judge, the appointing judge and even the chief justice. Such an act, however, always presumed that the case had not yet been tried before any judge's court, for once such a process had been initiated, the litigant was obliged to complete the proceedings within the jurisdictional purview of the presiding judge and to comply with his decision. Nor could any higher authority interfere in the process or alter the decision itself during the tenure of the presiding judge. In 135/752, for instance, on the testimony of a single witness, the Egyptian judge Khayr b. Nuʿaym placed in temporary custody a soldier who had been accused of defamation of character. In the meantime, to complete filing the evidence against the accused, the plaintiff was to present to the court a second witness. But before the proceedings were finalized, the governor of Egypt, ʿAbd Allāh b. Yazīd, released the soldier, an action that left Khayr with no option other than to resign. The latter made his return to office conditional upon the re-arrest of the soldier,

[9] Wakīʿ, *Akhbār*, II, 55.
[10] Ibid., III, 251.

a condition vehemently rejected by the governor, who soon appointed another judge in Khayr's place.[11]

This incident, unquestionably authentic, nicely illustrates the considerable independence of the early (and indeed later) judiciary in Islam, and accurately characterizes the stark contrast between the power of those who came to appoint and to dismiss, and that of the judge himself over his own jurisdiction. The judicial independence of the *qāḍī* must therefore be seen to stand outside the vertical process of delegation. Each *qāḍī*, from the lowest rung of the legal profession up to the chief justice, was judicially independent irrespective of the powers of the appointing agency. This independence began at appointment and ended with dismissal.

Beginning with the early years of the second century H., if not before, judicial independence became the hallmark of the Islamic legal tradition. As a rule, no authority could redirect cases (from one jurisdiction to another) or interfere in the process of adjudication. However low-ranking the judge might be, his court, his hearings and his decisions were sacrosanct, in both theory and practice, since evidence of interference in the process is rare in our sources. Furthermore, judicial independence was bolstered by the absence from the Islamic legal tradition of any system of appeal. Once a decision was rendered, it was considered final and irrevocable within the tenure of the presiding *qāḍī*. The system did, however, allow what might be termed successor judicial review within the same court. Accordingly, a newly appointed judge might reevaluate the decisions of his predecessor and revoke or reverse some of them. In 194/809, the Egyptian judge Hāshim al-Bakrī reversed two decisions rendered by his predecessor ʿAbd Allāh al-ʿUmarī.[12] Some three decades later, also in Fusṭāṭ, Ibn Abī al-Layth overturned a decision rendered by his predecessor, Hārūn b. ʿAbd Allāh. The same decision was reversed a few years later by al-Ḥārith b. Miskīn, who succeeded Ibn Abī al-Layth and affirmed Hārūn's verdict.[13]

It remains true, however, that the caliph, governor or their representatives possessed full authority to appoint and dismiss judges, an authority that encompassed the power to appoint a candidate without the latter's consent – or at least, such appointment was never conditional upon the candidate's willingness to serve in the capacity of a *qāḍī*. The literature is

[11] Ibid., III, 232; Kindī, *Akhbār*, 356.

[12] Kindī, *Akhbār*, 403, 404.

[13] Ibid., 474–75; for a similar case, see Ibn Ḥajar al-ʿAsqalānī, *Rafʿ al-Iṣr ʿan Quḍāt Miṣr* (printed with Kindī, *Akhbār*), 506.

replete with accounts of judges refusing to serve or politely excusing themselves from such a service, offering such pretexts as physical ailment or ignorance of the law. In chapter 8, we will have occasion to discuss the moral and religious predicaments that a career in the judgeship entailed for the Sharīʿa-minded, but for now it suffices to state that, at least theoretically, the candidate's wishes or readiness to take on the office were deliberately ignored. The rationale behind this practice stems from the assumption that a judge who has no personal interest in the office is less likely to be motivated by considerations of power and wealth, and hence more immune to corruption. Investiture therefore had to be – or to have the semblance of being – derived from the very act of appointment. The reasoning underlying this conception was also at the foundation of the power of dismissal.

At its core, the near-limitless power of the delegating office ultimately represented the legal authority of the caliphs – and later those who practically and theoretically acted on their behalf – to administer justice. As the deputies of God on Earth and of Muḥammad as Prophet, the caliphs were an integral part of the legal profession as it had developed by the first quarter of the second century (750 AD). But they also stood at the top of a hierarchy, themselves being rulers, judges and – in many cases – even jurists of some sort. We have seen that, in matters of substantive law, they advised judges but also received counsel from them. However, in administering law through judicial appointment, they reserved for themselves the prerogative to act as they wished, although even here they did not always do so without seeking counsel. The literature abundantly attests to the fact that they frequently sought the opinions of jurists and other men of learning about the best candidate for a specific post; and there is no doubt that such opinions mattered and were taken into serious consideration. It remains a fact, however, that the final decision rested in the hands of the political sovereign, be it the caliph or his (pretending) representative.

The same principle of delegation obtained under the early ʿAbbāsid caliphs, who acted on the assumption that they were administering the law of God, an assumption strengthened by the fact that the process of Islamicization came to a zenith in that era. Toward the end of the third/ninth century, however, the caliphs increasingly began to lose their supremacy to military commanders and powerful local dynasties who took over the responsibility of appointing judges in the lands under their dominion. But, as we have earlier mentioned, such appointments remained nominally caliphal, although at later times the caliph often had nothing whatsoever to do with such acts. In other words, the principle of delegation continued to be assumed even when the reality was quite otherwise.

2. THE COMPOSITION OF THE *QĀḌĪ*'S COURT

By the close of the second century (ca. 800–815 AD), the structure and make-up of the court had taken final shape.[14] All the basic personnel and logistical features had been introduced, and any enlargement or diminution of these elements were merely a function of the nature and needs of the *qāḍī*'s jurisdiction. Thus a *qāḍī* might have had one, two or more scribes depending on the size of his court and the demands placed on it, but the scribe's function itself was integral to the proceedings, whatever their magnitude. The same went for all other court officials and functions.

In terms of personnel, the court consisted of a judge and any number of assistants (*aʿwān*) who performed a variety of tasks. We have spoken of the *jilwāz* and the court chamberlain whose function it was to maintain order in the court, including supervising the queue of litigants and calling upon various persons to appear before the judge. Some courts whose jurisdiction included regions inhabited by various ethnic and linguistic groups were also staffed by an interpreter or a dragoman.

By the 130s/750s, if not earlier, witness examiners (*aṣḥāb al-masāʾil*) appear in our sources as a fully established institution even to the point of being taken for granted.[15] The basic elements of this institution must have been in operation since the middle of the first century (ca. 670 A.H.), when the proto-*qāḍī*s, who worked to resolve criminal, pecuniary and other disputes, called upon witnesses to attest to the truthfulness of claims and events. In this context, it must also have been the practice that, out of logical necessity, the proto-*qāḍī* had often to inquire into the rectitude of these witnesses or ask someone who did. The institution must therefore have taken shape prior to the 110s (730s AD) or thereabouts, which explains why it is such an established feature in historical accounts dating from the late 120s and 130s.

[14] For a general account of the workings of the *qāḍī*'s court during the post-formative period, see David Powers, *Organizing Justice in the Muslim World, 1250–1750*, Themes in Islamic Law, edited by Wael B. Hallaq, no. 2 (Cambridge: Cambridge University Press, in progress).

[15] In the courts of Ibn Shubruma (d. 144/761) and Ibn Abī Laylā (d. 148/765), the *aṣḥāb al-masāʾil* were apparently as permanent a feature as the *qāḍī* himself. See, e.g., Wakīʿ, *Akhbār*, III, 106, 138. It is to be noted that the function of the *muzakkī* (lit., he who establishes the integrity of witnesses) derived from the office of *aṣḥāb al-masāʾil* and appears to have been a later appellation for roughly the same function.

This dating is consistent with an account in which it is reported that the Egyptian judge Ghawth b. Sulaymān, who served during the first years of the ʿAbbāsids (and probably under the last Umayyads), insisted, more than any of his predecessors, upon a thorough examination of character witnesses in his court. The account explains that Ghawth's actions were precipitated by careless appointments of witnesses, which resulted in what had become a widespread practice of giving false testimony.[16] Ghawth is said to have conducted a confidential investigation of all the court's witnesses,[17] although it is not clear whether in this case he performed the task himself or delegated it to the witness inspectors. By 170/786 or thereabouts, the names of court witnesses investigated and certified by the *ṣāḥib al-masāʾil* were entered into the court records, thereby creating a list that became a permanent feature of the *qāḍī*'s register.[18]

By the last years of Umayyad rule, then, it was clear to everyone that the *aṣḥāb al-masāʾil* were part of every city's court, trusted by the judge to enquire into the integrity of character witnesses whose function it was in turn to attest to legal records, contracts and all sorts of transactions passing through the court. Inasmuch as they were the judge's assistants (*aʿwān*), they were also his *umanāʾ* – literally, trustees. They "asked around" about potential witnesses and, once they determined their rectitude to be unblemished, they recommended them to the judge who would then approve the *aṣḥāb*s' recommendation. At times the recommendation was rejected, but on other occasions, the judge would approve the witnesses after he had done his share of investigating. Around 212/827, the judge ʿĪsā b. al-Munkadir is reported to have acted upon the recommendation of his *ṣāḥib al-masāʾil*, ʿAbd Allāh b. ʿAbd al-Ḥakam, only after he himself had personally investigated the witnesses the former had proposed. ʿĪsā was said to have been in the habit of "walking at night in the streets with a [type of a] headgear masking his face, asking about the witnesses."[19]

Once recommendations of the *ṣāḥib* al-*masāʾil* were accepted, the judge appointed the witnesses to the court, an appointment that came to be known as *al-rasm bil-shahāda*.[20] That this expression had become common in the legal profession no later than 190/805 suggests an earlier origin extending back, perhaps, to the middle of the second century (ca. 770

[16] Kindī, *Akhbār*, 361.
[17] Ibid.
[18] Ibid., 386, 394, 395.
[19] Ibid., 437.
[20] Ibid., 422 (read *marsūmūn* not *mawsūmūn*), 494.

AD), if not earlier; for this highly technical usage could not have come into existence unless a practice had preceded it by a relatively long stretch of time.

Be this as it may, the work of the *ṣāḥib al-masāʾil* did not end with finding and recommending trustworthy witnesses. It was often the case that the character of appointed witnesses was periodically examined in order to ensure their continuing ability to perform in that capacity. It is reported that when Lahīʿa b. ʿĪsā was appointed as a judge in 199/814, he designated Saʿīd b. Talīd as his *ṣāḥib al-masāʾil* and ordered him to investigate the court's witnesses every six months. The latter is said to have received the former's approval to appoint thirty such witnesses.[21] Anyone found in the meantime to have engaged in behavior that would disqualify him was dismissed and his name removed from the list of witnesses. One such witness was disqualified and dismissed on the grounds that he was a Qadarite,[22] i.e., a member of a theological school associated with the rationalist Muʿtazila.

Our sources are less clear on the exact status and role of witnesses in the early period. It is fairly safe to say that by the middle of the second century (ca. 770 AD), evidential testimony was still somewhat undetermined. By this time, we learn, judges would occasionally accept the testimony of a single witness in situations where two would have been demanded at a later period. The Kūfan judge Ibn Shubruma, who served during the 130s (747 AD et seq.), even accepted the testimony of a wife in favor of her husband against a third party,[23] a practice totally at odds with later normative doctrine. Similarly, Ibn Shubruma's contemporary and colleague Ibn Abī Laylā accepted other judges' written instruments sent to him without the attestation of witnesses,[24] a practice likewise rejected during later periods.[25] However, toward the end of the second century H (beginning of the ninth century AD), the institution of witnesses became well established, allowing for little subsequent variation. Oral testimony became the linchpin of the system of evidence, rivaling in strength written attestation which in and of itself was insufficient as evidentiary proof. By the end of the second century, if not sometime before, it had become a universal doctrine that

21 Ibid., 422.

22 Ibid.

23 Wakīʿ, *Akhbār*, III, 80.

24 Ibid., III, 133, 137, although on p. 134, this report is contradicted by another to the effect that Ibn Abī Laylā did accept, and in fact insisted on, such an attestation.

25 On the much later changes in the Andalusian Mālikite law of procedure concerning the judges' written communications to each other, see Wael B. Hallaq, "*Qāḍī*s Communicating," at 453 ff.

all documents, in order to be deemed valid, had to be attested by at least two witnesses. It is very likely that by this time too the judge's decisions also had to be attested and signed by the court's witnesses, the *shuhūd ʿadl*. These witnesses also sat in court, and their presence, procedural in nature, was intended to confirm the lawful conduct of all concerned.

Historical reports also make it clear that by the middle of the second century (ca. 770 AD), witnesses, however they were used, became not only a fixture of the court but also paid employees of the *qāḍī*, who always controlled the budget of the court. In the early 140s/late 750s, the Baṣran judge Sawwār b. ʿAbd Allāh is reported to have allotted regular salaries for assistants and witnesses.[26] That such an item was thought worthy of being noted in historical and biographical works suggests the novelty of the practice. Sawwār comes down in historical narratives as a judge who endeavored to enhance the standing of the court in the public eye by giving it prestige and credibility.[27] But this should in no way imply that the social standing of court witnesses suffered in any form or manner. The sources permit us to conclude that the witnesses came mostly from the upper classes, whose social prestige intermeshed with the judicial valuation of rectitude. In fact, generally speaking, they seem to have belonged to a social stratum higher than that of the typical judge. When in 212 or thereabouts (ca. 827 AD) Ibn ʿAbd al-Ḥakam chose, in his capacity as *ṣāḥib al-masāʾil*, a number of witnesses for the court of the judge ʿĪsā b. al-Munkadir, he exposed himself – together with the judge he was serving – to the severe charge of "dishonoring the institution of testimony" because he "allowed into the House of Justice people who do not belong to it, people who possess neither social standing nor property, such as tailors, grocers, etc."[28]

The court's prestige and authority was also enhanced by the presence in it of men learned in the law. These were the legal specialists (*fuqahāʾ*, *muftī*s) who, mostly out of piety, made the study and understanding (lit. "fiqh") of religious law their primary private concern, and it was this knowledge that lent them what I have elsewhere called epistemic authority.[29] The sources are frequently unclear as to whether or not these specialists were always physically present in the court, but we know that from the beginning of the second century (ca. 720 AD) judges were encouraged to seek the counsel of these learned men and that, by the

26 Wakīʿ, *Akhbār*, II, 58.
27 Ibid.
28 Kindī, *Akhbār*, 436.
29 Hallaq, *Authority*, ix, 166–235.

120s/740s, they often did.[30] From an abundance of later writings on this issue, one can assert with some confidence that the legal specialists were regularly consulted on difficult cases and points of law, although evidence of their *permanent* physical presence in the court is meager (which is not to say that absence of this evidence necessarily means that they did not frequent the courts). However, it is likely that they attended the court often, frequently accompanied by students or apprentices aspiring to a career in the judiciary. What is certain is that from the very beginning, even while Islamic law was still forming during the first century, the proto-*qāḍī*s and *qāḍī*s were in the habit of asking "people who know" about difficult cases they faced[31] – a practice highly encouraged by the Quran itself. In other words, the legal specialists were and remained for many centuries a fixture of the court even when they were not physically present in it. When they were not attending hearings, it was common practice for judges to write to them asking their opinion with regard to matters of law that they found abstruse. And although the judges were not legally bound by the expert opinions of these jurists, in reality they conformed to them nearly always.

This practice was therefore normative, without any official sanction by recognized authority, or at least this was the case in the east. In Andalusia, on the other hand, soliciting the opinions of legal specialists – properly called *mushāwar*s – was mandatory. There it became something of a formal matter, insisted upon by both the legal profession and the political sovereign. Thus, generally speaking, an Andalusian judge's decision was considered invalid without the prior approval of the *mushāwar*s.

The practice may have begun before the middle of the second/eighth century, when the Umayyads established their rule in Andalusia after their defeat by the ʿAbbāsids in the east; but there is no doubt that the obligatory character of the *mushāwar* institution had been fairly established by the beginning of the third/ninth century. During this latter century and the next, the number of *mushāwar*s for each judge seems to have varied according to time and place, although soon thereafter two *mushāwar*s became standard for each court. As in the east, the *mushāwar*s were *muftīs*, chosen by the judge for their mastery of the law. (This fact explains why the greatest bulk of the surviving *fatwā* literature consists mainly of opinions issued by *muftī*s for the benefit of judges.)

30 Wakīʿ, *Akhbār*, II, 423; III, 86.

31 See chapter 3, section 1, above.

Together with the witnesses, bailiffs, chamberlains, and often the legal specialists, the courts of the second/eighth century also included a number of other functionaries, also generally known as the *qāḍī*'s assistants (*aʿwān*). Among these were men whose function it was to search out and apprehend persons charged with a felony or to bring in defendants against whom plaintiffs had presented the court with claims. They were also sent out by the judge to look for witnesses who might have seen, for example, an illegal act being committed. It is possible that at times these functions were discharged in part by *ṣāḥib al-masāʾil* himself, although we have reason to believe that, in larger courts dealing with a considerable volume of cases, there would have been other officials assigned specifically to perform such tasks. Some of these assistants specialized in "public calling," thus acquiring the technical title *munādī*s. These *munādī*s usually went to the markets and public spaces and spoke out loud on court-related matters. They "called" on certain individuals, sought either as witnesses or as defendants, to appear before the judge. Occasionally, they were used as a means of communicating the judge's messages to the public. Thus, in 226/840, immediately upon receiving appointment to the office, Fusṭāṭ's judge, Muḥammad b. al-Layth, dispatched his *munādī* to announce in public that anyone in possession of property belonging to an orphan or absentee should, to avoid the penalty of the law, immediately surrender it to the court. Our source reports that this announcement was effective, in that it resulted in many people surrendering such properties to the Treasury.[32] A decade later, another judge in the same city sent his *munādī* to the Grand Mosque to invite people who might have knowledge of a case of embezzlement to come forth to testify to this effect before him. This call was also effective, for it resulted in many individuals appearing before the *qāḍī* to act as witnesses. [33] It was also the practice for the *munādī*s to be dispatched by a judge merely to announce that the court was in session and that it was open for those who needed to bring a claim before the court.[34] They similarly acted in the same capacity as the chamberlain or *jilwāz*, calling plaintiffs and defendants present in the vicinity of the court to stand before the judge when their turn came.[35] Thus, by the middle of the second century (ca. 770 AD), "calling" in public spaces had become an established practice. To what extent this practice continued beyond the third/ninth century we do not know.

[32] Kindī, *Akhbār*, 450.
[33] Ibid., 462–63. See also Wakīʿ, *Akhbār*, II, 20.
[34] Kindī, *Akhbār*, 76; Wakīʿ, *Akhbār*, II, 52.
[35] Wakīʿ, *Akhbār*, III, 168.

The judge's assistants also included a number of *umanā' al-ḥukm* (lit., trustees of the court) whose tasks involved the safekeeping of confidential information, property and even cash. One category of these officials was responsible for the court's treasury, known as the *tābūt al-quḍāt* (the judge's security chest). The judge who is associated with first establishing such a chest was ʿAbd Allāh al-ʿUmarī who, sometime in the 180s (ca. 800 AD), ordered its construction at the cost of four *dīnār*s. Its location was in the state Treasury but the key to it remained with the judge and/or his trustee placed in charge of it. We know that all sorts of monies were kept in it, especially those belonging to heirless deceased persons, to orphans and to absentees.[36] It is in no way clear how or where such monies had been kept before that time, but we may surmise that the judge himself may have safeguarded them, either on his person or in the state Treasury, without this involving any separate arrangement. At any rate, it was the judge who ultimately was responsible for the *tābūt*'s contents as well as for the conduct of his trustee. For instance, the judge Hārūn b. ʿAbd Allāh was jailed by his successor, Muḥammad b. Abī al-Layth, on the charge that Hārūn's trustee had embezzled large amounts of money from the *tābūt* during his tenure.[37]

Another type of trustee was the *qassām*, who was responsible for dividing cash and property among heirs or disputed objects among litigants. This official was usually hired for his technical skills and knowledge of arithmetic. We are not certain, however, as to the origins of this court institution, although it is fairly safe to say that the function itself may have started during the second half of the first century at the latest (between 670 and 715 AD), this being a reasonable estimate because the division of inherited property was one of the earliest functions assigned to proto-*qāḍī*s, when they still were dealing with estates left by soldiers who had participated in the early conquests. Nonetheless, it is uncertain when judges began to delegate this function to their trustees. As late as the 160s (ca. 780 AD), Sharīk b. ʿAbd Allāh, the judge of Kūfa, was assigned this function himself by the caliph al-Mahdī, although whether it was understood that the duty would automatically be handed over to trustees is hard to say. [38]

Last, but by no means least, a major official of the court was the judge's scribe, of whom we spoke in the previous chapter. By the early portion of

36 Kindī, *Akhbār*, 405.
37 Ibid., 450.
38 Wakīʿ, *Akhbār*, III, 158.

the second/eighth century, his function had become an established feature in all courts. He usually sat immediately to the right or left of the judge, recorded the statements, rebuttals and depositions of the litigants, and, moreover, drew up legal documents on the basis of court records for those who needed the attestation of the judge to one matter or another. His appointment to the court appears to have been the first to be made when a new judge assumed office, and he was required to be of just character, to know the law and to be skilled in the art of writing.[39]

The scribe's function as a court notary must be distinguished from the private notary (*muwaththiq* or *shurūṭī*), who operated outside the court and who drafted legal documents for private parties entering into contracts. This notarial function seems to have become standard legal practice around the middle of the second/eighth century, a good half century after the scribe's function had become fairly established. But its rudimentary origins – in the sense that some proto-experts wrote down legal or quasi-legal documents for the benefit of people – extend back perhaps to the middle of the first century (if not even before, as it must have been an ancient Near Eastern practice). We have seen, for example, that Khārija b. Zayd, who flourished during the last three decades of the first century, was acknowledged to have been expert in the field.

Be that as it may, the *shurūṭī* did not sit in the court; his function was private, not public, unlike that of the court scribe. In contrast to the latter, whose activity was limited to writing in, and copying from, the *qāḍī*'s register, and whose salary the *qāḍī* himself paid, the *shurūṭī* wrote contracts and legal documents of all types and forms, and was retained, for a fee, as a legal expert for this specific purpose by individuals transacting outside the purview of the court.

Thus, the scribe's function was established at an early date, and it did not take long for the institution of the *dīwān* to follow suit and to attain its full form by the third quarter of the second century or immediately thereafter (780 AD et seq.). The *dīwān* represented the totality of the records (*sijillāt*) kept by a judge, and these were normally filed in a bookcase termed a *qimaṭr*.[40] The first judge associated with the notion of a consistent and perhaps systematic keeping of court records was the Baṣran judge Sawwār

39 Hallaq, "*Qāḍī*'s *Dīwān*," 423.

40 Wakīʿ, *Akhbār*, II, 159. The word *qimaṭr* seems to have acquired a variety of meanings, depending on time and place. It may have been "that in which books are preserved," and in a more specifically legal context "the register (*zimām*) in which documents are recorded." See, e.g., Muḥammad al-Ḥaṭṭāb, *Mawāhib al-Jalīl li-Sharḥ Mukhtaṣar Khalīl*, 6 vols. (Ṭarāblus, Libya:

b. ʿAbd Allāh, who was appointed to office in the 140s/760s. In an effort to enhance the authority and prestige of the court, he initiated a series of reforms that included a fairly elaborate keeping of records pertaining to court business.[41] But his *dīwān* does not seem to have been sufficiently inclusive. His near-contemporary Ibn Shubruma is reported to have begun the practice of writing down the claims of the litigants, including a summary of all evidence relevant to the case.[42] The sixth-/twelfth-century jurist al-Ḥusām al-Shahīd b. Māza observed that prior to Ibn Shubruma, judges were not in the habit of reducing to writing the claims of parties to the suit, but instead depended on their memory of who said what. With the benefit of hindsight, Ibn Māza was able to state that the practice initiated by Ibn Shubruma had been imitated by judges ever since.[43] Still, there was room for yet further expansion. It is reported that the practice of *systematic* recording of court affairs was initiated by al-Mufaḍḍal b. Faḍāla, the judge of Fusṭāṭ in around 168/784. He is said to have expanded, as never before, the contents of the *dīwān* so as to include in it records of inheritance, bequests, debts, and much else.[44]

Thus, it is safe to say that before the second/eighth century came to a close, the *qāḍī*'s *dīwān* included the following documentation:

(1) The *maḥāḍir* and *sijillāt*. The former term referred to records of actions and claims made by two parties in the presence of the judge, who usually signed them before witnesses in order for them to be complete and confirmed. It also referred to records of statements made by witnesses to the effect that a certain action, such as sale or a pledge, had taken place. The practice of writing down such testimonies appears to have been in place prior to the middle of the second/eighth century, and is associated with the name of the Kūfan judge and jurist Ibn Abī Laylā, among others.[45] It was on the basis of these *maḥāḍir* that the judge's decision was based. The term *sijillāt*, on the other hand, referred to witnessed records of the contents of *maḥāḍir* together with the judge's decision on each case. The *maḥāḍir* were therefore the basis

Maktabat al-Najāḥ, 1969), VI, 116. It may also be defined as "the sealed register in which cases are recorded." See Taqī al-Dīn Ibn al-Najjār, *Muntahā al-Irādāt*, ed. ʿAbd al-Mughnī ʿAbd al-Khāliq, 2 vols. (Cairo: Maktabat Dār al-ʿUrūba, 1381/1962), II, 582.

41 Wakīʿ, *Akhbār*, II, 58.

42 Ibn Māza al-Ḥusām al-Shahīd, *Sharḥ Adab al-Qāḍī lil-Khaṣṣāf* (Beirut: Dār al-Kutub al-ʿIlmiyya, 1994), 486.

43 Ibid., 487.

44 Kindī, *Akhbār*, 379; Wakīʿ, *Akhbār*, III, 237.

45 Wakīʿ, *Akhbār*, III, 136, 137.

from which the *sijillāt* were constructed.[46] The scribe of the Egyptian judge Ibrāhīm b. al-Jarrāḥ (ca. 205/820) is reported to have described the process of preparing the *sijillāt*. He would prepare the *maḥḍar* and read it to Ibrāhīm who would examine, and then comment on, it. When a decision was required, Ibrāhīm would ask him to "construct a *sijill* on the basis of it." The scribe would usually find inscribed on the back of the sheet statements by Ibrāhīm such as "Abū Ḥanīfa held such-and-such opinion" and on the second line "Ibn Abī Laylā opined such-and-such" and, on yet another line, "Mālik said such-and-such." One of the opinions recorded would be underlined, signaling to the scribe the opinion on the basis of which the case was to be decided. The *sijill* would be composed accordingly.[47]

(2) A list of court witnesses whose just character was confirmed by the *ṣāḥib al-masāʾil* and/or the judge, along with the date of confirmation and the name(s) of the *ṣāḥib al-masāʾil*. The recording of such dates was important because, as we have seen, judges required a review of the character of these witnesses periodically. Six months seems to have been the commonly accepted period between reviews, an interval confirmed by second-/eighth-century accounts as well as by numerous later ones.[48]
(3) A register of trustees over *waqf* properties, orphan's affairs and divorcées' alimonies. Also included here were lists of *waqf* properties, their budgets and the names and salaries of those who worked to maintain them.[49]
(4) A register of bequests.[50]
(5) *Ṣukūk*, which included contracts, pledges, acknowledgments, gifts, donations, written obligations as well as other written instruments.[51]
(6) Copies of letters sent to, and received from, other judges (*kitāb al-qāḍī ilā al-qāḍī*), including any relevant legal documents attached to such letters.[52]

[46] Al-Ḥusām al-Shahīd, *Sharḥ*, 372; Hallaq, "*Qāḍī*'s *Dīwān*," 420.
[47] Kindī, *Akhbār*, 432.
[48] Ibid., 394, 422; Abū Naṣr al-Samarqandī, *Rusūm al-Quḍāt*, ed. M. Jāsim al-Ḥadīthī (Baghdad: Dār al-Ḥurriyya lil-Ṭibāʿa, 1985), 39 ff.
[49] Kindī, *Akhbār*, 355, 424, 444, 450; Abū al-Qāsim al-Simnānī, *Rawḍat al-Quḍāt*, ed. Ṣalāḥ al-Dīn Nāhī, 4 vols. (Beirut and Amman: Muʾassasat al-Risāla, 1404/1984), I, 112.
[50] Kindī, *Akhbār*, 379; Aḥmad b. ʿAlī al-Qalqashandī, *Ṣubḥ al-Aʿshā fī Ṣināʿat al-Inshā*, 14 vols. (Beirut: Dār al-Kutub al-ʿIlmiyya, 1987), X, 284.
[51] Wakīʿ, *Akhbār*, II, 136; Kindī, *Akhbār*, 319, 379; al-Ḥusām al-Shahīd, *Sharḥ*, 57–62; on written obligations, see Michael Thung, "Written Obligations from the 2nd/8th to the 4th Century," *Islamic Law and Society*, 3, 1 (1996): 1–12.
[52] Kindī, *Akhbār*, 410; Samarqandī, *Rusūm al-Quḍāt*, 46.

In addition to these items, the *qāḍī*'s *dīwān* may have contained several other types of registers, such as: a record of prisoners' names and the terms of their imprisonment; a list of guarantors (*kufalā*ʾ), those who had been guaranteed and the objects or matters in question; and/or a list of legally empowered agents (*wukalā*ʾ), those who had bestowed on them such powers of representation, the terms of each agency and the lawsuits involved, and the dates of cases involving such representation.[53] These registers are abundantly attested in later works and their entry into the *qāḍī*s' *dīwān*s may have in part been a later development. However, despite the silence of the early sources, it is conceivable that they may well have crept into the *qāḍī*s' *dīwān*s during the second/eighth century or, almost certainly, immediately thereafter.[54]

The *dīwān* was acknowledged to be the backbone of legal transactions and the means by which the judge could review his decisions as well as all cases and transactions passing through his court. It therefore embodied the complete record of the judge's work in the court, and represented the chief tool by which judicial practice preserved its continuity. By the middle of the second/eighth century, it had become the established practice of outgoing judges to deliver their *dīwān*s over to the newly appointed *qāḍī*s succeeding them, a practice that was to undergo gradual change thereafter when, beginning with the last decade of the second century (805–815 AD) or thereabouts, the new judge began by having his predecessor's *dīwān* copied by his own scribe. This transfer or copying is said to have been the second step taken by judges upon receiving investiture, the first being his appointment of a scribe. In 140/757, Ghawth b. Sulaymān took over the post of Yazīd b. Bilāl (who had just died), and when the *dīwān* failed to be delivered to him, he went to Yazīd's residence and received it there (presumably from one of his relatives).[55] Some three decades later, however, the mode of transferring the *dīwān* began to change. Khālid b. Ḥusayn al-Ḥārithī, who served as a judge sometime between 158/774 and 169/785, was reportedly one of the first, if not the first, to insist on retaining the original copy of his *dīwān*, and on having the incoming judge make two copies of it, both attested by witnesses.[56] But Ḥārithī's action does not seem immediately to have become the norm. At about the same time, the judge ʿĀfiya

[53] Qalqashandī, *Ṣubḥ al-Aʿshā*, X, 274, 291–92; Samarqandī, *Rusūm al-Quḍāt*, 34, 39 ff.; Hallaq, "*Qāḍī*'s *Dīwān*," 421, 428–29.
[54] Hallaq, "*Qāḍī*'s *Dīwān*," 433.
[55] Kindī, *Akhbār*, 360.
[56] Wakīʿ, *Akhbār*, II, 125.

submitted his resignation to the caliph al-Mahdī, and to finalize this process he gave up his *qimaṭr*, the bookcase containing his *dīwān*.[57] Even during the early part of the fourth/tenth century, some *dīwān*s were surrendered to the new judge, presumably without having been copied.[58] This practice, however, was to change soon, when transcribing the predecessor's *dīwān* became the rule.

Whatever the means of transferring the *dīwān*, access to predecessors' records was essential not only for continuing the new judge's work in protracted cases but also for reviewing the work of earlier judges, especially the immediate predecessor. Such a review was usually prompted either by complaints against the outgoing judge or by reasonable suspicion on the part of the new judge of abuse, corruption or one form or another of miscarriage of justice that might be associated with his predecessor. It was access to the *dīwān*s that allowed judicial review in Islam to take on a meaningful role, a role that was, to some limited extent, equivalent to appeal in western judicial systems.

Finally, we turn to the judge himself, who was the backbone of the court. In the course of chapters 2 and 3, we had more than one occasion to discuss the evolution of his office and function. There, we saw that by the very end of the first/seventh century, the judge's office had undergone a degree of specialization whereby it became increasingly confined to legal matters and dissociated from strictly administrative, policing and fiscal tasks. With this development, the judges began to represent a distinct sphere of governance, a class of professionals largely associated with the growing independence of a province of law. I say largely, because the *Islamic* non-judicial functions were not completely and irrevocably removed from the judge's sphere of duties until the middle of the third/ninth century, if not later. In the 150s/770s, Sawwār was appointed by the caliph al-Manṣūr as the judge of Baṣra, and also its prayer-imam as well as its chief of police.[59] As late as 204/819, Ibrāhīm b. Isḥāq was appointed as both judge and story-teller of Fusṭāṭ.[60] Nonetheless, as a general rule, by the middle of the second/eighth century the function of *qaḍā'* became increasingly restricted to duties that, for many centuries thereafter, were to be regarded as appropriate to a judge. This was not only a matter of specialization but also a register of growing

[57] ʿAlī b. al-Muḥassin al-Tanūkhī, *Nishwār al-Muḥāḍara*, 8 vols. (n.p., n.p., 1971–), VIII, 151; al-Ḥusām al-Shahīd, *Sharḥ*, 86.
[58] Ibn Ḥajar al-ʿAsqalānī, *Rafʿ al-Iṣr ʿan Quḍāt Miṣr*, ed. Ḥāmid ʿAbd al-Majīd, 2 vols. (Cairo: al-Hay'a al-ʿĀmma li-Shu'ūn al-Maṭābiʿ al-Amīriyya, 1966), II, 269.
[59] Wakīʿ, *Akhbār*, II, 60.
[60] Kindī, *Akhbār*, 427.

professionalization, further marked by increasing attention that the government paid to the judges' hierarchies, appointments and dismissals. But a no less important indicator of this evolving phenomenon was the investment by the government in their salaries.

Before the middle of the second/eighth century, judges were mostly part-time officials of the government, even if they served it in other, non-judicial capacities. The occasional references in the sources allow us to conclude that a great many – if not most – of them had other jobs, apparently more often manual than clerical. The *nisba*s that formed part of their names point to the manual and other non-judicial professions they practiced.[61] The Egyptian judge Khuzayma b. Ibrāhīm, for example, was otherwise a maker of halters, and the sources confirm that he continued to practice this profession during his tenure as judge (ca. 135/752). In fact, a man is said to have approached him during a court session and to have asked him if he could buy a halter from him. Khuzayma got up, went home (which must have been within a short distance), came back with a halter, sold it to the man, and immediately resumed his court business.[62] However, as time went on, there was a tendency among those who served (or wished to serve) as judges to adopt professions more akin to legal practice, the most notable of these being teaching (the Quran and other subjects) or, more often, copying books and manuscripts. In the middle of the second/eighth century or sometime thereafter, the Kūfan judge Sharīk b. ʿAbd Allāh reportedly was in the business of copying books, teaching the Quran and selling yogurt![63] Similarly, Muḥammad al-Khuwārizmī was a copyist working in Iraq before he was assigned to the judgeship of Fusṭāṭ in 205/820.[64]

The changes in the *qāḍī*s' salaries functioned as both cause and effect in their growing professionalization: they gradually abandoned other concurrent professions and engaged themselves exclusively in judicial work. It appears that even as late as the ninth decade of the first century, judges were still receiving military–administrative stipends (*ʿaṭāʾ*) – to be sharply distinguished from judicial salaries, referred to by the common expression "*ujriya ʿalayhi*" (roughly: "he was paid"). Under the caliph al-Walīd (r. 86/703–96/714), the judge of Damascus was receiving an *ʿaṭāʾ* in the handsome

[61] Hayyim Cohen, "The Economic Background and the Secular Occupations of Muslim Jurisprudents and Traditionists in the Classical Period of Islam (Until the Middle of the Eleventh Century)," *Journal of the Economic and Social History of the Orient*, 13 (1970): 16–61.
[62] Wakīʿ, *Akhbār*, III, 233, 234.
[63] Ibid., III, 150, 151.
[64] Kindī, *Akhbār*, 449.

amount of 200 *dīnārs* a month.[65] This was an extraordinarily high stipend, unique in our sources, and it can perhaps be explained by the fact that the appointee was the judge of the imperial capital. By contrast, the average salary of Egyptian *qāḍīs* ca. 140/757, a much later date, was close to 30 *dīnārs* a month, although smaller salaries are documented from the same period.[66] Still, such an income was far better than the average salary of an artisan or a craftsman. The monthly income of a tailor or an embroiderer during this period does not seem to have exceeded 10 *dīnārs* a month,[67] and a family would have needed some 60 *dīnārs* a year in order to maintain a modest standard of living at this time.[68] By the end of the second/eighth century, the judges' salaries seem to have increased dramatically, an indication that the process of professionalization of the judiciary had reached a certain point of culmination. The salary of Fusṭāṭ's judge, al-Faḍl b. Ghānim, was 168 *dīnārs* a month in 198/813,[69] a generous income considering that this was a provincial appointment. The sources make it clear that this pay was unprecedented for an Egyptian judge,[70] but that it became more or less the standard for later appointments. Thus, we might well take it as an index of the growing specialization and professionalization of the office of *qaḍā'* which, by the end of the third/ninth century, became much coveted and as such developed into a possible source of corruption and competition among the learned hierarchy.

The specialization-cum-professionalization of the *qāḍī*'s office meant that by the beginning of the third/ninth century, and certainly by the middle of it, the judge's functions were defined once and for all. Story-telling, policing and tax collection were, as a rule, removed from his purview, while litigation in all its aspects became his major concern. For in addition to arbitrating disputes, deciding cases and executing verdicts,[71] he supervised the performance of all his assistants – the scribe, the witness examiner, the chamberlain, the trustees and the *munādī*. His functions, however, did not exclude other normative duties performed by *qāḍīs* in earlier periods. Thus, directly or indirectly, he (1) supervised charitable trusts (*awqāf*), their material condition, their maintenance and the performance of those who managed them;[72]

[65] Wakī', *Akhbār*, III, 202.
[66] Ibid., III, 233, 235.
[67] Ibid., III, 169.
[68] Ibid., III, 246.
[69] Kindī, *Akhbār*, 421. For other salaries, see ibid., 435 and Wakī', *Akhbār*, III, 187, 242.
[70] Kindī, *Akhbār*, 421.
[71] Wakī', *Akhbār*, II, 415; III, 89, 135.
[72] Kindī, *Akhbār*, 383, 424, 444, 450.

(2) acted as guardian for orphans, administering their financial affairs and caring for their general wellbeing;[73] (3) took care of the property of absentees, as well as that of anyone who died heirless;[74] (4) heard petitions for conversion from other religions to Islam, and signed witnessed documents to this effect for the benefit of the new Muslims;[75] (5) attended to public works; and (6) often led Friday prayers and prayers at funerals, and announced the rising of the moon, signaling the end of the fast of Ramadan.

3. EXTRA-JUDICIAL TRIBUNALS

Roughly around the time that the ʿAbbāsids created a centralized judicial hierarchy, there appeared a new set of tribunals that stood at the margins of the Sharīʿa courts. These were the *maẓālim* tribunals (lit. "boards of grievances"), generally instated by governors and viziers, theoretically on behalf of the caliph, and presumably for the purpose of correcting wrongs committed by state officials. Theoretically, too, they were sanctioned by the powers assigned to the ruler to establish justice and equity according to the religious law (*siyāsa sharʿiyya*). In reality, however, they at times represented his absolutist governance and interference in the Sharīʿa, however marginal this may have been. Marginal, because the jurisdiction of these tribunals was both limited and sporadic: they were neither permanent nor could they be sustained in the manner the Sharīʿa courts were.

It must be noted, however, that the precise nature of these tribunals is not clear, especially during the formative period. The sources say little about the qualifications of the judges who presided over them, and even less about the procedures and rules they applied. Generally speaking, they tended to apply a wide range of procedural laws – wider, at any rate, than those procedures adopted by the Sharīʿa court judges. They seem to have adopted a far less stringent procedure – admitting, for instance, coercion and summary judgments. Their penalties, furthermore, exceeded the prescribed laws of the Sharīʿa. They thus applied penal sanctions in civil cases, or combined civil and criminal punishments in the same case.

By all indications, the *maẓālim* tribunals functioned less as an encroachment on the Sharīʿa courts than as a supplement to their jurisdiction. Characterized as courts of equity, where the sovereign showed himself to

[73] Wakīʿ, *Akhbār*, II, 58; Kindī, *Akhbār*, 444.
[74] Wakīʿ, *Akhbār*, II, 58; Kindī, *Akhbār*, 444.
[75] Wakīʿ, *Akhbār*, II, 65.

be conducting justice, the *maẓālim* tribunals operated within four main spheres: (1) they prosecuted injustices committed in the performance of public services, such as unfair or oppressive collection of taxes, or non-payment of salaries by government agencies; (2) they dealt with claims against government employees who transgressed the boundaries of their duties and who committed wrongs against the public, such as unlawful appropriation of private property; (3) they heard complaints against Sharīʿa judges that dealt mainly with questions of conduct, including abuses of office and corruption (the *maẓālim* tribunals did not arrogate to themselves the power to hear appeals against Sharīʿa court decisions, which as we have seen were to all intents and purposes final);[76] and (4) they enforced Sharīʿa court decisions that the *qāḍī* was unable to carry out.

References to the *maẓālim* tribunals are rare in our sources. It seems certain that they began to appear after the middle of the second/eighth century, especially during the reign of the caliph al-Mahdī (158/775–169/785). Their function may have been to adjudicate extra-judicial matters, but our sources portray these tribunals as a sort of temporary substitute for the Sharīʿa courts, specifically during periods when a city or a region was left without a Sharīʿa *qāḍī* to sit on the bench. For example, the first reference – to the best of my knowledge – to *maẓālim* in the province of Egypt appears for the year 211/826. In that year, the judge Ibrāhīm b. al-Jarrāḥ died, leaving the bench empty. Unable to find a *qāḍī*, ʿAbd Allāh b. Ṭāhir, then governor of Egypt, appointed ʿAṭṭāf b. Ghazwān as a *maẓālim* magistrate. But once the *qāḍī* ʿĪsā b. al-Munkadir was found willing to serve in Egypt, ʿAṭṭāf was immediately dismissed, having served for less than a year. Again, when ʿĪsā was himself dismissed in 215/830, it was said that Egypt had no *qāḍī*, and Muḥammad b. ʿAbbād was appointed as a *maẓālim* magistrate for about a year, until Hārūn b. ʿAbd Allāh assumed office as Sharīʿa judge. In fact, later on – between 270/883 and 277/890, and between 280/893 and 292/904 – Egypt was exclusively under *maẓālim* jurisdiction, apparently because no *qāḍī* could be found (at least no *qāḍī* who would accept the office).[77]

Judging from the Egyptian experience in the third/ninth century, there appears to have been a great deal of overlap between the *maẓālim* tribunals and the Sharīʿa courts. First of all, during this period, the *maẓālim* tribunals were instituted not in addition to, but instead of, the Sharīʿa courts,

76 For a general discussion of successor review, see David Powers, "On Judicial Review in Islamic Law," *Law and Society Review*, 26 (1992): 315–41.

77 Kindī, *Akhbār*, 432–33, 441, 479–81.

and the reason for this substitution was (by all indications) not judicial interference on the part of the sovereign but rather the absence of men qualified or willing to serve as Sharīʿa judges. If this substitution was meant to bridge the gap left by the absence of a functioning Sharīʿa court, then it is plausible to assume that these tribunals dealt with the same issues that normally came before the Sharīʿa court. Second, some *maẓālim* tribunals were staffed by Sharīʿa judges, no less. In 270/883, Muḥammad b. ʿAbdah was appointed to the *maẓālim* court for seven years, but in 292/904, he was recalled to serve in the joint appointment of a *maẓālim*-cum-Sharīʿa *qāḍī*.[78] Such appointments, and more so, appointments of Sharīʿa judges to *maẓālim* tribunals, were a common phenomenon throughout Islamic history. Third, at least in the Egyptian experience under discussion – and offering an excellent example of jurisdictional overlap – a Sharīʿa judge had the power to rescind decisions of the *maẓālim* magistrate. When Hārūn was appointed as a *qāḍī* in 216/831, he reviewed the decisions of the *maẓālim* magistrate Muḥammad b. ʿAbbād and "revoked many of them."[79] This judicial review may have been sparked by Ibn ʿAbbād's judicial incompetence, but it is more likely that it was a reaction to the extraordinarily wide discretion of the *maẓālim* procedures and the nature of the penalties its tribunals imposed. Be that as it may, during the entire formative period and long thereafter, the standard and dominant law court was the *qāḍī*'s Sharīʿa court. The *maẓālim* tribunals were both sporadic and ephemeral.

[78] Ibid., 480–81.
[79] Ibid., 441.

CHAPTER 5

Prophetic authority and the modification of legal reasoning

1. SUNNAIC PRACTICE VS. PROPHETIC *ḤADĪTH*

It is by now clear that during most of the first century H, the concept of Prophetic Sunna was part and parcel of the *sunan*, i.e., instances of model, binding precedent established by a long list of venerated predecessors. References to *sunna* and *sunna māḍiya* were not always made with the Prophet alone in mind; it was not infrequently the case that other *sunna* founders were, as individuals, the point of such references. Nor was it unusual for *sunna* to refer to the collective conduct of individuals belonging to successive generations, it being assumed that they were all prominent figures who had, by their actions, sanctioned an earlier *sunna* and thereby bestowed their authoritative approval on it. As we have seen, the Prophet himself became the ultimate source of otherwise ancient Arabian *sunan* by virtue of the fact that he merely adopted them (later on, this became the third sub-type of Prophetic Sunna, known as "tacit approval"; the other two were based on the Prophet's own statements and actions, respectively). In other words, in the Muslim tradition, Muḥammad became the initiator of a multitude of *sunan* that were ultimately disconnected from their pre-Islamic past to form an integral part of Prophetic Sunna.

The dramatic increase in Prophetic authority also meant projecting on Muḥammad post-Prophetic *sunan* as well. Legal practices and legal doctrines originating in various towns and cities in the conquered lands, and largely based on the Companions' model, began to find a representational voice in Prophetic Sunna. The projection of the Companions' model back onto the Prophet was accomplished by a long and complex process of creating the narrative of *ḥadīth*. Part of this narrative consisted in the Companions' recollection of what the Prophet had said or done, but another part of it involved extending the chain of authority back to the

Prophet when it in fact had previously ended with a Companion. The creation of massive quantities of *ḥadīth* – including fabrications that had little to do with what the legal specialists knew to be the continuous tradition of legal practice – began to compete not only with Arabian, caliphal and Companion *sunan*, but also with those of the Prophet that had become the basis of legal practice.

Before we proceed, a fundamental point with regard to the proliferation of Prophetic *ḥadīth* must be made. Until recently, modern scholarship seems to have agreed on the notion that the rise of this genre signified the emergence of Islamic law out of secular beginnings, what Joseph Schacht has labeled the "administrative" and "popular" practices of the Umayyads.[1] In other words, law could become Islamicized only upon the creation of a link between secular legal doctrine and the verbal expression of Prophetic Sunna, namely, the *ḥadīth*. This understanding can be validated only if we assume that the *sunan* that appeared prior to Prophetic *ḥadīth* were not conceived by the new Muslims as being religious in nature, namely, that they were disconnected from any religious element that may be defined as Islamic, however rudimentary. But this assumption can in no way be granted since the *sunan*, which preeminently included Prophetic *sīra* and Sunna, were religious and furthermore inspired by the early Muslims' interpretation of what Islam meant to them. They also included *sunan* of the Companions and early caliphs that must be seen, *on their own*, as representations of Islam's religious experience. That these *sunan* and interpretations constituted a rudimentary form of Islam made them no less Islamic than other, later, discourses. That they were dynamic and constantly evolving is self-evident; but to dismiss them as non-religious or non-Islamic just because they underwent significant changes that made them unrecognizable as predecessors of the later, "settled" religious forms is to miss the meaning and historical significance of Islam's first century.

If one accepts the fact that Abū Bakr and ʿUmar I's *sunan*, to use only two examples, were established by these two men in the spirit of the then understood Quranic and Prophetic mission – as two leading Companions who understood best what the Prophet and "Islam" meant to achieve – then one cannot argue that these *sunan* were secular and thus lacking in Islamic, religious content. To argue thus would amount to reducing Islam to a monolith, excluding from it anything that does not fit into our

[1] Schacht, *Origins*, 190–213; Schacht, *Introduction*, 23–27.

conception of what mainstream Islam is or should be. And it was these *sunan* – many of them the genuine *sunan* of the Prophet himself – that constituted much of what later became known as Prophetic *ḥadīth*. Modern research has shown that the emergence of *ḥadīth* involved a lengthy process that involved projecting back Companion and other post-Prophetic narrative onto the Prophet himself, thereby attributing the *sunan* of the former to the latter. This very process in fact attests to how the ancient *sunan* were viewed as embodying a sufficient degree of Islamic content so as to qualify for substitution by Prophetic narrative. To argue that it was only with the emergence of Prophetic *ḥadīth* that Islamic, religious law arose amounts therefore not only to constructing a myth but also to overlooking the entirety of the first Hijri century as one of religious history, however inchoate the Islamic values may have been during that time.

Nor is it reasonable to argue that the body of *ḥadīth* that began to proliferate at the turn of the second century H was fabricated in its entirety, for this argument would overlook the Prophetic *sunan* that had existed from the very beginning. Yet, it is undeniable that much of the *ḥadīth* is inauthentic, representing accretions on, and significant additions to, the Prophetic *sīra* and *sunan* that the early Muslims knew. As we have seen, many of these additions were the work of the story-tellers and tradition-(al)ists, who put into circulation a multitude of fabricated, even legendary, *ḥadīth*s. Indicative of the range of such forgeries is the fact that the later traditionists – who flourished during the third/ninth century – accepted as "sound" only some four or five thousand *ḥadīth*s out of a corpus exceeding half a million. This is one of the most crucial facts about the *ḥadīth*, a fact duly recognized by the Muslim tradition itself.

For reasons that are not entirely clear, but which may have been connected with the rise of political and theological movements in Iraq – the centre-stage of the empire – much of the *ḥadīth* fabrication seems to have occurred in that region's garrison towns which, by the beginning of the second/eighth century, had developed into full-fledged urban centers. As literary narrative that had undergone tremendous growth, the *ḥadīth* was no longer an authentic expression of the fairly modest range of genuine Prophetic *sunan* and *sīra*. Masses of *ḥadīth*s, all of them equipped with their own chains of transmission, were put into circulation throughout the Muslim lands, but they often contradicted the memory and practice of Muslim communities in some regions. Nowhere was this more obvious than in the case of the Hejaz, especially Medina, where the legal scholars believed that their memory of the Prophet's actions – performed there as part of his Sunna – still survived amongst them. For these scholars, the Prophetic Sunna and their own practice were identical, and reference to one was nearly always a reference to the other, although it was often the case that the Prophetic example was both implied and even taken for granted rather than explicitly mentioned. With the rapid proliferation of *ḥadīth* narratives during the course of the second/eighth century, significant differences between *ḥadīth* and Prophetic Sunna frequently became apparent – especially to those living in the Prophet's homeland. For the latter, these *ḥadīth* could be an importation from Iraq or elsewhere (including some probably originating in Medina itself), having nothing to do with what they viewed as the "true" and "authentic" Sunna preserved by the actual practice of their own community. For Medinan scholars then, the true Sunna of the Prophet was attested by their own practice, the ultimate proof of past Prophetic *sunna* (*sunna māḍiya*), and not by a literary narrative that had nothing to commend it except its own affirmation of itself.

Ibn al-Qāsim (191/806), a Medinese scholar, explains this duality in the Prophetic model. Speaking of one *ḥadīth*, he says:

> This tradition [*ḥadīth*] has come down to us, and if it were accompanied by a practice passed to those from whom we have taken it over by their own predecessors, it would be right to follow it. But in fact it is like those other traditions which are not accompanied by practice . . . These things could not assert themselves and take root, [for] the practice was different, and the whole community and the Companions themselves acted on other rules. So the traditions remained neither discredited nor adopted in practice, and actions were ruled by other traditions which were accompanied by practice.[2]

The continuous practice of the Medinese, as reflected in the cumulative, common opinion of the scholars, thus became the final arbiter in determining the content of the Prophet's Sunna. The literary narrative of *ḥadīth* acquired validity only to the extent that it was supported by this local usage. In other words, *ḥadīth* lacking foundations in practice was rejected, while established, past practice (*sunna māḍiya*, *al-amr al-mujtamaʿ ʿalayhi ʿindanā*, etc.)[3] constituted an authority-statement fit to serve as the basis of legal construction even if not backed by *ḥadīth*.

It would be a mistake, however, to view the Medinese doctrine as a categorical rejection of *ḥadīth* in favor of local practice, as some modern scholars have done. What was at stake for the Medinese was not a

[2] Cited in Schacht, *Origins*, 63.
[3] Mālik b. Anas, *al-Muwaṭṭa'* (Beirut: Dār al-Jīl, 1414/1993), 664, 665, 690, 698 and *passim*.

distinction between Prophetic and local, practice-based authority, but rather one between two competing conceptions of Prophetic sources of authority: the Medinan scholars' conception was that *their own* practice represented the logical and historical (and therefore legitimate) continuation of what the Prophet lived, said and did, and that the newly circulating *ḥadīths* were at best redundant when they confirmed this practice and at worst, false, when they did not accord with the Prophetic past as continuously documented by their own living experience of the law. Nor is it to say that the sunnaic practice itself stood as the ultimate authority, as a self-justifying body of doctrine. Rather, it was clearly based on Companion and, consequently, Prophetic authority. Mālik's *Muwaṭṭa'* – an accurate account of Medinese doctrine as it stood by 150/767 or before –[4] contains 898 Companion reports, but as many as 822 for the Prophet alone. The latter were deemed authentic by virtue of the fact that they – or most of them – reflected the actual practice of the Medinese.

The Iraqians, and particularly the Kūfans, also displayed a duality in their conception of *sunna*, but this conception was different from the one held by the Medinese in at least two respects. First, the Kūfan practice could not (and did not) claim the continuity of Prophetic practice that the Medinese were able to do. In fact, the term "practice" (*'amal*), including any expression connoting notions of "practice," was virtually nonexistent in the Kūfan discourse, although "*sunna*" for them at times referred to legal practice. Nor were references to uninterrupted past practices as frequent as those made by the Medinese. Second, the Iraqians could never claim the consensual unanimity that the Medinese easily claimed for their practice. At the same time, however, the Iraqian concept of Prophetic Sunna was not always expressed in *ḥadīth* from the Prophet. Their *sunna* was embedded in the legal realia of practice and, like that of Medina, did not always need to be identified as Prophetic. It was nearly always understood to have emanated from the Prophetic past, although the scope of this past often exceeded that of the Prophet himself to include the experience of some of his Companions. The formal narrative that came to be known as *ḥadīth* not only excluded non-Prophetic elements but included, in addition, variants to the then-existing local practice.

The Iraqians rationalized their reliance on Prophetic Sunna by accepting as part of their doctrine those Prophetic traditions that were widespread in the community, together with others that were deemed reliably

[4] Wael Hallaq, "On Dating Mālik's *Muwaṭṭa'*," *UCLA Journal of Islamic and Near Eastern Law*, 1, 1 (2002): 47–65, at 53.

transmitted by individuals (what we will call "solitary" reports). More importantly, the Iraqians, like the Medinese, saw themselves as connecting their own practice with the Prophetic past through an appeal to the Companions, many of whom had left the Hejaz to settle in the garrison towns of southern Iraq. They accepted as authoritative those Companion reports or rulings not contradicted by the reports of other Companions or by those of the Prophet. The operative assumption here was that the absence of contradictory information from other Companions was a decisive argument in favor of the reports' truth, since this silence in their view demonstrated not only the Companions' unanimous approval of the practice but also their certain knowledge of what the Prophet's Sunna was. For the Iraqians, therefore, this mode of documentation established a link, however indirect, between their practice, or "living tradition," and the Prophet's Sunna.

Like the Medinese notion of Prophetic Sunna, the Syrian concept, as reflected in the doctrine of Awzāʿī, was the uninterrupted practice of Muslims, beginning with the Prophet and maintained by the early caliphs and later scholars. Awzāʿī refers to the practices of the Prophet without adducing *ḥadīth* accompanied by chains of transmission, all as part of an uninterrupted practice that came down to him and to his contemporaries from Prophetic times.

This picture of legal practice as Prophetic Sunna is the hallmark of developments at least until the end of the second century (ca. 815 AD). Each locale, from Syria to Iraq to the Hejaz, established its own legal practices on the basis of what was regarded as the *sunna* of the forefathers, be they the Companions or the Prophet, although the latter more often than not merely sanctioned the ancient Arabian *sunan*. Medina was the abode of the Prophet, whose own actions contributed to the formation of a fairly unified practice. In Kūfa, Baṣra and Damascus, the Prophetic example was embodied in his Companions who migrated to these regions and who carried with them the Prophetic legacy, however this legacy might have been interpreted or applied in one place or another. Thus the ancient Arabian concept of *sunna*, largely if not exclusively secular, was transformed into a religious paradigm, undergoing a process whereby it increasingly focused on the Prophet as person. The pre-Islamic *sunan* adopted by the Prophet, like those *sunan* sanctioned by the post-Prophetic generations, in time became lodged within the realm of Prophetic authority. The Prophet, in time, was to emerge as the single axis of this authority.

The logic of the Prophet's centricity appeared on the scene soon after his death, and started to assert itself by the sixth or seventh decade of the Hijra (ca. 680 AD). But its most obvious manifestation occurred during the second half of the second century (770–810 AD) and thereafter, when his authority became most paramount. The central phenomenon associated with this process was, however, the proliferation of formal *ḥadīth* which came to compete with the practice-based *sunan* – what we call here sunnaic practice. The competition was thus between a formal and nearly universal conception of the Prophetic model and those local practices that had their own view of the nature of Prophetic Sunna. With the emergence of a mobile class of tradition(al)ists, whose main occupation was the collection and reproduction of Prophetic narrative, the formal, literary transmission of *ḥadīth* quickly gained the upper hand over sunnaic practice. The tradition(al)ists were not necessarily jurists or judges, and their impulse was derived more from religious ethic than from the demands and realities of legal practice; nevertheless, at the end of the day, their *ḥadīth* project proved victorious, leaving behind a distant second the local conceptions of Prophetic Sunna – a Sunna that did not have the overwhelmingly personal connection to the Prophet claimed by the tradition(al)ist version. That many of the local jurists participated in the tradition(al)ist project to the detriment of their own sunnaic practice is eloquent testimony to the power of the newly emerging *ḥadīth*.

The power of the formal *ḥadīth* to captivate the minds of Muslims can be explained in at least two ways: First, unlike the sunnaic practice, which had no objectively defined pedigree, *ḥadīth documented*, or *attempted to document*, the Sunna as a historical event, attested by persons who had themselves engaged in transmitting it. This mode of documentation not only proved successful for the tradition(al)ists, but also captured the imagination even of the historians who recorded the annals of Islam. Second, the *ḥadīth* was a universal body of knowledge, borne and worked out by a large and mobile class of scholars who, on the whole, had no particular loyalty to a regionally based practice. It is no coincidence that the rise of *ḥadīth* occurred simultaneously with the evolution of Muslim communities in the vast, non-Arab regions of the empire, especially in the eastern provinces of the Iranian world. Urban Muslim communities in these regions did not possess practice-based *sunna* (as had developed in the Hejaz, Iraq and Syria), and the *ḥadīth* was a convenient means through which these communities could acquire a source for their own legal practice. Thus, both documentation and lack of particular practice-based loyalties rendered the *ḥadīth* universally appealing, except to those jurists and judges who remained loyal to their own version of sunnaic practice. (This is not to suggest that the latter version was less faithful to the

Prophetic example, for in all likelihood it was more consistent with actual Prophetic history than the extremely rich, but highly contradictory and inconsistent, narrative of formal *ḥadīth*. It would be ironic, therefore, if the very narrative that claimed the authority to unravel the true Prophetic example ended by masking rather than revealing this Prophetic history.)

By the end of the second/eighth century, it had become clear that the tradition(al)ist movement was in a position to permit it to achieve significant victory over sunnaic practice, a victory that would be complete about half a century – or more – later. For Shāfiʿī (d. 204/819), who was one of the most vocal *ḥadīth* protagonists of his day, Prophetic Sunna could be determined only through formal *ḥadīth*. He attacked the sunnaic practice as a mass of inconsistencies, decidedly inferior to what he saw as the authentic *ḥadīth* of the Prophet. His theory – and he was no doubt the first to theorize in this regard to any significant degree – is to be expected, since by his time Prophetic *ḥadīth* had become rampant and the tradition(al)ist movement dominated to an unprecedented degree. The most distinctive feature of his theory was the paramount importance of this form of *ḥadīth*, which he took to override the authority of Iraqian, Medinese and Syrian sunnaic practices. Yet, his insistence on the supremacy of Prophetic *ḥadīth* (and the Quran) as the paramount sources of the law did not gain immediate acceptance, contrary to what some modern scholars have argued.[5] It took more than half a century after his death for the *ḥadīth* to become (with the Quran, of course) the exclusive material source of the law, thereby once and for all trumping sunnaic practice.[6]

What strengthened the case of the traditionalists was the crucial development of the science of *ḥadīth* criticism, known as *al-jarḥ wal-taʿdīl*. This science, which focused mainly on establishing the credibility of traditionists, had as its central task the scrutinizing of the chains of transmission, thereby establishing for "sound" *ḥadīth*s a continuous series of trustworthy transmitters going back to the Prophet himself. This "scientific" documentation of *ḥadīth*, we have said, proved to be an attractive feature and one that was conducive to the propagation and success of *ḥadīth* over and against sunnaic practice.

[5] For a revision of this position, see the important article by Susan Spectorsky, "*Sunnah* in the Responses of Isḥāq B. Rāhawayh," in Bernard Weiss, ed., *Studies in Islamic Legal Theory* (Leiden: Brill, 2002), 51–74.

[6] Although – as we shall see in chapter 6, section 2 below – the later Mālikites continued to uphold a revised form of the sunnaic, consensual practice of Medina. See Abū al-Walīd al-Bājī, *Iḥkām al-Fuṣūl fī Aḥkām al-Uṣūl*, ed. ʿAbd al-Majīd Turkī (Beirut: Dār al-Gharb al-Islāmī, 1986), 480–85.

2. CONSENSUS

During the first two centuries H (seventh–eighth centuries AD), the concept of consensus could hardly be distinguished from sunnaic practice, since the sanctioning authority of the latter resided in the overwhelming agreement of the legal specialists who collectively upheld this practice. Conversely, general acceptance by the community at large, and by the community of specialists in particular, were deemed two of the most essential features of sunnaic practice. Agreement on this practice – what we call here, somewhat anachronistically, "consensus" – was often employed as argument against *ḥadīth*s that were not transmitted "by many from many" – namely, "solitary" or "individual" *ḥadīth*s. At times, this agreement was invoked to sanction the authenticity of a *ḥadīth* that supported a particular doctrine of sunnaic practice. The point to be made here is that by deeming consensual sunnaic practice to be determinative of which *ḥadīth*s were credible and which were not, this practice was raised in effect to the first source of law, save perhaps for the Quran.

During most of the first two centuries H, the notion of consensus was expressed by various verbs or through compound expressions, rather than by the later technical term *ijmāʿ* (lit., agreement, and thus consensus). The Medinese often expressed it in terms such as "the matter on which we agree." The Kūfans characterized it as the "opinion on which the people of Kūfa agree."[7] More frequently, however, claims for consensus were neither direct nor positive. Medinese consensus was often reflected in statements about the unanimity of sunnaic practice, such as "this is the matter that the people [of Medina] have continuously upheld," or "the Sunna on which there is no disagreement among us."[8] Thus, the lack of a fixed technical term for consensus does not mean that during this period the notion of consensus was rudimentary or even underdeveloped; on the contrary, it was seen as binding and, furthermore, determinative of *ḥadīth*.

As the other side of the coin of sunnaic practice, consensus represented the final argument on all matters. In other words, it could not be conceived as being subject to error, since any acknowledgment that sunnaic practice was fallible would have cast the entire edifice of legal doctrine into doubt. This epistemic quality of certitude placed consensus in diametrical opposition to *raʾy* which, by definition, represented the opinion of an individual jurist. Thus, whereas consensus generated a unity of doctrine, *raʾy*

[7] Ibid. See also Mālik, *Muwaṭṭaʾ*, 452, 454, 456; Ansari, "Islamic Juristic Terminology," 285, 287.
[8] Mālik, *Muwaṭṭaʾ*, 463, 558, and *passim*.

generated disagreement (to develop later as a field of study on its own, designated by the technical expression *ikhtilāf* or *khilāf*.)

As an expression of sunnaic practice, consensus was not conceived merely as "the agreement of recognized jurists during a particular age," a definition that became standard in later legal theory. Rather, consensus during this early period strongly implied the agreement of scholars based on the continuous practice that was, in turn, based on the consensus of the Companions. It should be stressed here that the latter was viewed as essential to the process of foregrounding later doctrine in Prophetic authority, since the consensus of the Companions, *ipso facto*, was an attestation of Prophetic practice and intent. The Companions, after all, could not have unanimously approved a matter that the Prophet had rejected or prohibited. Nor, in the conception of early jurists, could they have pronounced impermissible what the Prophet had declared lawful.

The conviction of the Medinans that their city and its law were the locus of Prophetic action seems to have affected their conception of both their sunnaic practice and consensus. The chief Medinan scholar, Mālik, emphasized that it was Medina that the Prophet had made his home, and that it was in Medina that the Quran was revealed. This city had been led by the Prophet, who ordered its life and who set examples (*sunan*) to be followed by its community of believers. What these believers and the succeeding generations of Medinans had accomplished was upholding the Prophetic example through, in effect, living it. With this conception in mind, Mālik declared Medinan consensus to be binding on all jurists, local or otherwise.[9] The Medinese certainty of their ways, Prophetically inspired and dictated, allowed them to declare the Medinese example – expressed in its consensus – as the standard norm from which deviation could not be allowed.

Thus understood, Medinan consensus cannot be viewed as a provincial concept, as some modern scholars have argued.[10] If the Medinans referred to their own consensus exclusively, as they did, it was because they believed that theirs represented the ruling consensus. The Iraqians, on the other hand, did not have the benefit of a direct Prophetic foregrounding, since their highest authorities were Companions (although these latter did forge the necessary link with the Prophetic past). In their polemical bid for doctrinal legitimacy, the Iraqian jurists often – but by no means always – claimed universal consensus for certain of their doctrines, bringing in

[9] Ansari, "Islamic Juristic Terminology," 284–85.
[10] Schacht, *Origins*, 83–85.

the Medinese, Meccans, Kūfans and Baṣrans. Such doctrines, however, were Iraqian, and if a universal consensus was claimed for them, it was by virtue of the fact that they represented a common denominator of the sunnaic practices of the Companions. In other words, Iraqian consensus, no less than was the case with Medina (and, for that matter, Syria), was the other side of the coin of Iraqian sunnaic practice.

The force of Medinese sunnaic-consensual practice as the supreme model manifested itself in the fundamental issue of rationalizing consensus. The growth in the religious values and impulse of Islam, coupled with the development of technical legal thought, produced – as part of the theoretical sophistication of Islamic jurisprudence – the need to justify what came to be considered "secondary" sources of the law, sources that did not directly issue from the Divine. Consensus, originating in pre-Islamic Arab tribal conduct, was one of these. By the middle of the second/eighth century, it had inextricably merged with the sunnaic practices of various Muslim communities, thus acquiring a religious character. It was at that time that Muslim jurists felt the need to anchor their consensus in religious texts. Shaybānī appears to have been among the first to do so, invoking the *ḥadīth*: "What Muslims consider to be good is good in the view of God."[11] (This *ḥadīth* was soon classified as weak, and consensus was justified by other means.)[12] Shaybānī's reliance on *ḥadīth* reflected the rising importance of textual sources as competitors of sunnaic, consensual practice. But it also reflected the Kūfan knowledge that the pedigree of their sunnaic practice did not extend directly down to the Prophet himself, but only to his Companions who, by implication and extension, connected the Prophetic past with the practice of the present. This the Medinese had no problem with. They could claim the Prophet as their final, direct authority, one who created the Sunna for the Companions by means of actually applying it before them. Mālik therefore did not feel the need to invoke *ḥadīth*s as an integral part of his reasoning, for the sunnaic, consensual practice of his city was in itself evidence of the authoritative character of consensus. If the Medinese adopted a doctrine by virtue of their agreement on it, then everyone had to adopt it, for by definition it was embedded in the continuing Prophetic experience that the Medinese put into practice each day of their lives.

[11] On Shaybānī and the larger issue of grounding consensus in revelation, see Wael Hallaq, "On the Authoritativeness of Sunni Consensus," *International Journal of Middle East Studies*, 18 (1986): 427–54, at 431.

[12] Ibid.

3. LEGAL REASONING

In chapter 2, we saw that *ra'y* represented the opinions of the proto-*qāḍīs* and legal scholars, as well as of the caliphs. Nearly all those who were involved in matters legal, from the very beginning until the end of the second/eighth century (and for decades thereafter), employed it in their reasoning. Whether based on knowledge of precedent (*ʿilm*) or not, *ra'y* encompassed a variety of inferential methods that ranged from discretionary and loose reasoning to arguments of a strictly logical type, such as analogy or the *argumentum a fortiori.* The Medinese, the Iraqians and the Syrians made extensive use of it during the second/eighth century, subsuming under it nearly all forms of argument.

However, with the development of the circles of legal specialists and with the evolution of new forms of scholarly debate and dialogue, legal reasoning was soon to become more and more elaborate. Sophisticated techniques of reasoning began to surface by the very beginning of the second/eighth century, although much of the old, and somewhat archaic, juristic formulations were not phased out completely. *Ra'y,* therefore, became the umbrella term for a wide variety of legal arguments, and it remained for nearly a century thereafter the standard term designating legal inferences.

During the second half of the second/eighth century, a new generation of scholars was reared in an environment permeated by Prophetic *ḥadīth,* which had come to assert, more than at any time before, the personal authority of the Prophet. The more pronounced this authority became, the less freedom the jurists had in expounding discretionary opinion. For, after all, the *raison d'être* of Prophetic authority was its ability to induce conformity of conduct to the Prophetic model. Insofar as it included discretionary and personal opinion, *ra'y* stood as antithetical to this notion of authority.

Because it included what later came to be considered loose methods of reasoning, *ra'y* inevitably acquired negative connotations, and as a result suffered a significant decline in reputation toward the end of the second/eighth century. It was not fortuitous that this decline coincided with the rise of *ḥadīth* as an incontestable expression of Prophetic Sunna. The latter, in other words, could leave no room for human discretion, since its very existence demanded that a choice be made between human and Prophetic/Divine authority. The former obviously was no match for the latter.

But by the middle of the second century (ca. 770 AD), and long before *ḥadīth* asserted itself as an unrivaled entity, *ra'y* had incorporated systematic and logical arguments of the first rate, arguments that were in turn far from devoid of sunnaic support. These types of argument could not have declined with *raʾy*, and had to be protected as valid forms of reasoning. In a gradual process of terminological change that began immediately after the middle of the second/eighth century and which reached its zenith sometime before the middle of the next century, *raʾy* appears to have been broken down into three categories of argument, all of which had originally been offshoots of the core notion.

The most general of these categories was *ijtihād*, which term, during the first/seventh and most of the second/eighth century, appeared frequently in conjunction with *raʾy*, namely, *ijtihād al-raʾy*. In this early period, whenever *ijtihād* stood alone, it denoted the "estimate" of an expert, i.e., the evaluation of damages in terms of financial or other compensation.[13] But when combined with *raʾy*, it meant the exertion of mental energy for the sake of arriving, through reasoning, at a considered opinion. Later, when the term "*raʾy*" was dropped from the combination, *ijtihād* came to stand alone for this same meaning, but this terminological transformation was short lived, as we shall see in due course.

The second category of arguments to emerge out of *raʾy* was *qiyās*, signifying disciplined and systematic reasoning on the basis of the revealed texts, the Quran and *ḥadīth*. This is not to say that *qiyās* as a procedure became known only after *raʾy* experienced a decline, for the concept was already known, without its later name, as early as (if not long before) the beginning of the second/eighth century. The Iraqians used it, without calling it such, extensively; indeed, Shāfiʿī repeatedly calls them the "Folk of *Qiyās*."[14] In fact, they seem to have employed this procedure more extensively than others did, and all indications point to the likelihood that the legal culture of Islamic (and very possibly pre-Islamic) Iraq favored this method of reasoning. Long before Shāfiʿī, Kūfan jurists realized that *qiyās* had to rest on the texts and that it could not be used in the presence of established sunnaic and textual rules.[15]

A characteristic feature of jurisprudential terminology before Shāfiʿī is that most *qiyās* reasoning was not labeled as such but operated under the general guise of the term "*raʾy*" and its derivatives. When later jurists, including Shāfiʿī, looked back at the contents of earlier *raʾy*, they discerned therein unambiguous forms of *qiyās*. However, by the end of that century,

[13] Schacht, *Origins*, 116. This meaning of *ijtihād* was to persist for many centuries thereafter.
[14] Ibid., 109.
[15] Ansari, "Islamic Juristic Terminology," 290–91.

qiyās as a distinct term had become fairly widespread, and Shāfiʿī began using it in a technical sense.[16] But for Shāfiʿī, *qiyās* was a near synonym of *ijtihād*, involving specific methods of legal reasoning. As explained earlier, however, *ijtihād* lost this sense at a point soon after, or probably during, Shāfiʿī's lifetime. In the legal theory (*uṣūl al-fiqh*) of the later schools, *ijtihād* universally came to mean the effort exerted by the jurist in exercising his interpretive and reasoning faculties – an elaborate process that included *qiyās* as well as more general and wide-ranging methods of a hermeneutical or linguistic nature. In other words, *ijtihād* after Shāfiʿī ceased to be equated simply with *qiyās*, and indeed this jurist seems to have been alone in equating the two concepts.

For jurists after Shāfiʿī, *ijtihād* encompassed, among many other things, *qiyās*. The latter, on the other hand, emerged as the standard term designating those strictly and systematically reasoned arguments of *raʾy* that were based on the revealed texts. The most common argument subsumed under *qiyās* is analogical reasoning, which can range from the simplest to the most complex of forms. Thus, if grape-wine is textually prohibited because of its intoxicating quality, then date-wine, by analogy, would also be prohibited, since the latter is an inebriating substance.[17] A more complex analogy may be seen in a case involving the purchase of a married female slave. The Iraqians argued that the buyer had the option (*khiyār*) of canceling the sale within three days, and of recovering the price from the seller. The reasoning behind this ruling is that the goods purchased (in this case the female slave) contained a defect entitling the buyer to exercise the option of cancellation. The defect, analogically inferred, lay in the buyer's inability to exercise his full rights of ownership over the slave since the fact that she was married ruled out the possibility of having sexual intercourse with her. The marriage of the slave therefore constituted – in this particular context – an impediment similar to an actual defect rendering her unfit for sexual relations with her master.[18]

Qiyās encompassed other forms of argument that had been known – again without being designated by technical terms – as early as the first century H.[19] One of the most common of such arguments was the *a fortiori*,

[16] Muḥammad b. Idrīs al-Shāfiʿī, *al-Risāla*, ed. M. Kīlānī (Cairo: Muṣṭafā Bābī al-Ḥalabī, 1969), 205–19, trans. M. Khadduri, *Islamic Jurisprudence: Shafiʿi's* Risala (Baltimore: Johns Hopkins University Press, 1961), 288–303.

[17] Mālik, *Muwaṭṭaʾ*, 737–38.

[18] Muḥammad b. al-Ḥasan al-Shaybānī, *al-Aṣl*, 5 vols. (Beirut: ʿĀlam al-Kutub, 1990), V, 173; see also Mālik, *Muwaṭṭaʾ*, 544–45.

[19] Schacht, *Origins*, 99, 110, 124 f.

in both of its forms, the *a maiore ad minus* and the *a minore ad maius*. If the consumption of any quantity of wine, however small, is prohibited in the revealed texts, then a larger quantity would obviously be equally prohibited. The same is the case with selling it: if drinking it is unlawful, then selling it, though less offensive, would be equally impermissible.[20]

The third and final category of arguments that came under the heading of *raʾy* was *istiḥsān*, commonly translated as "juristic preference." We have no adequate definition of this reasoning method from the period before Shāfiʿi, most of our knowledge of it being derived either from Shāfiʿī's polemics against it (which are hardly trustworthy) or late Ḥanafite theoretical reconstructions of it (which involve an ideological remapping of history). It seems, however, safe to characterize the second-/eighth-century meaning of *istiḥsān* as a mode of reasoning that yields reasonable results, unlike strictly logical inference such as *qiyās* which may lead to an undue hardship. But it was also employed as a method of equity, driven by reasonableness, fairness and commonsense. For example, according to strict reasoning, punishment for thievery (cutting off the hand) is to be inflicted on the person who moves the stolen goods from the "place of custody" (*ḥirz*), irrespective of whether or not he had accomplices. According to *istiḥsān*, if a group commits theft, but only one person moves the stolen object from its *ḥirz*, then all must face the same penalty.[21] This latter mode of reasoning was deemed preferred, for, since the rationale of punishment is deterrence, all participating thieves should be held accountable.

The Iraqians used *istiḥsān* extensively (again mostly without giving it this designation) as early as the beginning of the second/eighth century, and the Kūfan jurist Shaybānī, half a century later, would devote an entire chapter to it in his *Aṣl*, entitled, significantly, "The chapter of *istiḥsān*," in which a large number of such cases are included.[22] This does not mean, however, that all these cases fell under the "loose" reasoning which later non-Ḥanafite jurists accused the Iraqians of employing, since many were textually based and, furthermore, exhibited the systematic and strict arguments of *qiyās*. Nor does the existence of such a chapter mean that other sections of Shaybānī's work were devoid of cases of *istiḥsān*, since such cases can be found throughout Iraqian works, whether penned by Shaybānī or

[20] Mālik, *Muwaṭṭaʾ*, 737–39. For a more detailed discussion on how these arguments developed in later legal theory, see Hallaq, *History*, 96–99.

[21] Cited in Ansari, "Islamic Juristic Terminology," 294.

[22] Shaybānī, *Aṣl*, III, 43–137.

by others. Like *ra'y*, which acquired a bad name by virtue of its having included personal opinions that lacked formal grounding in the revealed texts, *istiḥsān* too shared a similar fate of rejection. But unlike *ra'y*, it survived in the later Ḥanafite and Ḥanbalite schools as a secondary method of reasoning, though not without ingenious ways of theoretical rehabilitation.[23]

The jurist whose work best exemplifies this transition from what we may call the pre-*ḥadīth* to the *ḥadīth* period was Shāfiʿī. This is not to say, however, that he effected any significant change in Islamic legal development, for he was merely one among many who contributed to this process. It is a mistake – which Joseph Schacht and others[24] have committed – to credit him with having transformed Islamic jurisprudence into what came to be its mature form. But we shall return to this theme later.[25]

Shāfiʿī is important chiefly because his later work represents a defense of Prophetic *ḥadīth* as an exclusive substitute for sunnaic practice. Of almost equal importance in this context, however, is what this defense entailed in terms of legal reasoning. In respect of *ra'y*, his work is remarkable because it manifests a stage of development in which *ra'y* meets with the first major attack in an offensive that ultimately led to its ouster (terminologically and to a certain extent substantively) from Islamic jurisprudence. Categorically labeling *ra'y* as arbitrary, he excluded it, along with *istiḥsān*, from the domain of reasoning altogether. *Ḥadīth* at the same time comes to reflect divine authority, leaving no room for human judgment. As a methodical inference dictated by textual imperatives, *qiyās* (or *ijtihād*) thus became the exclusive method of legal reasoning, based on the Quran, the Sunna of the Prophet (as expressed by *ḥadīth*) and the consensus of the scholars.[26] It was to be used, however, only in the absence of a relevant text, and then sparingly. By virtue of the fact that it was based on such sources, *qiyās* could not repeal or supersede them.

Shāfiʿī appears to have been the first jurist consciously to articulate the notion that Islamic revelation provides a full and comprehensive evaluation of human acts. The admittance of *qiyās* (*ijtihād*) into his jurisprudence was

[23] Hallaq, *History*, 107–13. See also chapter 5, section 3 and chapter 6, section 1 below.

[24] Schacht, *Origins*; N. J. Coulson, *A History of Islamic Law* (Edinburgh: Edinburgh University Press, 1964), 53 ff.

[25] In chapters 6 and 7, below. But see also Wael Hallaq, "Was al-Shafiʿi the Master Architect of Islamic Jurisprudence?" *International Journal of Middle East Studies*, 25 (1993): 587–605.

[26] The view that Shāfiʿī upheld the concept of community consensus has been revised by Joseph Lowry, "The Legal–Theoretical Content of the *Risāla* of Muḥammad b. Idris al-Shāfiʿī," (Ph.D. dissertation, University of Pennsylvania, 1999), 471 ff.

due to his recognition of the fact that this divine intent is not completely fulfilled by the revealed texts themselves, since these latter do not afford a direct answer to every eventuality. But to Shāfiʿī, acknowledging the permissibility of *qiyās* does not bestow on it a status independent of revelation. If anything, without revelation's sanction of the use of this method it would not have been allowed, and when it is permitted to operate it is because *qiyās* is the only method that can bring out the meaning and intention of revelation regarding a particular eventuality. *Qiyās* does not itself generate rules or legal norms; it merely discovers them from, or brings them out of, the language of revealed texts.

Much of Shāfiʿī's theory ultimately harks back to his vehement defense of Prophetic *ḥadīth* as the universal substitute for sunnaic practice. His careful definition of *qiyās* and the limit beyond which it cannot be employed was little more than a veiled attack against *istiḥsān*, which he saw as being part of the arbitrary, personal opinions characteristic of the dangerously speculative *raʾy*. If the *ḥadīth* was to thrive and be given a definite and enduring place in the law, it had to be taken seriously as the foundation of reasoning. The semiotic structure, so to speak, of sunnaic practice made it too vague as a medium for deriving rules, for it lacked textual specificity and left too much room for human deliberation and intervention. In other words, the latitude accorded to human interpretation was too great for Shāfiʿī, whose reformulation of divine authority required taking the Prophet's life as the exclusive model. And the best way to know what that model represented was the *ḥadīth*s – that is, those traditions that could be studied, verified as reliable and then exploited as text and language. *Qiyās* (and *ijtihād*), therefore, must be a systematic and well-defined method that is fully controlled as an interpretive and inductive/deductive tool. This mode of reasoning is the only guarantee that one is adhering closely to God's intentions, and the only way to achieve compliance with these intentions is through the study of the Prophet's *ḥadīth*, namely, *a study of texts* that will lead to reasoning and, finally, inference of rules.

The centrality of the *ḥadīth* thesis to Shāfiʿī's theory led him to formulate, and indeed articulate, other principles of interpretation. One such principle was that *qiyās* must be based on the outward meaning (*ẓāhir*) of the texts, thus excluding the possibility of overinterpretation that allows for arbitrary reasoning – a characteristic feature of *raʾy*. Furthermore, *qiyās* cannot be based on an exception, and *ḥadīth*s reflecting exceptions in the Prophetic conduct thus had to be excluded from the realm of reasoning. These two cardinal principles of interpretation proved permanent, and were adopted by the mainstream theory that prevailed during later centuries.

4. CONCLUSION: THE HIERARCHY OF LEGAL SOURCES

As we shall see in chapter 6, there was no question in the legal theory that emerged during the fourth/tenth century as to the correct hierarchy of legal sources. The Quran came first, at least formally and in terms of prestige and sanctity. The Sunna, wholly represented by *ḥadīth*, formed the second material source of the law, followed, in order of importance, by consensus and *qiyās*. The first two may be described as material sources, while the latter two (especially *qiyās*) are procedural, drawing on the former. This typology was distinctly of later provenance, and Shāfiʿī knew it only in outline and without conscious articulation. Part of the reason why he did not articulate this theory, or for that matter any such comprehensive theory, was the fact (as we have stressed) that his central theoretical concern was to install Prophetic *ḥadīth* as the exclusive source of Sunna that emerged as a substitute for sunnaic practice. Installing *ḥadīth* in this central position entailed the elaboration of a new theoretical construct that would account, from various perspectives, for this somewhat new idea. As we remarked earlier, the introduction of *ḥadīth* into a paramount position would have remained meaningless without a redefinition of the methods of legal reasoning that reveals, after all, the intent of *ḥadīth*; hence the emphasis on, and (re)definition of, *qiyās* over and against more liberal modes of *raʾy* reasoning, modes that suited the non-textual nature of sunnaic practice. The fact that *ḥadīth* was text-based required of Shāfiʿī that he elaborate a theory of linguistic–legal interpretation in order to accommodate this genre in a larger theoretical framework, one that reflected the *unmediated* authority of the Prophet. The attack on *raʾy* and the advocacy of a controlled method of *qiyās* were expressions of this accommodation. We would do well to keep in mind that Shāfiʿī's writings carried this specific agenda; and once the fight for the cause of *ḥadīth* was won, Shāfiʿī's theoretical construct became irrelevant and thus fell into disuse.[27] Shāfiʿī thus could hardly have elaborated a general legal theory that anticipated what was to be accomplished much later. Since his concern was not the elaboration of a general legal theory, his discourse lacked a conscious articulation of the sources and their hierarchy.

[27] Hallaq, "Was al-Shafiʿi the Master Architect?"

This is not to say, however, that he operated without some assumption of source-hierarchy, for even the jurists before him, such as Shaybānī, did. A close look at his writings reveals that this hierarchy (lacking, as expected, any express formulation) was, from top to bottom: the Quran; the Sunna of the Prophet; consensus; and *qiyās/ijtihād*. His understanding was that inasmuch as the Quran can explain the Sunna, the Sunna can in turn explain ambiguous provisions in the Quran. *Qiyās* can make sense only when based on the two primary sources, as well as on the substantive law sanctioned by consensus. Finally, the latter can come into operation on the basis of the three other sources, always assuming that *qiyās* is textually supported.

If Shāfiʿī's theory did not consciously articulate a hierarchy of sources, the same can be said of any other works written prior to this jurist's death, for legal theorization had not yet emerged. The absence of theoretical discussion, however, does not necessarily mean that jurists worked without operative assumptions, and it is these assumptions that allow us to reconstruct an outline of their hierarchy of sources. It is obvious, I think, that the Quran was generally deemed as the first and highest source of the law from the beginning. This position not only has the support of the overwhelming body of evidence, but is the only position that makes sense within the historical context of formative Islamic history. The primacy of the Quran must therefore be taken for granted, as it was by the Companions, by the legal specialists who flourished at the end of the first century and by later jurists before and after Shāfiʿī.

The next legal source during the second/eighth century was, as we have seen, sunnaic practice. Although it may not have determined the meaning of Quranic provisions, it certainly influenced – by the nature of things – their interpretation. But it did determine which *ḥadīth*s should be accepted and which not. As a rule, only *ḥadīth*s not contradicted by sunnaic practice were accepted as credible and thus fit as bases for legal construction. The force of this sunnaic practice could not, however, be separated from the concept of consensus. The former could not have risen to paramountcy without unanimous or near-unanimous agreement, and this is precisely the phenomenon of consensus. Sunnaic practice therefore presupposed consensus.

This is why we must insist that the second source of second-/eighth-century jurisprudence was a compound construct of sunnaic–consensual practice. It represented a unitary source that was almost invariably and often interchangeably expressed by both sunnaic and consensual terms, as evidenced in the aforementioned language of Mālik's

Muwaṭṭaʾ.[28] It was only with the introduction of *ḥadīth* as the exclusive representation of Prophetic Sunna – which entailed the dismemberment of sunnaic practice – that consensus was conceptually dissociated from the sunnaic elements. Sunnaic, consensual practice stood then *en bloc* between the Quran and *raʾy*, the third source of second-/eighth-century jurisprudence. But *raʾy* too was to undergo a fate similar to that of sunnaic practice, with the result that many of its liberal methods of reasoning were gradually suppressed. Shāfiʿī was one of those who contributed to this process, but he could never have accomplished such a historical feat single-handedly and, more importantly, could not have anticipated developments nearly a century after his death.

[28] See n. 3, above.

CHAPTER 6

Legal theory expounded

From our discussions thus far, we have seen that by the beginning of the third/ninth century, the judiciary had reached a mature stage of development, with all its essential features having taken final shape. By this time, legal doctrine (or substantive law) had also become more comprehensive and detailed in coverage, with virtually no eventuality or case escaping the domain of religious legal discourse. Yet, while in other circumstances these two developments would have allowed us to declare a given legal system complete and fully developed, in the case of Islamic law it would be premature to do so; for the beginning of the third/ninth century set the stage for what might be called the pivotal scene in this legal drama. Put differently, while legal developments during the first two centuries of Islam were no mean feat, they were only the foundation of what was to be erected later. For there remained two absolutely essential and fundamental features of the law that had yet to emerge, or at least had not done so in any meaningful form. And it was not until a century and a half later – namely, until the middle or second half of the fourth/tenth century – that these two features took final hold and shape. These features were, first, the emergence and fundamental articulation of legal theory and, second, the formation of the doctrinal schools. This chapter will treat the first of these, while the second will be taken up in the next chapter.

I. THE GREAT RATIONALIST–TRADITIONALIST SYNTHESIS

The genealogy of legal theory, the so-called *uṣūl al-fiqh*, dates back to the momentous conflict between the rationalists (*ahl al-raʾy*) and the traditionalists (*ahl al-ḥadīth*). We have said that the latter movement experienced an unprecedented upsurge during the last quarter of the second/eighth century, thereby subjecting the former to immense pressure that resulted in partial decline. Shāfiʿī's project signaled the need for readjustment, namely, to account for both the rising tide of Prophetic *ḥadīth* and for the hermeneutical implications of this new phenomenon. His project thus reflected not so much the emergence of a legal theory as his interpretive reaction to the traditionalist challenge. We will do well to remember that, up to the middle of the second/eighth century, *raʾy* was the driving trend in legal reasoning – in effect, the standard. The traditionalists began to assert themselves after this period, becoming a force to contend with by the end of the century. By the middle of the third/ninth century, *ḥadīth* had won the war against *raʾy*, leaving only a few battles to be fought and won thereafter. Long before this century ended, there emerged six "canonical" *ḥadīth* collections, designed – in their contents and arrangement – to service the law.

Furthermore, a clear pattern of scholarly affiliation with these two movements began to manifest itself. Whereas a few jurists of the second/eighth century were seen as traditionalists (and many of these acquired such descriptions *ex post eventum*, decades after the century came to a close), the third/ninth century produced more traditionalists and traditionists than rationalists, and they were clearly identified as such. It is also significant that, during this century, migration (or conversion) from the rationalist to the traditionalist camp was frequent, whereas movement in the opposite direction was rare to nonexistent. An illustrative case is that of Ibrāhīm b. Khālid Abū Thawr (d. 240/854), who is reported to have been trained in the *raʾy* school of the Iraqians, and who became a traditionalist and a "school founder" in the latter part of his career.[1] While we are unable to unearth examples of conversion to the rationalist camp from this century, the sources tell of such movement for the preceding century. The famous Zufar b. al-Hudhayl, for example, began his career as a traditionalist (again, an *ex post eventum* characterization), but before long he was attracted by the Kūfan rationalists, one of whose leaders he became.[2]

While exclusive affiliation to one or the other camp was common by the early part of the third/ninth century, the standard affiliation among jurists had shifted dramatically by the end of that century. Most jurists are reported to have combined the two in some way, and the Muslim historians and biographers made it a point to mention this synthesis in

[1] Taqī al-Dīn Ibn Qāḍī Shubha, *Ṭabaqāt al-Shāfiʿiyya*, 4 vols. (Hyderabad: Maṭbaʿat Majlis Dāʾirat al-Maʿārif al-ʿUthmāniyya, 1398/1978), I, 3–4.
[2] Ibn Khallikān, *Wafayāt*, I, 342.

the biographies of jurists who flourished between ca. 250 and 400 H (ca. 870–1000 AD). After this period, however, only a few are described as exclusively belonging to one camp or the other. Even fewer jurists who lived before and after this period are described as having "combined" the ideologies of the two camps. In other words, this designation was most relevant during the period in question, and, as we will show, for a good reason.

On both the ideological and legal levels, the history of Islam between 150 and 350 H (ca. 770 and 960 AD) can be characterized as a process of synthesis, with the opposing movements of traditionalism and rationalism managing (though not without a considerable struggle) to merge into one another so as to produce a "third solution" – what we have called here the "Great Synthesis." But the Synthesis was not reached without sharp swings of the pendulum. After Shāfiʿī, the traditionalist movement gained significant strength, attracting many jurists who can easily be described as staunch opponents of rationalism. Aḥmad b. Ḥanbal (d. 241/855), the reputed founder of the Ḥanbalite legal school, was amongst the most renowned of this group. So was Dāwūd b. Khalaf al-Ẓāhirī (d. 270/883), the reputed founder of the literalist Ẓāhirite school, which did not survive for long. The doctrines of these two scholars, as reflected in their attitudes to rationalism, signified the constantly increasing power of traditionalism. While both generally approved of Shāfiʿī, they went much further in their emphasis on the centrality of scripture and on the repugnant nature of human reasoning. For them, the latter detracted from knowledge of revelation which, in Dāwūd's eyes, could be gleaned from the revealed language itself without impregnating these texts with human meaning. Yet, the respective positions of Ibn Ḥanbal and Dāwūd on reasoning – perhaps the best gauge of their legal tendencies – were by no means identical. Ibn Ḥanbal, who was most active some three decades before Dāwūd and three decades after Shāfiʿī, accepted *qiyās* only when absolutely necessary, placing far more restrictions on its use than Shāfiʿī did. But Dāwūd rejected it categorically, and in fact refuted it as a flawed method.

Thus, during the seven decades between Shāfiʿī and Dāwūd, the traditionalist movement took a sharp turn towards a total opposition to rationalism, including its use of the method of *qiyās*. The Inquisition (Miḥna), pursued by the caliphs and rationalists between 218/833 and 234/848, was not only about whether or not the Quran was created, but also about the role of human reason in interpreting the divine texts. The final defeat of the rationalists was exemplified both in the withdrawal of the Miḥna and in the emergence of its victims as heroes, with Ibn Ḥanbal standing at the forefront. With this defeat, there was implied an acknowledgment that human reason could not stand on its own as a central – much less exclusive – method of interpretation and was, in the final analysis, subservient to revelation. The Miḥna thus brought to a climax the struggle between two opposing movements: the traditionalists, whose cause Ibn Ḥanbal was seen to champion; and the rationalists, headed by the caliphs and the Muʿtazilites, among whom there were many Ḥanafites. The forms that these two movements took by the end of the Miḥna represented the most extreme positions of the religious/hermeneutical spectrum, and if conflict between them was about anything fundamental, it was, at the end of the day, about hermeneutics.

The majority of the Muslim intellectual and religious elite did not necessarily subscribe to either of the two positions as they emerged at the end of the Miḥna or even later. The traditionalism of Ibn Ḥanbal was seen as too austere and rigid, and the rationalism of the Muʿtazila and their supporters among the *ahl al-raʾy* as too libertarian. When Ibn Ḥanbal and the traditionalists won the Miḥna, moreover, they did not prevail on account of their interpretive stand, or by virtue of their doctrinal and intellectual strength (although their tenacious piety no doubt won them popular admiration). Rather, their victory was due in part to the weakening of pronounced rationalism and in part to the withdrawal of political support from a stance that was becoming unpopular. Hence, the limited success of the traditionalists was largely a function of the weakness of the rationalists. Indeed, if the conflict represented by the Miḥna signified anything, it was that extreme forms of traditionalism and rationalism did not appeal to the majority of Muslims. It was the midpoint between the two movements that constituted the normative position of the majority; and it was from this centrist position that Sunnism, the religious and legal ideology of the majority of Muslims, was to emerge. Later Muslims were right when, with the benefit of hindsight, they called this majority "the middle-roaders" (*al-umma al-wasaṭ*).

The middle point between rationalism and traditionalism was thus the happy synthesis that emerged and continued, for centuries thereafter, to represent the normative position. The end of the Miḥna was the take-off point of this synthesis. By the middle of the fourth/tenth century, the synthesis was fully in place, not to be questioned again until the second half of the nineteenth century.

But how did the synthesis come about? Or, at least, how did it manifest itself? By the middle of the third/ninth century, it became clear that

Prophetic *ḥadīth* was there to stay. The internationalization of legal scholarship – i.e., the intense geographical mobility of legal scholars within the wide expanse of Muslim territory, from Andalusia in the west to Transoxania in the east – began early on, but became a truly normative practice by the end of the second/eighth century. And with this crucial phenomenon in place, loyalty to the sunnaic practice diminished. A scholar who traveled far and wide found the variations in regional sunnaic practice difficult, if not impossible, to transpose. A Kūfan jurist who moved to Old Cairo and then to Khurāsān would expect to be less bound by the Kūfan sunnaic practices in towns and cities that did not abide by traditions that had evolved in the Iraqian garrison towns from the earliest phase of Islam. In other words, the Islamicization of such regions as Khurāsān or Transoxania could not depend on the sunnaic practices of the Kūfans, Baṣrans or Medinese. A universally transmitted *ḥadīth* from the Prophet proved more appealing as a material and textual source of the law than the living sunnaic practice as defined by specific cities or legal communities, since the latter had developed their own judicial and juristic peculiarities in keeping with their own particular environment (peculiarities that all Muslim regions were to develop later). Prophetic *ḥadīth* was free of these peculiarities, and was, as a *textual entity*, more amenable to use in new environments. Medina, Mecca, Kūfa, Baṣra and Damascus ceased to be the only major centers of the Muslim empire, and came to be rivaled, after the first century of Islam came to a close, by major new centers, such as those in Khurāsān, Transoxania, Egypt and North Africa, not to mention Baghdad.

The *ḥadīth* thus emerged as a dominant, even paradigmatic, genre that defined the Prophetic exemplary conduct for all places and times. More specifically, it provided cities and towns all over the Muslim lands with a textual source that did not need to be culled from the living juridical experiences of a particular community. Even the latter were finally to succumb to this genre, acknowledging that their doctrines could not continue to withstand the mounting pressure from the *ḥadīth*. Their positive legal doctrine may not have undergone significant change due to the influx of *ḥadīth*, but it needed to be anchored afresh in the rock of this imposing material.

Among the rationalists, the jurist who seems to have initiated this process of re-grounding was Muḥammad b. Shujāʿ al-Thaljī (d. 267/880), an Iraqian jurist whose training and scholarly interests reflected the new reality in which not only *ḥadīth* had to be reckoned with but where acceptance within mainstream Islam meant espousing a middle-of-the-road stance between traditionalism and rationalism. Thaljī was a master of both *raʾy* and *ḥadīth* and he is identified in the biographical sources clearly as such. Although he was more inclined to rationalism than to traditionalism (sufficiently so to anger the radical traditionalists), he seems to have understood that espousing one or the other might be harmful to the cause of his school, in this case the Iraqian Ḥanafites. If there is any contribution for which he is remembered in the sources, it was his grounding of Ḥanafite positive law in Prophetic *ḥadīth* and his recasting of legal reasoning according to this new genre.[3]

On the other hand, the radical traditionalists had to moderate their ways of thinking at the peril of extinction. They, too, had to meet rationalism halfway. Ibn Ḥanbal's jurisprudence – restrictive and rigid – was soon abandoned by his immediate and later followers. The later Ḥanbalite school adopted not only *qiyās*, abhorrent to Ibn Ḥanbal, but also, in the long run, *istiḥsān*, originally a Ḥanafite principle that Shāfiʿī had severely attacked as amounting to "human legislation."[4] In other words, for the Ḥanbalite school to survive, it had to move from conservative traditionalism to a mainstream position, one that accepted a synthesis between traditionalism and rationalism. The Ẓāhirite school, by contrast, which remained steadfast in its literalist/traditionalist stand and adamantly refused to join this synthesis, was left behind and before long expired.

The end of the third/ninth century thus marked the beginning of the final compromise between rationalism and traditionalism (which is not to say that a minority of scholars of either camp abandoned their strong leanings toward one position or the other). The majority had come to embrace the synthesis, and it is with this development that *uṣūl al-fiqh* (legal theory) was at last defined. Expressed differently, though somewhat tautologically, legal theory emerged as a result of this synthesis, which itself embodied, and was reflected by, this theory.

One of the first groups to begin propounding legal theory in its organic and comprehensive form was a circle of Baghdadian Shāfiʿites, headed by the distinguished jurist Ibn Surayj (d. 306/918). He and his disciples were tradition(al)ists, jurists and speculative theologians, a combination that was uncommon in the preceding periods, but that had now become largely normative. This group was to conceptualize legal theory as a synthesis between rationality and the textual tradition, that is, between reason and

[3] Ibn al-Nadīm, *al-Fihrist* (Beirut: Dār al-Maʿrifa lil-Ṭibāʿa wal-Nashr, 1398/1978), 291; ʿAbd al-Ḥayy al-Laknawī, *al-Fawāʾid al-Bahiyya fī Tarājim al-Ḥanafiyya* (Benares: Maktabat Nadwat al-Maʿārif, 1967), 171–72.

[4] On *istiḥsān*, see section 2 below.

revelation. Thus, Ibn Surayj must be credited with paving the way for his students, who would discourse on this synthesis and elaborate it in greater detail. This explains why the earliest Shāfiʿite authors to write works on *uṣūl al-fiqh* were his students, such as Abū Bakr al-Fārisī (fl. ca. 350/960), Ibn al-Qāṣṣ (d. 336/947), Abū Bakr al-Ṣayrafī (d. 330/942) and al-Qaffāl al-Shāshī (d. 336/947). However, it must be emphasized that the legal theory produced by this circle of scholars was not the product of an ongoing process of elaboration based on an established tradition, as later theory came to be. Instead, it was largely the product of the specific historical process that had begun a century or more earlier, and that had culminated under the influence of the Synthesis formed at the close of the third/ninth century and the first half of the fourth/tenth. Their theory can thus be characterized as the child of its environment, and it owed little more to Shāfiʿī than nominal affiliation.

In the next chapter, we will show how the authority of Shāfiʿī as founder of the Shāfiʿite school (as well as that of others) was both constructed and augmented, but for now we must be content to assert that the achievements of Ibn Surayj, of his generation and of the generation to follow were projected back onto Shāfiʿī as the first synthesizer – namely, as the architect of the all-important *uṣūl al-fiqh*. The fact is that Shāfiʿī had very little to do with the elaboration of *uṣūl al-fiqh*, although he happened to advocate the Synthesis in a rudimentary form. But his theory was not accepted by the community of jurists, and his followers, until Ibn Surayj's time, remained few. It is likely, however, that it was his own modest thesis that made it convenient for Ibn Surayj and his students to impute the achievement of *uṣūl al-fiqh* to him.[5]

By the middle of the fourth/tenth century, therefore, an elaborate and comprehensive theory of *uṣūl* had emerged. The next century and a half witnessed a phase in the history of this theory that produced the standard works on which later expositions heavily depended, but the essential developments had already occurred by 350/960 or thereabouts. We shall now attempt to sketch the outlines of this theory as they stood by that time.

2. LEGAL THEORY ARTICULATED

Along with legal development, Islamic civilization saw a major advance in the theological sciences. The synthesis that law accomplished was likewise

[5] For a detailed discussion of these issues, see Hallaq, "Was al-Shafiʿi the Master Architect?"

matched by a theological synthesis, represented in part by the Ashʿarite and Māturidite schools (both standing somewhere between the rationalist Muʿtazilites and the early Ḥanbalites and other traditionalists). *Uṣūl al-fiqh*, by its very nature theoretical, was not impervious to theological influences. During the fourth/tenth century, law was already seen as an integral part of a universal scheme. Theology established the existence, unity and attributes of God, as well as the "proof" of prophecies, revelation and all the fundaments of religion. Law presupposed these theological conclusions and went on to build on them. The Quran was shown by theology to be the Word of God, and the Prophetic Sunna was established as a religious foundation by virtue of the demonstrative proofs of Muḥammad's Prophecy. These two sources were therefore shown to be demonstratively true by means of theological argument – a process with which legal theory had no direct concern. Thus established, the two primary sources were taken for granted, and constituted in principle the final authority on all matters legal.

Consensus, on the other hand, was a purely juristic tool, requiring, from within the law, conclusive authorization as the third legal source. Since the Quran and the Sunna logically constituted the only demonstrative, certain sources, it was from these two veins that arguments for the authority of consensus were to be mined. As it turned out, and after several initial attempts to support consensus with Quranic provisions, the jurists realized that the Quran did not possess the arguments necessary to accomplish the task. It was finally through Prophetic *ḥadīth*, which supplied the premise that the Islamic community as a whole could never err, that consensus found its textual support as a certain source of law.[6] Similar was the case of *qiyās*, the fourth formal source of the law. While the Quran proved somewhat more useful here, it was again the Sunna and the practices of the Companions (perhaps as an extension of Prophetic authority) that permitted the jurists to formulate an authoritative basis for this source.

Clearly, certainty was a juristic desideratum, at least insofar as the legal sources (rather than the individual opinions of positive law) were concerned. Islamic law, it must be stressed, rests squarely on the distinction between probability and certainty. Knowledge of God must be certain for one to be a true Muslim; in other words, one cannot claim membership in the Islamic faith if one is not sure that, for example, God exists or whether or not He created the world or sent Muḥammad as His Messenger. Nor

[6] For a detailed discussion of juristic developments on this issue, see Hallaq, "On the Authoritativeness of Sunni Consensus."

can one claim such membership if one entertains doubts about the Quran as the Word of God, or the Sunna of Muḥammad as that of a true prophet. By the same token, there is no place for doubt about consensus or *qiyās*, whose certainty must be accepted without any qualification. Doubts raised about any of these sources would mean that the entire edifice of the law, the foundation of the community, is subject to uncertainty; and any such doubt would therefore give rise to the possibility that there is a disjunction between God and His creation, and that His followers constitute a community of pretenders.

Yet, while the sources themselves, as sources, had to be known with certainty, the particular legal conclusions or opinions drawn from them did not need to be more than probable, i.e., more likely true than not. Outside the four sources, therefore, probability dominated. As a set of rules applied to society, positive law was mostly an exercise in probability, since a jurist could only conjecture what the law might be in a particular case. For God did not reveal a law but only texts containing what the jurists characterize as indications (or indicants: *dalīl*s). These indications guide the jurist and allow him to *infer* what he thinks to be a particular rule for a particular case at hand. And since each qualified jurist (*mujtahid*) employs his own tools of interpretation in undertaking the search for God's law, his conclusions might differ from those of another. One jurist's inference is therefore as good as that of another, hence the cardinal maxim: "All qualified jurists are correct." All jurists are assumed to be "doing the right thing" in exerting their juristic effort (*ijtihād*) in reaching a rule or an opinion. This individual *ijtihād* explains the plurality of opinion in Islamic law, known as *khilāf* or *ikhtilāf*. Each case may elicit two, three, sometimes up to eight or more opinions, all of which remain "opinions" that are equally valid, although one of them must be viewed as superior to the others (considered weak) and is thus chosen by a jurist or his school to be the authoritative opinion to be applied in law courts and issued in *fatwā*s. The "weak" opinions, on the other hand, are subject to verification or revision, although for other jurists or schools these very opinions are deemed to possess the highest authority. In theory and logic, however, a given problem can have only one correct solution, irrespective of whether or not the community of jurists knows which one it is. Obviously, in all cases outside the purview of consensus, the jurists cannot decide which is the correct solution, for the matter remains inherently subjective. Hence the other cardinal maxim: "The *mujtahid* whose opinion is correct is rewarded twice [i.e., both for exercising his effort and for getting it right], while the *mujtahid* whose opinion is incorrect is rewarded only once [for his effort]."

As accurately reflected in legal theory, Islamic law is thus a hermeneutical system of the first order. Using the tools of interpretation prescribed in legal theory, the jurist goes about finding solutions for hitherto unsolved problems, i.e., the acknowledged purpose of *uṣūl al-fiqh* (although reevaluation and reinterpretation of existing solutions was also a discrete part of this theory's function).[7] The purpose of the jurist is thus to work out the legal indications (*dalīls*) in the sources in order to arrive at a normative rule which was seen to fall into one of five categories: the obligatory (*wājib*), the recommended (*mandūb*), the permissible or indifferent (*mubāḥ*), the repugnant (*makrūh*), and the prohibited (*ḥarām*). The obligatory represents an act whose performance entails reward, and whose omission requires punishment. The recommended represents an act whose performance entails a reward but whose omission does not require punishment. The permissible or indifferent, as the name suggests, requires neither reward nor punishment for commission or omission, respectively. This category was intended to deal with situations in which textual indications are either silent on an issue or lacking in clear provisions as to the status of the case. The principle underlying the indifferent is that whenever the texts fail to provide clear indications as to the commission or omission of an act, the Muslim has a free choice between the two. An act falling into the fourth category, the repugnant, is rewarded when omitted, but is not punished when committed. Finally, the prohibited obviously entails punishment upon commission.

All human acts must thus fall into one or another of these categories, although juristic opinions would differ as to the value of a particular act. One jurist may reach the opinion that a certain act is prohibited, while another may declare it merely repugnant. However, it was relatively rare that opinions differed dramatically, where one jurist would deem a certain act prohibited while another jurist would declare it permissible.

The classifiability of human acts into the five norms did not cover another group of legal acts pertaining to validity, invalidity or nullity. For example, a contract – say of lease – concluded in a lawful transaction is not, in terms of validity, subject to the taxonomy of the five norms. Although itself classifiable in terms of the five norms (in this case permissible), a lease's effects cannot be deemed either valid or invalid. As long as a contract of this type is valid, it is binding and produces full legal effects, such as delivery of the leased object and the payment of the fee. But when

[7] Further on this, see section 3 below.

invalid, it ceases to be binding. Being invalid, however, does not necessarily mean that it is entirely null and void, i.e., productive of no effect whatsoever, a category known as *bāṭil.*

But how does the jurist arrive at a legal norm or a ruling regarding a specific act? In other words, what are the materials and interpretive tools at his disposal that permit him to derive one rule or opinion but not another? To answer these questions, we begin with a brief account of legal language and the hermeneutical principles that govern its use.

Legal language

In attempting to find a solution to a hitherto unresolved legal problem, the jurist begins with texts that constitute his ultimate frame of reference. His analysis of these texts comprises, first, the identification of passages applicable to the case at hand and, second, the determination of the semantic force and implication of these passages as they bear on that case. This latter constitutes part of *qiyās*, which we shall take up later. The former, however, involves a linguistic interpretation in preparation for *qiyās*, with a view to determining whether words within the relevant text are univocal, ambiguous, general, particular or metaphorical. In other words, before any inference is made, the text must be established as relevant and fit for such an inference.

Despite its problematic nature, language often does contain univocal, clear expressions that engender certitude in the mind. For instance, when we hear the word "four" we understand, without a shade of doubt, that it is not five, three or seven. To know what "four" means, we need not resort to any principles of interpretation, nor to other explicative language. The language is self-evident. The clarity and certitude it generates makes it the most evincive, a category labeled as *naṣṣ*.

But most expressions are not so clear, even when they appear to be so. One such linguistic type is metaphorical terms. It is the general assumption of jurists that words are originally coined for a real meaning, e.g., "lion" signifies a member of the species of big cats. A word is used in a metaphorical sense when applied by extension to something that is not the original referent; thus, the expression "lion" may be applied in the Arabic language to a man who is courageous. Legal examples of this use of language include words such as "today" or "tomorrow," which may be used metaphorically when promising to perform a duty at a certain time. In their real usage, the expressions "today" or "tomorrow" can include late night hours, but they normally mean – in business transactions, for instance – daytime hours.

The challenge for the jurist here is to determine whether a particular word in legal language is used as a metaphor or in its real sense.[8]

Metaphorical or otherwise, words may also be clear or ambiguous. When ambiguous, they can brook different interpretations, due to the fact that the referent of such words includes several attributes or different genera. One such ambiguity is found in homonymous nouns, which refer to more than one object, such as the word "spring," which may refer to the season of the year, an artesian well or a coil of wire. Yet, a word may not be a homonym and still retain ambiguity. For example, Quran 17:33 reads: "And he who kills wrongfully, we have given power to his heir." The term "power" here is markedly ambiguous, since it may include pardoning, the right to retaliate or entitlement to monetary compensation. If the ambiguity can be solved by seeking the help of another text, then the ambiguity is resolved in favor of one meaning or another. If not, the rule would by necessity encompass all possible meanings, as in the case of Quran 17:33. In the absence of further clarification, the heirs in the case of homicide are in fact given the full range of the term "power," granting them the free option of choosing which of the three "rights" they should exercise.

General terms are also problematic in the sense that they refer to two or more individuals, as in the case of plural nouns and general statements that include more than one genus. When confronted with such language, the jurist is faced with the task of particularization, namely, determining which genus or genera is meant by the general statement. A classic example of particularization occurs in Quran 5:3, where it is stated: "Forbidden unto you [for food] is carrion." This was particularized by a Prophetic *ḥadīth* allowing the consumption of dead fish. That the Quran can be particularized by a *ḥadīth*, as this example illustrates, is obvious; so can a *ḥadīth* be particularized by the Quran, epistemologically a more secure source of law.

Imperative and prohibitive forms

As a system of obligations, law depends heavily on prescriptive textual expressions of the type "Do" or "Do not do," known, respectively, as imperatives and prohibitives. Such expressions were not devoid of interpretive problems either, as their effects were often ambiguous. For example, when someone commands another, telling him "Do this," should this command be construed as falling only within the legal value of the

[8] Abū ʿAlī al-Shāshī, *Uṣūl* (Beirut: Dār al-Kitāb al-ʿArabī, 1402/1982), 42–50.

obligatory norm, or could it also be within that of the recommended and/or the indifferent? The position of the majority of legal theorists seems to have been that imperatives, as a rule, are assumed to engender obligation, unless shown otherwise by circumstantial or contextual evidence. Furthermore, an imperative form that is non-specific does not require performance at a particular time, as long as what is commanded is performed within the widest definition of the allotted time.

Some theorists viewed prohibitives as encompassing commands not to do either of two types of acts: sensory and legal acts. An example of the former is "Do not drink wine," and of the latter, "Do not sell one gold coin for two gold coins" (since this would involve prohibited usury). The former acts are prohibited because they are inherently evil, whereas the latter are prohibited for a reason external to themselves. Drinking wine or fornication are inherently evil acts, but selling gold is not, since it is prohibited only when it is transacted in a particular situation resulting in unlawful consequences.[9]

Transmission of revealed texts

The jurist's interpretation of legal language would be meaningless without knowledge that this language has been transmitted with a certain degree of credibility. A text that has been transmitted via a dubious or defective chain of transmitters, or transmitters who are known to be untrustworthy, was held to lack any legal effect even though its language may be clear and unequivocal. Thus all texts must pass the test of both linguistic analysis and transmission before they are employed as the raw material of legal reasoning.

The general principle with regard to the duality of interpretation/transmission is that probable conclusions of legal reasoning are the result of lack of certainty in either the denotation of a term or the transmission of the text encompassing that term. A particular language may thus be univocal (*naṣṣ*) in meaning, but transmitted by a chain of transmission that is merely probable, rendering its overall legal effects probable. The same is true of a text transmitted by a multiplicity of channels that render the text certain in terms of knowledge that it originated with the Prophet, but deemed only probable if its language is equivocal or ambiguous, since the certainty gained in transmission is lost through its lack of clarity.

[9] Ibid., 165 ff.

The Quran is deemed to be wholly certain in terms of transmission, since it has been consistently transmitted by multitudes of Muslims who could not conceivably have conspired in either forging or distorting it. Thus, for a text to be deemed credible beyond a shadow of doubt (i.e., to have certainty), it must meet this requirement of multiple transmission, or recurrence, known as *tawātur*. Any text transmitted through channels fewer than *tawātur* is termed *āḥād* (lit., solitary), although the actual number of channels can be two, three or even more. The Quranic *tawātur*, however, cannot guarantee that all its language is certain, since the meanings of many of its provisions were acknowledged to be ambiguous or lacking in decisive clarity.

Unlike the Quranic text, Prophetic material generally did not possess the advantage of *tawātur*.[10] As we saw earlier, there were far more fabricated, and thus weak, *ḥadīth*s than there were sound ones. But even these latter did not always engender certainty, since most were of the solitary kind and therefore yielded only probable knowledge.

In order for a report to yield probable knowledge, i.e., to be deemed fit to be applied in practice, all its transmitters, from beginning to end, must be reliable and trustworthy, and each must have met the next link in person, so as to make it credible that transmission did occur. Throughout the third/ninth century, and probably the fourth/tenth, the jurists held that interrupted *ḥadīth*s are nonetheless sound, "interrupted" meaning that one or more transmitters in the chain are unknown. But this was predicated on the assumption that the transmitter with whom the report resumes after the interruption had the reputation of transmitting only those *ḥadīth*s that are sound. This assumption rests on another, namely, that such a person would not have transmitted the *ḥadīth* had he known it to be inauthentic or fabricated. The later jurists, however, seem to have rejected such *ḥadīth*s, classifying them as unsound or defective.

It is thus clear that the trustworthiness of individual transmitters played an important role in the authentication of *ḥadīth*s. The attribute that was most valued, and in fact deemed indispensable and determinative, was that of being just (*ʿadl*), namely, being morally and religiously righteous. A just character also implied the attribute of being truthful (*ṣādiq*; n. *ṣidq*), which made one incapable of lying. This requirement was intended to preclude either outright tampering with the wording of the transmitted text, or interpolating it with fabricated material. It also implied that the

[10] See Wael Hallaq, "The Authenticity of Prophetic Ḥadīth: A Pseudo-Problem," *Studia Islamica*, 89 (1999): 75–90.

transmitter could not lie as to his sources by fabricating a chain of transmitters or claiming that he had heard the *ḥadīth* from an authority when in fact he did not. He had also to be fully cognizant of the material he related, so as to transmit it with precision. Finally, he must not have been involved in dubious or sectarian religious movements, for should he have been so involved, he would have been liable to produce heretical material for the sake of the movement to which he belonged. This last requirement clearly suggests that the transmitter must be seen to be loyal to Sunnism, to the exclusion of any other community. (This latter requirement suggests that many – though not all – of the fabricated *ḥadīth*s originated with sectarian scholars, as modern scholarship has demonstrably shown.)

Transmitters are also judged by their ability to transmit *ḥadīth*s verbatim, for thematic transmission may run the risk of changes in the wording, and thus the original intent, of a particular *ḥadīth*. Furthermore, it was deemed preferable that the *ḥadīth* be transmitted in full, although transmitting one part that is not thematically connected with the rest was acceptable.

In attempting to arrive at a solution to a particular case, the jurist may encounter more than one *ḥadīth* relevant to that case. The problem that arises is when these *ḥadīth*s are contradictory or inconsistent with one another. If he cannot reconcile them, the jurist must seek to make one *ḥadīth* preponderant over another by establishing that a particular *ḥadīth* possesses attributes superior to, or lacking in, another. The criteria of preponderance are relative to the mode of transmission as well as to the subject matter of the *ḥadīth* in question. For example, a *ḥadīth* transmitted by mature persons known for their prodigious ability to retain information is superior to another transmitted by young narrators who may not be particularly known for their memory or precision in reporting. Similarly, a *ḥadīth* whose first transmitter was close to the Prophet and knew him intimately is superior to another whose first transmitter was not on close terms with the Prophet. The subject matter also determines the comparative strength or weakness of a *ḥadīth*. For instance, a *ḥadīth* that finds thematic corroboration in the Quran would be deemed preponderant over another that finds no such support. But when preponderance proves to be impossible, the jurist resorts to the procedure of abrogation, whereby one of the *ḥadīth*s is made to repeal, and thus cancel out the effects of, another.

Abrogation

Abrogation was unanimously held as an authoritative method of dealing with contradictory texts. Just as Islam as a whole came to abrogate earlier religions without denying their legitimacy, abrogation among and between revealed Islamic texts was also admitted and in fact practiced, without this entailing the diminution of the status of the repealed texts as divine scripture. This method was specifically approved in Quran 2:106: "Such of Our Revelation as We abrogate or cause to be forgotten, We bring [in place of it] one better or the like thereof."

It is important to stress that the Muslim jurists espoused the idea that it is not the texts themselves that are actually abrogated, but rather the legal rulings embedded in these texts. For to admit that God revealed contradictory and even conflicting statements would mean that one of the statements is false and that God, therefore, revealed an untruth.

The basic principle of abrogation is that a text repeals another contradictory text that was revealed prior to it in time. But abrogation may be propelled by a decidedly clearer consideration, especially when the text itself is made to supersede another. An example in point is the Prophet's statement: "I had permitted for you the use of the carrion leather, but upon receipt of this writing [epistle], you are not to utilize it in any manner." Yet another consideration is the consensus of the community as represented by its scholars. If one ruling is adopted in preference to another, then the latter is deemed abrogated, since the community cannot agree on an error. However, in the post-formative period, a number of jurists tended to object to this principle, arguing that a consensus that lacks textual support does not possess the power to abrogate. Consensus, they asserted, must rest on revealed texts, and if these texts contain no evidence of abrogation, then consensus cannot decide the matter. Consensus, in other words, cannot go beyond the evidence of the texts, for it is only the texts that determine whether or not one ruling can abrogate another. If a ruling subject to consensus happened to abrogate another conflicting ruling, then the assumption is that abrogation would be due to evidence existing in the texts, not to consensus.

The epistemological strength of texts also plays a central role in abrogation. A text deemed presumptive or probable cannot repeal another having the quality of certitude. On the other hand, texts that are considered of equal epistemological value may abrogate one another. This principle derives from Quran 2:106 which speaks of abrogating verses and replacing them by similar or "better" ones. Hence, Quranic verses, like recurrent *ḥadīth*s, can repeal each other. The same is true of solitary *ḥadīth*s. Furthermore, by the same principle, the Quran and recurrent *ḥadīth*s may abrogate solitary *ḥadīth*s, but not vice versa.

That the Quran can abrogate *ḥadīth* is evident, considering its distinguished religious and epistemological stature. And it is perfectly understandable, on the basis of the epistemological principles just outlined, why solitary *ḥadīth* cannot abrogate Quranic verses (although a minority of jurists permitted this type of abrogation). However, the question that remained controversial was whether or not recurrent *ḥadīth* can abrogate Quranic verses. Those who denied this power to the *ḥadīth* argued their case on the basis of Quran 2:106, in effect claiming that *ḥadīth* can never acquire a status equal to the Quran. Its proponents, on the other hand, couched their arguments in epistemological terms, maintaining that both recurrent *ḥadīth* and Quranic materials enjoy the status of *mutawātir*, and since this rank yields certainty, they are both equal in status, and thus can repeal one another. (It must be said, however, that in practice there are a few cases where both solitary and recurrent *ḥadīth* have abrogated Quranic verses.[11])

Consensus

In its mature form, consensus was defined as the agreement of the community as represented by its *mujtahid*s living in a particular age or generation, an agreement that bestows on those rulings or opinions subject to it a conclusive, certain knowledge. But this nearly universal understanding of consensus was not to be reached until the end of the fourth/tenth century, if not later.

In the previous chapter, we saw that by the end of the second-/eighth-century practice-based *sunna* was intertwined with the local consensus of scholars. This consensus, in turn, frequently was based on the idea that unanimous legal practice issued, and continued with regularity, from the conduct and ways of the Companions.

The traces of this sort of consensus may be found in the legal theory of the early fourth/tenth century, which represents a middle point between the untheorized second-/eighth-century practice and the fully mature and developed theory of the post-formative period. For the Ḥanafite Shāshī (d. ca. 344/955), consensus constitutes an authority for practice, meaning that an opinion subject to it permits an individual to adhere to it in religious works, such as prayer, sale transactions, marriage and the like. But it cannot constitute a basis for theological belief, such as the existence of God and the

11 For a detailed discussion of recurrent and solitary traditions, see Bernard Weiss, "Knowledge of the Past: The Theory of *Tawātur* According to Ghazālī," *Studia Islamica*, 61 (1985): 81–105; Wael Hallaq, "On Inductive Corroboration, Probability and Certainty in Sunnī Legal Thought," in N. Heer, ed., *Islamic Law and Jurisprudence* (Seattle: University of Washington Press, 1990), 3–31.

validity of Muḥammad's Prophethood, both of which must be demonstrated by rational argument.

In Shāshī's theory, consensus consists of four types that epistemologically and chronologically represent a descending order. The first is the Companions' consensus, which in turn consists of two sub-types: (1) their unanimous consensus on a rule clearly stipulated in the revealed sources; and (2) the consensus of some of them, and the silence of, and absence of objection by, the rest. (These two sub-types, it must be said, seem to justify and rationalize a good part of Ḥanafite law that was originally based on the Iraqian practice-based and Companion-inspired *sunna*.) The second is the consensus of the next generation either on an opinion that was reached by the Companions or on one reached by that generation itself. Here, the former type yields certitude equivalent to that generated in a ruling stipulated by a clear Quranic text, whereas this second type of consensus – which does not involve the Companions – also yields certitude even though it was reached by some scholars and tacitly approved by the rest (i.e., no objections to it are known to have been voiced). Its certitude, according to Shāshī, amounts to knowledge generated by *tawātur*, namely, the recurrent narration of *ḥadīth*. The third type is the consensus of the third generation of scholars, which yields knowledge equivalent to that generated through the transmission of *ḥadīth* in the so-called widespread (*mashhūr*) form, a distinctly Ḥanafite category of transmission that stands between the solitary and the recurrent modes. Finally, the fourth type of consensus is that of subsequent generations on an opinion reached by (but remaining subject to the disagreement of) earlier generations of scholars. This type yields a probable degree of knowledge, amounting to that generated by the sound solitary reports.[12]

Shāshī's theory of consensus hardly reflects a mature stage in the development of the doctrine in *uṣūl al-fiqh*, in terms of either substance or coverage. Later theory, in other words, differed substantively from Shāshī's discourse and was far more comprehensive, encompassing countless other issues. Although some traces of Shāshī's Ḥanafite understanding is to be found in the writings of a minority of much later theorists, the common doctrine as it stood by the early fifth/eleventh century – and probably somewhat earlier – was different, at least epistemologically. The later theory granted the instrument of consensus the authority of certitude, no matter how or by whom consensus is reached.

[12] Shāshī, *Uṣūl*, 287–91.

But the Ḥanafites were not the only jurists to attempt to rationalize their own, perhaps unique, experience of the Iraqian past. Mālikite legal theory too invoked the history of the school in Medina, attempting to rationalize that experience by fitting it within that school's development during later centuries. The Mālikite jurists insisted that the consensus of the scholars of Medina, the hometown of Mālik, constituted a binding authority, an insistence that gave rise to a discussion of whether or not any region of Islamdom could independently form a consensus. Against the Mālikites, theorists of other schools argued that the Quran and, particularly, the Sunna attest to the infallibility of the entire community, and that there is nothing in these texts to suggest that any segment of the community can alone be infallible. Furthermore, they maintained that the recognition of the consensus of a particular geographical area would lead to a paradox, since the opinion of a *mujtahid* who partook, say, in a Medinese consensus would be authoritative in Medina but not so once he left the city. The Mālikite claims, these jurists argued, give rise to another objectionable conclusion, namely, that a particular geographical locale possesses an inherent capacity to bestow validity and authority upon the products of *ijtihād*, the cornerstone of consensus. This claim not only makes no sense rationally, but also cannot be justified by the revealed texts: consensus is either that of the entire community (as represented by all its *mujtahid*s who live in a particular generation) or it is not a consensus at all.[13]

Qiyās

Before embarking on inferential reasoning, the jurist must establish the meaning and relevance of the text employed and ascertain its validity insofar as it was not abrogated. Knowledge of cases subject to consensus was required in order to ensure that his reasoning did not lead him to results different from, or contrary to, the established agreement in his school or among the larger community of jurists. The importance of this requirement stems from the fact that consensus bestows certainty upon the cases subject to it, raising them to the level of the unequivocal texts in the Quran and the recurrent *ḥadīth*; thus, reopening such settled cases to new solutions would amount to questioning certainty, including conclusive texts in the Quran and recurrent *ḥadīth*. Inferential reasoning is therefore legitimate only in two instances, namely, when the case in

[13] On this theoretical discussion, see Hallaq, *History*, 80.

question had not been subject to consensus (having remained within the genre of juristic disagreement – *khilāf*) or when it was entirely new. Shāshī defines *qiyās* as "a legal rule resulting – with regard to a case unstipulated in the revealed texts – from a meaning that constitutes the *ratio* for a legal rule stipulated in the texts."[14]

Now, the most common and important form of reasoning that is generally subsumed under the term *qiyās* is analogy. As the archetype of all legal argument, *qiyās* was seen to consist of four elements: (1) the new case that requires a legal solution; (2) the original case that may be found either stated in the revealed texts or sanctioned by consensus; (3) the *ratio legis*, or the attribute common to both the new and original cases; and (4) the legal norm that is found in the original case and that, due to the similarity between the two cases, must be transposed to the new case. The archetypal example of legal analogy is the case of wine. If the jurist is faced with a case involving date-wine, requiring him to decide its status, he looks at the revealed texts only to find that grape-wine was explicitly prohibited by the Quran. The common denominator, the *ratio legis*, is the attribute of intoxication, in this case found in both drinks. The jurist concludes that, like grape-wine, date-wine is prohibited due to its inebriating quality.

Of the four components of *qiyās*, the *ratio legis* (*ʿilla*) occasioned both controversy and extensive analysis, since the claim for similarity between two things is the cornerstone and determinant of inference. Great caution, therefore, was to be exercised in determining the *ratio*.

Locating and identifying the *ratio legis* is not always an easy task, for although it may be stated explicitly, more often it is either merely intimated or must be inferred from the texts. When the Prophet was questioned about the legality of bartering ripe dates for unripe ones, he asked: "Do unripe dates lose weight upon drying up?" When he was answered in the affirmative, he reportedly remarked that such a barter is unlawful. The *ratio* in this *ḥadīth* was deemed explicit since prohibition was readily understood to be predicated upon the dried dates losing weight, and a transaction involving unequal amounts or weights of the same object would constitute usury, clearly prohibited in Islamic law.

On the other hand, the *ratio* may be merely intimated. In one *ḥadīth*, the Prophet said: "He who cultivates a barren land acquires ownership of it." Similarly, in 5:6, the Quran declares: "If you rise up for prayer, then you

[14] Shāshī, *Uṣūl*, 325.

must wash." In these examples, the *ratio* is suggested in the semantic structure of this language, reducible to the conditional sentence "If . . . , then . . . ." The consequent phrase "then . . . " indicates that the *ratio* behind washing is prayer, just as the ownership of barren land is confirmed by cultivating it. It is important to realize here that prayer requires washing, not that washing is consistently occasioned by prayer alone. For one can wash oneself without performing prayer, but not the other way round. The same is true of land ownership. A person can possess a barren land without cultivating it, but the cultivation of – and subsequent entitlement to – it, is the point.

The sequence of events in Prophetic narrative may also help in unraveling the *ratio* of a rule. If it is reasonably clear that the Prophet behaved in a certain manner upon the occurrence, for example, of an event, then it is assumed that the *ratio* of his action is that particular event. Similarly, any act precipitating a ruling by the Prophet is considered the *ratio* behind that ruling.

The *ratio legis* may also be known by consensus. For example, it is the universal agreement of the jurists that the father enjoys a free hand in managing and controlling the property of his minor children. Here, minority is the *ratio* for this unrestricted form of conduct, whereas property is the new case. Thus, the *ratio* may be transposed to yet another new case, such as the free physical control of the father over his children.[15]

Whether explicitly stated or inferred, the *ratio* may either bear upon a class of cases belonging to the same genus, or it may be restricted in its application to individual cases. In other words, the *ratio* may not be concomitant with the entire genus, but only some cases subsumed under that genus. In homicide, for example, capital punishment is meted out when the elements of both intentionality and religious equality (i.e., that the murderer and victim, for instance, are both Muslim or both Christian) are present. But it must not be assumed that capital punishment is applicable only where homicide is involved. For example, adultery committed by a married person as well as apostasy also elicit this punishment.

To be sure, analogy is not the only method of inference subsumed under *qiyās*. Another important argument is that of the *a fortiori*. For instance, Quran 5:3 states: "Forbidden unto you are carrion, blood, flesh of the pig." The jurists took "flesh of the pig" to include all types of pork, including that of wild boars, although the original reference was to domestic pigs.

[15] Ibid., 333.

Furthermore, it was argued that "the flesh of wild boars is forbidden" is a proposition that needs no inference since it is clearly understood from the very language of the Quran.

The *a fortiori* also includes other varieties of argument, namely, the *a minore ad maius* and the *a maiore ad minus*, thought to be the most compelling forms of *qiyās*. An example of the former type may be found in Quran 99:7–8: "Whoso has done an atom's weight of good shall see it, and whoso has done an atom's weight of evil shall see it." From this verse, it was understood that the reward for doing more than an atom's weight of good and the punishment for doing more than an atom's weight of evil are greater than that promised for simply an atom's weight. An example of the latter type, the *a maiore ad minus*, is the Quranic permission to kill non-Muslims who engage in war against Muslims. From this permission, it was understood that acts short of killing, such as confiscation of the unbeliever's property, are also lawful.

A third argument subsumed under *qiyās* is that of the *reductio ad absurdum*. This argument represents a line of reasoning in which the converse of a given rule is applied to another case on the grounds that the *ratio legis* of the two cases are contradictory. The cornerstone of this argument is the determination of a rule by demonstrating the falsehood or invalidity of its converse. In other words, if a rule standing in diametrical opposition to another is proven invalid or unwarranted, then the latter emerges as the only sound or valid rule. Of the same type is the argument that proceeds from the assumption that the nonexistence of a *ratio* leads to the absence of the rule that must otherwise arise from that *ratio*. For example, in the case of a usurped animal, the usurper – according to the Ḥanafites – is not liable for damages with regard to the offspring of the animal since the offspring, unlike its mother, was not usurped.[16]

From a different perspective, *qiyās* may be typified not according to the logical structure of its arguments but rather according to the strength of the *ratio legis*. From this perspective, *qiyās* is classified into two major types of inference, the causative and indicative. In the former, the *ratio* and the rationale behind it are readily identifiable, but in the latter, the rationale is merely inferred or not known at all. Wine is pronounced prohibited because of its intoxicating quality, and the rationale behind the prohibition is that intoxication leads to repugnant behavior, including carelessness and neglect in performing religious duties. Here the rationale is known. In

[16] Ibid., 388.

indicative inferences, however, the rationale is known merely by conjecture, such as positing that the *ratio* behind the prohibition of usury is edibility (according to the Shāfiʿites) or measurability by weight (according to the Ḥanafites). But no revealed text clearly states that one or the other (or both) constitutes the rationale behind the prohibition. Nonetheless, the difference between the two types is often one of form, not substance. God could have said: "Pray, because the sun has set," or he could have said "When the sun sets, pray." The former injunction gives rise to a causative inference, whereas the latter merely allows for an indicative one. The relationship between prayer and sunset is not, at any rate, causal but rather a matter of concomitance.

Istiḥsān

In the preceding chapter, we saw that second-/eighth-century Iraqian reasoning was not always based directly on the revealed texts, a fact that prompted Shāfiʿī to launch a scathing criticism of what he labeled "human legislation." A substantial part of this reasoning – which originally fell under the rubric of *ra'y* – became known as *istiḥsān.*

With the traditionalization of the Ḥanafite school, a process whose beginnings seem to have been associated with the contributions of Muḥammad b. Shujāʿ al-Thaljī, Ḥanafite theorists after the third/ninth century took steps to dissociate themselves from the reputation of being arbitrary reasoners. Following the normative practice that had evolved as the unchallenged paradigm of juridical reasoning, they insisted that no argument of *istiḥsān* can rest on any grounds other than the texts of revelation. In fact, they never acknowledged that discretionary reasoning had ever existed in their methodology. The resulting technical modifications that were introduced into *istiḥsān,* however, rendered it acceptable to other schools, notably, the so-called conservative Ḥanbalites.

In legal theory, *istiḥsān* was little more than another form of *qiyās,* one that was deemed to be – in some cases – "preferred" to the standard form. Simply stated, *istiḥsān* is reasoning that presumably departs from a revealed text but that leads to a conclusion that differs from another that would have been inferred through *qiyās.* If a person, for example, forgets what he is doing and eats while he is supposed to be fasting, *qiyās* dictates that his fasting becomes void, since food has entered his body, whether intentionally or not. But *qiyās* in this case was abandoned in favor of a Prophetic *ḥadīth* which pronounced the fasting valid if eating was the result of a mistake.

Istiḥsān is not always grounded in revealed texts, however (and it was this fact that earned it Shāfiʿī's wrath). It can also be based either on consensus or the principle of necessity. For example, to be valid, any contract involving the exchange of services or commodities requires immediate payment. But some contracts of hire do not fulfill the condition of immediate payment, a fact that would render them void if *qiyās* were to be used. But the common practice of people over the ages has been to admit these contractual forms in their daily lives, and this is viewed as tantamount to consensus. This latter, as an instrument that engenders certainty, becomes tantamount to the revealed texts themselves, thereby bestowing on the reasoning involved here the same force as the Quran or the *ḥadīth* would bestow on it.

Likewise, necessity often requires the abandonment of conclusions by *qiyās* in favor of those generated by *istiḥsān*. Washing with ritually impure water would, by *qiyās*, invalidate prayer, but not so in *istiḥsān*. Here, *qiyās* would lead to hardship in view of the fact that fresh, clean water is not always easy to procure. The acceptance of necessity as a principle that legitimizes departure from strict reasoning is seen as deriving from, and sanctioned by, both the Quran and the Sunna, since necessity, when not met, can cause nothing but hardship. Thus, *istiḥsān* in the context of necessity is viewed as legitimized by the revealed texts, reflecting the reasoned distinction of textual evidence.

Maṣlaḥa

Like the Iraqian Ḥanafites of the second/eighth century, the Medinese, including their chief jurist Mālik b. Anas, resorted to reasoning that did not appear to be directly based on the revealed texts. This procedure became known as *istiṣlāḥ/maṣlaḥa*, loosely translated as "public interest." Later Mālikite theory even denied that their Medinese predecessors had ever reasoned without such a support. They argued that to proceed thus on the grounds of public interest must, at the end of the day, boil down either to a universal principle of the law or to a specific, revealed text. On the basis of a comprehensive study of the law, the jurists came to realize that there are five universal principles that underlie the law, namely, protection of life, mind, religion, private property and offspring. In one sense, therefore, the law has come down to protect and promote these five areas of human life, and nothing in this law can conceivably run counter to these principles or to any of their implications, however remotely. Thus, in a case appertaining to private ownership a choice may be made not to judge it according to the letter of a particular revealed text, but instead to solve it by *istiṣlāḥ*, on the principle that private property is sacred in the law and must therefore be protected.

Ijtihād *and* Mujtahids

Of prime concern to legal theory is the idea that only qualified jurists can perform legal reasoning, especially when new cases arise. But what are the conditions that a jurist must fulfill to rise to the rank of *mujtahid*? Or, to put it differently, what legal qualifications are required to allow a jurist to perform *ijtihād*? It must first be stated that *ijtihād* is an epistemic attribute, revolving around the quality and quantity of knowledge that a jurist must have accumulated. First, he must have expert knowledge of about 500 Quranic verses that embody legal subject matter. Second, he must know all legal *ḥadīth* and must acquire proficiency in *ḥadīth* criticism, so as to be able to sort out credible and sound *ḥadīth*s from those that are not. But he may also rely on those canonical works that have already recorded the *ḥadīth*s that are considered sound. Third, he must be knowledgeable in the Arabic language so that he can understand the complexities involved, for example, in metaphorical usages, the general and the particular, and in equivocal and univocal speech. Fourth, he must possess a thorough knowledge of the theory of abrogation and of those verses that have been abrogated by others. Fifth, he must be deeply trained in the art of legal reasoning, in how *qiyās* is conducted and in the principles of causation (i.e., establishing the *ratio legis* and using it in inferences). Sixth, he must know all cases that have been sanctioned by consensus, as he is not permitted to reopen any of these cases and subject them to fresh legal reasoning. However, he is not required to know all cases of positive law, although this is recommended, especially those cases subject to disagreement. Nor is he required to be of just character, even though the absence of the quality of rectitude does have an effect on the authoritativeness of his opinions, for judges and laymen are perfectly permitted to ignore them.

Once a jurist rises to the rank of a *mujtahid*, he can no longer follow the *ijtihād* of others and must exercise his own reasoning and judgment. This requirement stems from the assumption that all *mujtahid*s in principle are correct in their legal reasoning, and that his opinion is as valid as that of any other. Yet another rule that follows from the principle of equality of *ijtihād* is that a *mujtahid* must never follow the opinion of another less learned than he is.

Taqlīd

Any jurist who is not a *mujtahid* is, by definition, a *muqallid*, someone who practices *taqlīd*. A *muqallid* is a jurist who follows the *mujtahid* and who cannot perform *ijtihād* by himself (although juristic discourse outside legal theory did recognize various levels of qualification ranging between the two, thus allowing for middle-range *mujtahids* or *muqallids* capable of partial *ijtihād*).[17]

In the terminology of legal theory, laymen are also *muqallids* . It is their inability to reason independently on the basis of the revealed texts that consigns them to the status of jurist-*muqallids*. The laymen's access to the law can be had only through referring to the opinion of the *mujtahid*, whose opinion is transmitted to them by the jurist-*muqallid* and which they must follow.

The jurisconsult

Theorists generally equate the *mujtahid* with the *muftī*, or jurisconsult, who issues expert legal opinions (*fatwās*). Whatever scholarly credentials the *mujtahid* must possess, the *muftī* must possess too, but with a single difference: the latter must be pious and of just character and must take religion and law seriously. A person who meets all these requirement falls under the obligation to issue a legal opinion to anyone who solicits it from him. As a master of legal science, he is even under the obligation to teach law to anyone interested, this being considered as meritorious as the issuing of *fatwās*.

3. CONCLUDING REMARKS

A bird's-eye view of the development of legal thought throughout the first four centuries H shows significant change. *Ra'y* during the first century after the Prophet's death was increasingly challenged by traditionalism, represented in the proliferation and gradual acceptance of a notion of Prophetic Sunna expressed in the narrative of *ḥadīth*. Between the end of the second/eighth century and roughly the middle of the third/ninth, this traditionalism was to gain the upper hand, to be tempered in turn by the acceptance of a restrained form of rationalism. By the end of the latter

[17] See Hallaq, *Authority*, 1–23.

century, a synthesis was struck between rationalism and traditionalism, manifested in the legal theory (*uṣūl al-fiqh*) that was beginning to emerge. The major preoccupation of this theory with *qiyās* (to which subject, on average, more than one-third of the works was allotted) no doubt reflected its importance as a carefully crafted hermeneutical method charting the role of human reason as exclusively dependent on the revealed texts. But this dependence found expression in virtually every other part of this theory. Legal language, abrogation, consensus and the very method of *qiyās qua* method were, among others, anchored (in terms of authoritativeness) in the two textual sources of the law, the Quran and Sunna. Thus, the main characteristic of legal theory was that human reasoning must play a significant role in the law, but can in no way transcend the dictates of revelation. It was this particular marriage – nay, balance – between a well-defined scope of human reasoning and a carefully sorted out body of revealed texts that marked the most distinctive characteristic of this theory. This characteristic balance proved untenable by the end of the third/ninth century, except perhaps in the case of Shāfiʿī, whose theory did propound a rudimentary version of this balance. The fact that his theory was neglected for nearly a century after his death shows that the community of jurists had not yet, as a legal community, reached that synthesis. Furthermore, by the middle of the fourth/tenth century, legal theory was sufficiently developed as to make of Shāfiʿī little more than a theorist *manqué*. In other words, by the time he was "rediscovered," his theory – in its outline – had not only come to be taken for granted, but must have also been seen as rudimentary and basic.[18]

As the product of a synthesis, *uṣūl al-fiqh* was articulated in a double-edged manner. It was both descriptive and prescriptive. It expounded not only the methods and *modus operandi* of juristic construction of the law as the later *mujtahid*s carried them out, but also the proper and sound ways of dealing with the law. In other words, the theory culled out what was seen as the best methods of actual legal practice and made them the prescribed methods of "discovering" the law; for, after all, the declared purpose of this theory was, in essence, to lay down the methodology by which new legal cases might be solved. It is curious that this theory never formally acknowledged any other purpose for its *raison d'être*.

This theory provided the jurists with a methodology that allowed them not only to find solutions for new cases, but also to articulate and maintain

[18] See n. 5 above.

the existing law. Even old solutions to old problems were constantly rehabilitated and reasoned anew. The later jurists belonged to legal schools which, as we shall see, each had a legal doctrine to maintain and protect. Maintenance of legal doctrine required defense, and this defense meant no less than the finest possible articulation of one's position regarding a point of law. A Shāfiʿite jurist, for example, might deem Shāfiʿī's opinion on a particular case of law to be, among many others, the authoritative one, but he might also find Shāfiʿī's reasoning in justification of that opinion wanting. Thus, he might retain the solution but give it a fresh line of reasoning based on evidence perhaps different from that originally adduced by Shāfiʿī himself. None of this could have been done without the tools of legal theory.

Nor could jurists handle anything but the most basic of cases without training in this methodology. Oftentimes, legal cases were unique and complex. For the jurist to be able to distinguish the nuances of such cases, he had to resort to his knowledge of this methodology and the principles of reasoning and hermeneutics that it offered. Most of the *fatwā* literature (which often includes the so-called "difficult" cases) exhibits unique variations of legal reasoning, all drawing heavily, if not exclusively, upon the principles of legal theory. Without this theory, therefore, not only could new cases not be solved, but already-established positive legal doctrine could not be maintained, articulated and renewed. Equally important, without this theory no law could be extended from within established positive legal doctrine (in contradistinction to a fresh confrontation with the revealed texts) to cover the multitudes of cases that seem to be variations on older ones, but that nonetheless require, owing to their complexity, the tools of the *mujtahid.*

CHAPTER 7

The formation of legal schools

With the emergence of legal theory by the middle of the fourth/tenth century or thereabouts, Islamic law can be said to have become complete, save for one essential and fundamental feature which we have not yet discussed. This is the phenomenon of the legal schools, one of the most defining characteristics of Islamic law. In order to understand this complex phenomenon, it is perhaps best to begin with a survey of the meanings that are associated with the Arabic term "*madhhab*," customarily translated into the English language as "school."

1. THE MEANINGS OF *MADHHAB*

Derived from the Arabic verb *dhahaba*/*yadhhabu* (lit. "went/to go"), the verbal noun *madhhab* generally means that which is followed and, more specifically, the opinion or idea that one chooses to adopt. It is almost never applied by a jurist to his own opinion, but rather used in the third person, e.g., the *madhhab* of so-and-so is such-and-such. The most basic meaning of the term is thus a particular opinion of a jurist. Historically, it is of early provenance, probably dating back to the end of the first/seventh century, but certainly to the middle of the second/eighth. By the early third/ninth century, its use had become frequent.

The *madhhab*s and their history, however, are not associated with this basic usage to any meaningful extent, for it is conceivable that the usage might have persisted without there being any schools at all. In fact, it was already in circulation before any developed notion of "school" had come to exist. The concept of *madhhab* – so significant in the history of Islamic law – is rather associated with four other meanings that have emerged out of, and subsequent to, this basic usage, and which contributed to, or reflected, the formation of schools. The first of these was the technical meaning of the term as a principle that underlies a set of cases subsumed under such a principle. For example, a posited assumption of the Ḥanafites is that usurpation, in order to qualify as such, must involve the unlawful removal of property from its original place, where it had been possessed by the owner. The Ḥanbalites, on the other hand, define usurpation as mere seizure of property, even if it is not removed from its original place of ownership. Thus, taking possession of a rug by sitting on it (without removing it) is considered usurpation by the Ḥanbalites, but not by the Ḥanafites. In terms of recovery of damages, this basic difference in definition has resulted in generating significant differences between the two *madhhab*s. Whereas the Ḥanbalites make the usurper liable to the original owner for all growth on, and proceeds of, the usurped object, the Ḥanafites place severe restrictions on the ability of the owner to recover his accruing rights – the reasoning being that the growth or proceeds of the usurped property was not yet in existence when the property was "removed" from the hands of the rightful owner, and since they had not been in existence, no liability on the part of the usurper is deemed to arise.

Now, this example illustrates a central meaning of the term *madhhab* as a legal doctrine concerning a group of cases, in this instance cases pertaining to the recovery of damages, which are subsumed under a larger principle. And it is in this sense that it can be said that one school's *madhhab* differs, sometimes significantly, from another. (Incidentally, the foregoing example, like so many others, also illustrates the falsehood of the notion, dominant in modern scholarship, that the differences between and among the schools are minor, or limited to matters of detail.[1])

The second meaning of *madhhab* represents a combination of the basic meaning outlined above and the first technical meaning, namely, a principle underlying a group of derivative cases, as exemplified in the case of damages. Once jurists consciously developed such principles, it was possible to use the singular term "*madhhab*" to refer to the collective doctrine of a school or of a *mujtahid*, first with reference to a segment of the law (e.g., the law of usurpation) and second, by implication, the entirety of a school's, or a *mujtahid*'s, positive law. Historically, it must be stressed, the reference to a *mujtahid*'s collective doctrine preceded reference to a school, since schools developed out of these *mujtahids*' doctrines.

The third sense in which the term "*madhhab*" was used was with reference to the *mujtahid*'s individual opinion as the most authoritative

[1] In a recent commercial dispute (Delaware Superior Court, Case no. 00C-07-161), a party arguing on the grounds of the Ḥanbalite law of usurpation (*ghaṣb*) was awarded damages in excess of three hundred million US dollars, whereas in Ḥanafite law, it would have been entitled to no damages under the facts of the case.

in the collective doctrinal corpus of the school, irrespective of whether or not this *mujtahid* was the school's so-called founder. While this term appeared in the Arabic legal sources without qualification or conjunction with other terms, we will here assign to it the compound expression "*madhhab*-opinion." The most fundamental feature of the *madhhab*-opinion was its general and widespread acceptance in practice, as reflected in the courts and *fatwā*s. Thus, when an opinion is characterized as "*al-madhhab*" (with the definite article added), it signifies that that opinion is the standard, normative doctrine of the school, determined as such by the fact that practice is decided in accordance with it. The emergence and use of this term entailed a unanimity of doctrine and practice, which in turn entailed the existence of a school that, by definition, shared a common doctrinal ground.

Finally, the fourth meaning of *madhhab* is a group of jurists and legists who are strictly loyal to a distinct, integral and, most importantly, *collective* legal doctrine attributed to an eponym, a master-jurist, so to speak, after whom the school is known to acquire particular, distinctive characteristics (usually emanating from the first and third meanings of the term). Thus, after the formation of the schools – our concern here – jurists began to be characterized as Ḥanafite, Mālikite, Shāfiʿite or Ḥanbalite, as determined by their *doctrinal* (not personal) loyalty to one school or another. This doctrinal loyalty, it must be emphasized, is to a cumulative and accretive body of doctrine constructed by generations of distinguished jurists, which is to say, conversely, that loyalty is never extended to the individual doctrine of a single jurist–*mujtahid*. This (fourth) meaning of *madhhab* must thus be distinguished from its rudimentary predecessor, namely, a group of jurists who followed (but who, as we shall see, were not necessarily loyal to) the doctrine of a single, leading jurist. The latter's doctrine, furthermore, was not only non-accretive and, *ipso facto*, non-collective (in the sense that it was the product of the labor of a single jurist), but also represented merely a collection of the individual opinions held by that jurist.

Now, these four definitions roughly represent the development of the concept of *madhhab*, from the basic meaning of a jurist holding a particular opinion to strict loyalty to a collective, cumulative and self-contained body of legal doctrine. Obviously, such a development did not mean that one meaning would supersede or cancel out another meaning from which the former issued. Rather, with the exception of the rudimentary form of the fourth meaning, these notions of "*madhhab*" operated alongside each other throughout Islamic history, and were used variably in different contexts. By the middle of the fourth/tenth century, or shortly thereafter, these meanings were all present. The question that poses itself is: How and when did the concept of *madhhab* evolve from its most basic meaning into its highly developed sense of a doctrinal school? In the course of our enquiry, we will also attempt to answer the question: Why did this uniquely Islamic phenomenon develop in the first place? But let us first turn to the first question.

2. FROM SCHOLARLY CIRCLES TO PERSONAL SCHOOLS

In chapter 3, we saw that the early interest in law and legal studies evolved in the environment of scholarly circles, where men learned in the Quran and the general principles of Islam began discussions, among other things, of quasi-legal and often strictly legal issues. By the early part of the second century (ca. 720–40 AD), such learned men had already assumed the role of teachers whose circles often encompassed numerous students interested specifically in *fiqh*, the discipline of law. Yet, by that time, no obvious methodology of law and legal reasoning had evolved, and one teacher's lecture could hardly be distinguished, methodologically, from another's. Even the body of legal doctrine they taught was not yet complete, as can be attested from each teacher's particular interests. Some taught family law and inheritance, while others emphasized the law of rituals. More importantly, we have no evidence that the legal topics covered later were all present at this early period.

By the middle of the second/eighth century, not only had law become more comprehensive in coverage (though still not as comprehensive as it would be half a century later) but also the jurists had begun to develop their own legal assumptions and methodology. Teaching and debates within scholarly circles must have sharpened methodological awareness, which in turn led jurists to defend their own, individual conceptions of the law. On adopting a particular method, each jurist gathered around him a certain following who learned their jurisprudence and method from him. Yet, it was rare that a student or a young jurist would restrict himself to one circle or one teacher, for it was not uncommon for aspiring jurists to attend more than one circle in the same city, and even perhaps several circles. During the second half of the century, aspiring jurists did not confine themselves to circles within one city, but traveled from one region to another in search of reputable teachers. "Travel in search of knowledge" became an activity indulged in by many, and one of the most impressive features of Islamic scholarship.

Each prominent teacher attracted students who "took *fiqh*" from him. A judge who had studied law under a teacher was likely to apply the teacher's doctrine in his court, although, again, loyalty was not exclusive to a single doctrine. If he proved to be a sufficiently promising and qualified jurist, he might "sit" (*jalasa*) as a professor in his own turn, transmitting to his students the legal knowledge he gained from his teachers, but seldom without his own reconstruction of this knowledge. The legal doctrine that Abū Ḥanīfa taught to his students was largely a transmission from his own teachers, notably Nakhaʿī (d. 96/714) and Ḥammād b. Abī Sulaymān (d. 120/737). The same is true of Mālik, Awzāʿī, Shāfiʿī and many others. None of these, however, despite the fact that they were held up as school founders, constructed their own doctrine in its entirety. Rather, all of them were as much indebted to their teachers as their teachers had been to their own masters.

During the second/eighth century, therefore, the term "*madhhab*" meant a group of students, legists, judges and jurists who adopted the doctrine of a particular leading jurist, such as Abū Ḥanīfa or Thawrī (d. 161/777) – a phenomenon that I will call here a "personal school." Those who adopted or followed a jurist's doctrine were known as *aṣḥāb*, or associates, namely, those who studied with or were scholarly companions of a jurist. Most leading jurists had *aṣḥāb*, a term that often meant "followers." Thus, Abū Ḥanīfa, Awzāʿī, Abū Yūsuf and Thawrī, to name only a few, each had *aṣḥāb*, and each was associated with having a *madhhab*, namely, a personal school revolving around his personal doctrine. This was true even in the cases of Abū Ḥanīfa and his student Abū Yūsuf who each initially had what seem to have been independent followings – even personal *madhhab*s – although these personal *madhhab*s were later brought together under one doctrinal (not personal) *madhhab*, that of the Ḥanafites.

Adopting the doctrine of a certain jurist did not involve any particular loyalty to that doctrine, however. It was not unusual for a judge or a layman to shift from one doctrine to another or simultaneously adopt a combination of doctrines belonging to two or more leading jurists. A group of Medinese legists, for instance, is reported to have adhered to the doctrine of Saʿīd b. al-Musayyab but to have subsequently abandoned some parts of it in favor of others.[2] ʿAbd Allāh b. Ṭāhir al-Ḥazmī, who presided as judge in Egypt from 169/785 to 174/790, applied in his court the doctrines of Ibn al-Qāsim (d. 191/806), Ibn Shihāb al-Dīn al-Zuhrī, Rabīʿa and a certain Sālim.[3] Serving also as a judge in Egypt between 184/800 and 185/801 was Isḥāq b. al-Furāt, who is said to have combined the doctrines of several

[2] See Schacht, *Origins*, 7.
[3] Kindī, *Akhbār*, 383.

jurists, foremost among whom were the Medinese legist Mālik, whose disciple he was, and the Kūfan Abū Yūsuf.[4]

As late as the second half of the third/ninth century, some jurists were not yet sure of their affiliation, a fact that was inconceivable once the doctrinal schools emerged. Muḥammad b. Naṣr al-Marwazī (d. 294/906) was said to have been for long unable to decide which doctrine he should follow: that of Shāfiʿī, that of Abū Ḥanīfa or that of Mālik.[5] The fact that he finally adopted Shāfiʿī's doctrine, without combining it with others, is significant, since by his time it had become normative practice to adopt a single doctrine, and the combination of parts of various doctrines had ceased to be acceptable conduct. This is to be contrasted with the widespread acceptance during the second/eighth century of the practice of combining various opinions or doctrines.

In sum, by the middle of the third/ninth century, numerous jurists had established themselves as leaders in their field and acquired personal followings through the scholarly circles in which they debated legal issues, taught jurisprudence to students, and issued *fatwā*s. Most of those who were attracted to legal studies were free to attend one circle or another, and when some of these became judges or jurists, they also had the choice of what doctrine they wished to apply or propound. Some chose to combine, but others, who were more loyal to a single teacher, insisted on teaching or applying his doctrine alone. The case of Marwazī is a case in point, but even earlier, some students were loyal to a single teacher. During his tenure as judge in Egypt in around 246/860, Bakkār b. Qutayba seems to have insisted on applying Abū Ḥanīfa's doctrine exclusively, although he studied it not from Abū Ḥanīfa himself, but from one of the latter's students.[6]

3. FROM PERSONAL TO DOCTRINAL SCHOOLS

If the leading jurists did not always command total loyalty from their followers, then, strictly speaking, no claim can be made for a normative presence of personal schools. Therefore, we must be cautious not to generalize by saying that the period spanning roughly 80/700–250/865 was characterized by the emergence and operation of personal schools. The latter existed in a narrow sense. Only when a leading jurist attracted

[4] Ibid., 393.

[5] Tāj al-Dīn al-Subkī, *Ṭabaqāt al-Shāfiʿiyya al-Kubrā*, 6 vols. (Cairo: al-Maktaba al-Ḥusayniyya, 1906), II, 23.

[6] Kindī, *Akhbār*, 477; Subkī, *Ṭabaqāt*, II, 213–14.

a loyal following of jurists who exclusively applied his doctrine in courts of law or taught it to students, or issued *fatwā*s in accordance with it, can we say that a personal school of his existed. This was indeed the case with a number of prominent jurists, including Abū Ḥanīfa, Ibn Abī Laylā, Abū Yūsuf, Shaybānī, Mālik, Awzāʿī, Thawrī and Shāfiʿī. All these had loyal followers, but they also had many more students who did not adhere exclusively to their respective doctrines.

It is clear, however, that such personal schools, even when limited to loyal followers, do not truly represent what is referred to, in Islamic law, as the "*madhhab*," the doctrinal school, which possessed several characteristics lacking in the personal schools. First, the personal school, when fulfilling the condition of exclusive loyalty, comprised the positive legal doctrine of a single leading jurist, and, at times, his doctrine as transmitted by one of his students. The doctrinal school, on the other hand, possessed a cumulative doctrine of positive law in which the legal opinions of the leading jurist, now the supposed "founder" of the school, were, at best, *primi inter pares*, and at least, equal to the rest of the opinions and doctrines held by various other jurists, also considered leaders *within* the school. In other words, the doctrinal school was a collective, authoritative entity, whereas the personal school remained limited to the individual doctrine of a single jurist. For example, in the Ḥanafite doctrinal school, three categories of doctrine were recognized. The first was the so-called *ẓāhir al-riwāya*, attributed to Abū Ḥanīfa and his two students, Abū Yūsuf and Shaybānī. This possessed the highest level of authority, since it was transmitted, and surely worked out, by jurists considered to have been among the most qualified in the school. The second, known as *al-nawādir*, also belonged to these three masters, but without the sanctioning authority of the later, distinguished jurists. The third, termed *al-nawāzil*, represented the doctrinal constructions of the later, prominent jurists.[7] In contrast with the personal school of Abū Ḥanīfa, where his own doctrine constituted the basis of his following, the later doctrinal school of the Ḥanafites was a composite one, in which Abū Ḥanīfa's personal doctrine was one among many.

Second, the doctrinal school was, as we shall see, as much a methodological entity as a positive, doctrinal one. In other words, what distinguished a particular doctrinal school from another was largely its legal methodology and the positive principles it adopted – as a composite school –

[7] For a more detailed discussion of these doctrines, see Hallaq, *Authority*, 47–48, 181 f.

in dealing with its own law. Methodological awareness on this level had not yet existed in the personal schools, although it was on the increase from the middle of the second/eighth century.

Third, a doctrinal school was defined by its substantive boundaries, namely, by a certain body of positive law and methodological principles that clearly identified the outer limits of the school as a collective entity. The personal schools, on the other hand, had no such well-defined boundaries, and departure from these boundaries in favor of other legal doctrines and principles was a common practice.

The fourth characteristic, issuing from the third, is loyalty, for departure from positive law and methodological principles amounted to abandoning the school, a major event in the life (and biographies) of jurists. Doctrinal loyalty, in other words, was barely present in the personal schools, whereas in the later doctrinal schools, it was a defining feature of both the school itself and the careers of its members.

These four major characteristic differences, among others, sharply differentiate between personal and doctrinal schools. These fundamental differences also beg the question: How did the latter emerge?

A central feature of the doctrinal school – yet a fifth characteristic distinguishing it from the personal school – is the creation of an axis of authority around which an entire methodology of law was constructed. This axis was the figure of what came to be known as the founder, the leading jurist, in whose name the cumulative, collective principles of the school were propounded. Of all the leaders of the personal schools – and they were many – only four were raised to the level of "founder" of a doctrinal school: Abū Ḥanīfa, Mālik, Shāfiʿī and Ibn Ḥanbal, to list them in chronological order. The rest, perhaps with the possible exception of the Ẓāhirite school, did not advance to this stage, with the result that they, as personal schools, never survived beyond a relatively short duration. Later in this chapter, we will discuss the reasons behind the failure of these schools.

The so-called founder, the eponym of the school, thus became the axis of authority construction; and as bearer of this authority he was called the imam, and characterized as the absolute *mujtahid* who presumably forged for the school its methodology on the basis of which the positive legal principles and substantive law were constructed. The legal knowledge of the absolute *mujtahid* was presumed to be all-encompassing and thus wholly creative. The school was named after him, and he was purported to have been its originator. His knowledge included mastery of legal theory (*uṣūl al-fiqh*), Quranic exegesis, *ḥadīth* and its criticism, legal language, the theory of abrogation, substantive law, arithmetic, and the all-important science of juristic disagreement.

All these disciplines were necessary for the imam because he was the only one in the school who could engage directly with the revealed texts, from which, presumably, he derived the foundational structure of the school's positive law. The imam's doctrine therefore constituted the only purely juristic manifestation of the legal potentiality of revealed language. Without it, in other words, revelation would have remained just that, revelation, lacking any articulation as law. Furthermore, his doctrine laid claim to originality not only because it derived directly from the revealed texts, but also, and equally importantly, because it was gleaned systematically from the texts by means of clearly identifiable hermeneutical and positive legal principles. Its systematic character was seen as a product of a unified and cohesive methodology that only the founding imam could have forged; but a methodology that is itself inspired and dictated by revelation. To all of this epistemic competence, the imam was viewed as having been endowed with exceptional personal character and virtues. He embodied pure virtue, piety, morality, modesty, and the best of ethical values.

Now, this conception of the founding imams cannot be considered historically accurate – at least not entirely – for although they were knowledgeable jurists, they were certainly not as accomplished as they were made out to be in the Muslim tradition. Yet, this conception of them as absolute *mujtahid*s amounted to nothing less than what we may call a process of authority construction that served, in turn, an important function, and can hardly be dismissed as either misrepresentation of history or historical myth. In order to elevate the founding imams to this sublime rank of absolute *mujtahid*s, each of whom could be made responsible for founding a school, a number of things had to happen. Two of these deserve special attention: First, as we have seen earlier, no leading jurist around whom a personal school evolved constructed his own doctrine in its entirety. Indeed, a substantial part of any doctrine was transmitted from teachers and other mentors. Yet, the doctrinal school founder is made – in the discourse of each school – solely responsible for forging his own doctrine directly out of the revealed texts and, furthermore, through his own methodologies and principles. This process was accomplished by dissociating the doctrines of the imams from those of their predecessors, to whom in fact they were very much in debt.[8] One example of this process must suffice

[8] For a detailed treatment of this process, see Hallaq, *Authority*, 24 ff.

here: In Mālik's *Muwaṭṭa'*, it is stated: "Mālik heard (*balaghahu*) that if the faculty of hearing in both ears is completely lost [due to injury], then the full blood-money [for such an injury] is due." It is clear that this opinion was not Mālik's, but rather one transmitted to him from some unnamed authority. About half a century later, in Saḥnūn's *Mudawwana* (a foundational Mālikite work), Mālik begins to acquire the prestige of an absolute imam. There, in commenting on this case, Saḥnūn declares the following: "Mālik said: If hearing in both ears is completely lost, then the full blood-money is due."[9] This example, however simple, is typical of the process of dissociating the imams' doctrines from those of their predecessors, and with it of constructing their authority as imam-founders.

The second is a process of attributing to the imams the juristic accomplishments of their successors. A salient case in point is Aḥmad b. Ḥanbal, the reputed founder of the Ḥanbalite school. Whereas Abū Ḥanīfa, Mālik and Shāfiʿī were, to varying extents, jurists of high caliber, Ibn Ḥanbal could hardly be said to have approached their rank, as many of his own followers would admit. For instance, the distinguished Ḥanbalite jurist Najm al-Dīn al-Ṭūfī (d. 716/1316) openly acknowledged that Ibn Ḥanbal "did not transmit legal doctrine, for his entire concern was with *ḥadīth* and its collection."[10] Yet, within less than a century after his death, Ibn Ḥanbal emerged as the founding imam of a legal school of some renown. We discuss the emergence of the Ḥanbalite school because it illustrates an extreme example of authority construction, a process through which a legal doctrinal school arose out of meager juristic beginnings.

We may suppose, despite Ṭūfī's statement, that Ibn Ḥanbal did address some legal problems as part of his preoccupation with *ḥadīth*. This is probably the nucleus with which his followers worked, and which they later expanded and elaborated. It is therefore reasonable to assume that the bare beginnings of legal Ḥanbalism, which had already established itself as a theological school, are to be located in the juristic activities of the generation that followed Ibn Ḥanbal, associated with the names of Abū Bakr al-Athram (d. 261/874), ʿAbd Allāh al-Maymūnī (d. 274/887), Abū Bakr al-Marrūdhī (d. 275/888), Ḥarb al-Kirmānī (d. 280/893), Ibrāhīm Ibn Isḥāq al-Ḥarbī (d. 285/898), and Ibn Ḥanbal's two sons, Ṣāliḥ (d. 266/880 ?) and ʿAbd Allāh (d. 290/903). But these scholars are said to have been

[9] Mālik, *Muwaṭṭa'*, 748; Saḥnūn b. Saʿīd al-Tanūkhī, *al-Mudawwana al-Kubrā*, ed. Aḥmad ʿAbd al-Salām, 5 vols. (Beirut: Dār al-Kutub al-ʿIlmiyya, 1415/1994), IV, 563.

[10] Najm al-Dīn al-Ṭūfī, *Sharḥ Mukhtaṣar al-Rawḍa*, ed. ʿAbd Allāh al-Turkī, 3 vols. (Beirut: Mu'assasat al-Risāla, 1407/1987), III, 626–27.

no more than bearers of Ibn Ḥanbal's opinions, however few in number. None of them, for instance, elaborated a complete or near-complete legal doctrine of the eponym. Rather, it was left to Abū Bakr al-Khallāl (d. 311/923) to bring together what was seen as the master's dispersed opinions. Khallāl was reported to have traveled widely in search of those of Ibn Ḥanbal's students who had heard him speak on matters legal, and he reportedly contacted a great number of them, including his two sons and Ibrāhīm al-Ḥarbī. A major Ḥanbalite biographer was to announce that Khallāl's collection of the eponym's opinions was never matched, before or after.[11]

That Khallāl managed to collect a sufficient number of opinions on the basis of which he could produce the first major corpus of Ḥanbalite law is remarkable, for the reputed founder had never interested himself in law per se, and when he did occasionally deal with legal issues, he did so in a marginal and tangential manner. That Ibn Ḥanbal emerged as a founder-imam is more a tribute to Khallāl's constructive efforts than to anything Ibn Ḥanbal could have contributed to the province of law. Khallāl, drawing on the increasing prestige of the Miḥna's hero, essentially transformed Ibn Ḥanbal into the author of a methodologically cogent legal doctrine that sustained all later doctrinal developments. To say that Khallāl and his associates (*aṣḥāb*) were the real founders of the Ḥanbalite school is merely to state the obvious.

But Khallāl would never have claimed for himself anything more than credit for having elaborated the law in a Ḥanbalite fashion – whatever that may have meant to him – and he himself possessed none of the prestige that was conveniently bestowed on Ibn Ḥanbal and that he efficiently used to construct a school in the master's name. That Khallāl long escaped notice as the real founder (or at least as the main contributor to the formation) of a doctrinal Ḥanbalite school illustrates the second process of authority construction we have alluded to earlier, namely, that the doctrines of the reputed founders were not only dissociated from those of their predecessors, but also expanded to include the juristic achievements of their followers, as we have seen in the case of Khallāl (and each school had its own Khallāl, so to speak).

The generation of Khallāl, as well as the following two generations, produced jurists who, by later standards, were known as the *mukharrijūn* (sing. *mukharrij*), a rank of legal scholars whose juristic competence was of

[11] Muḥammad b. Abī Yaʿlā Ibn al-Farrāʾ, *Ṭabaqāt al-Ḥanābila*, ed. Muḥammad al-Fiqī, 2 vols. (Cairo: Maṭbaʿat al-Sunna al-Muḥammadiyya, 1952), II, 113.

the first rank but who, nonetheless, contributed to the construction of a doctrinal school under the name of a reputed founder. The activity in which the *mukharrij* engaged was known as *takhrīj*, said to be exercised either on the basis of a particular opinion that had been derived by the founding imam or, in the absence of such an opinion, on that of the revealed texts, whence the *mukharrij* would derive a legal norm according to the principles and methodology of his imam. In both direct and indirect *takhrīj*, then, conformity with the imam's legal theory and his general and particular principles regarding the law was theoretically deemed an essential feature.

However, a close examination of this juristic activity during the formation of the doctrinal schools reveals that the imam's legal doctrine and methodology were by no means the exclusive bases of reasoning. For example, the early Shāfiʿite jurist Ibn al-Qāṣṣ (d. 336/947) reports dozens, perhaps hundreds, of cases in which *takhrīj* was practiced both within and without the boundaries of the imam's legal principles and *corpus juris*. In fact, he acknowledges – despite his clearly Shāfiʿite affiliation – that his work is based on both Shāfiʿī's and Abū Ḥanīfa's doctrines.[12] For example, in the case of a person whose speaking faculty is impaired, Shāfiʿī and Abū Ḥanīfa apparently disagreed over whether or not his testimony might be accepted if he knows sign language. Ibn Surayj (who was the Shāfiʿite equivalent of the Ḥanbalite Khallāl, and Ibn al-Qāṣṣ's professor) conducted *takhrīj* on the basis of these two doctrines, with the result that two contradictory opinions were accepted for this case: one that such testimony is valid, the other that it is void. What is significant about Ibn al-Qāṣṣ's report is that Ibn Surayj's *takhrīj* activity in deriving these two solutions was deemed to fall within the hermeneutical contours of the Shāfiʿite school. The two opinions, Ibn al-Qāṣṣ says, were reached "according to Shāfiʿī's way."[13] At times, however, Ibn Surayj's *takhrīj* became Shāfiʿī's own opinion. In the case of how the judge should deal with the plaintiff and defendant in the courtroom, Ibn al-Qāṣṣ reports that "*Shāfiʿī's opinion* is that the judge should not allow one of the two parties to state his arguments before the court without the other being present. *Ibn Surayj produced this opinion by way of takhrīj.*"[14]

Like Ibn Surayj, Ibn al-Qāṣṣ, in his practice of *takhrīj*, also drew heavily on the Ḥanafite tradition, and to some extent on that of the Mālikites.

12 Aḥmad b. Muḥammad Ibn al-Qāṣṣ, *Adab al-Qāḍī*, ed. Ḥusayn Jabbūrī, 2 vols. (Ṭā'if: Maktabat al-Ṣiddīq, 1409/1989), I, 68.
13 Ibid., I, 306.
14 Ibid., I, 214 (emphasis added).

Although most of his *takhrīj* cases are drawn from Shāfiʿite–Ḥanafite materials, he frequently relies exclusively on Abū Ḥanīfa's opinions. What is striking here is that even when Abū Ḥanīfa's doctrine is the sole basis of his reasoning, he and his successors considered these *takhrīj* cases to be of Shāfiʿite pedigree, and they were in fact often attributed to Shāfiʿī himself. This practice of drawing on the doctrinal tradition of another school and attributing the resulting reasoning to one's own school and its founder was by no means limited to the Shāfiʿites, although they were known to have engaged in it, together with the Ḥanbalites and Ḥanafites, more than did the Mālikites. It is quite common, for instance, to find Ḥanbalite opinions that have been derived through *takhrīj* exclusively from the Ḥanafite, Mālikite or, more frequently, the Shāfiʿite school.[15]

Generally speaking, *takhrīj*, as a process through which later opinions were attributed to the so-called founding imams, was not recognized either in practice or in theory. The legal literature is by and large silent on this feature of constructing doctrine (which may explain modern scholarship's near-total neglect of this important phenomenon). One of the rare exceptions, however, is found in the work of the later Shāfiʿite jurist Abū Isḥāq al-Shīrāzī (d. 476/1083), who devotes to this issue what is for us a significant chapter in his monumental *Sharḥ al-Lumaʿ*. The chapter's title is revealing: "Concerning the matter that it is not permissible to attribute to Shāfiʿī what his followers have established through *takhrīj*."[16] What is significant in Shīrāzī's discussion is that his school was divided between those who permitted such an attribution and those who did not. The former saw it as normal to place a *takhrīj* opinion fashioned by a later *mukharrij* in the mouth of the founding imam, as if he himself had formulated it. In defense of their position, they argued that everyone agrees that conclusions reached on the basis of *qiyās* are considered part of the Sharīʿa, attributed to God and the Prophet, when in fact they are fashioned by individual *mujtahid*s. Just as this is true, it should also be valid that the conclusions of *qiyās* drawn by other jurists on the basis of Shāfiʿī's opinions be attributed to Shāfiʿī himself. Be this as it may, it is clear that the general silence over the matter of attribution – itself a significant process in the doctrinal construction of the schools – bespeaks the significant weight of the juristic community that found this attribution "permissible." Furthermore, this process of attribution, which is one of back-projection, both

[15] For a detailed discussion of this phenomenon, see Hallaq, *Authority*, 46 ff.

[16] Abū Isḥāq al-Shīrāzī, *Sharḥ al-Lumaʿ*, ed. ʿAbd al-Majīd Turkī, 2 vols. (Beirut: Dār al-Gharb al-Islāmī, 1988), II, 1084–85.

complemented and enhanced the other process of attribution by which the so-called founding imams were themselves credited with a body of doctrines that their predecessors had elaborated. Out of all of this, the figure of the imam emerged as a focal point around which not only positive doctrine originated, but (and more importantly) an entire methodology and a system of principles came to be fashioned. Therefore, the imam's doctrine in fact represents the collective contributions of his predecessors and successors, a cumulative juristic history that, in theory, is reduced to the experience of one individual: the founding imam or the school master.

Now, it is important to realize that the *madhhab* – as explained in section 1 of this chapter – meant not only the doctrine of the reputed founding imam but also the cumulative positive doctrine propounded by his predecessors and, no less so, by his successors. The term referred to the authoritative doctrine of the school, while the eponym's positive doctrine – when seen to stand independently and separately – was held to be no more than a *primus inter pares*. In other words, in practical terms, his doctrine (as a collection of positive legal opinions) carried no greater weight than did that of each of his followers who came to be recognized as pillars of the *madhhab* – this last being not only a doctrinal school but a group of jurists loyal to an integral doctrine. For although the authoritative body of opinion that defined the *madhhab* doctrinally was certainly the work of the later jurists, in addition to that of the eponym, this body of opinion rested on an interpretive methodology or on an identifiable and self-sufficient hermeneutical system that not only permitted the derivation of individual opinions but also, and more importantly, bestowed a particular legitimacy and, therefore, authority on them.

The *madhhab*, therefore, was mainly a body of authoritative legal doctrine existing alongside individual jurists who participated in the elaboration of, or adhered to, that doctrine in accordance with an established methodology attributed exclusively to the eponym. The latter (whose knowledge was presumed to have been all-encompassing, and to have been utilized by him to confront revelation directly) thus becomes the absolute and independent *mujtahid*, and all subsequent *mujtahid*s and jurists, however great their contributions, remain attached by their loyalty to the tradition of the *madhhab* that is symbolized by the figure of the founder. What made a *madhhab* (as a doctrinal school) a *madhhab* is therefore this feature of authoritative doctrine whose ultimate font is presumed to have been the absolute *mujtahid*-founder, not the mere congregation of jurists under the name of a titular eponym. This congregation would have been meaningless without the polarizing presence of an authoritative, substantive and methodological doctrine constructed in the name of a founder. Education and transmission of legal knowledge from teacher to student cannot therefore explain the formation of the *madhhabs*, as one modern scholar has recently contended.[17] For without the authoritative doctrinal feature of the school, there would have been no rallying doctrine around which loyalty to a *madhhab* can be manifested. Teaching and transmission were thus a vehicle for passing the school tradition from one generation to the next, but by themselves did not, as pedagogical mechanisms, contribute to the creation of the *madhhab* as defined in the three sentences opening this paragraph. In other words, the formation of the *madhhabs* – as we have conventionally come to recognize them, and which we have dubbed here as doctrinal schools – was very much, if not entirely, an internal process of doctrine-building, and for this process to have a sociological context (as all law must indeed rest in a sociological substrate), there had to be groups of jurists who participated in the creation of, and adherence to, that doctrine. This participation would give the *madhhab* its meaning as an association of jurists loyal to an eponym's doctrine (our fourth meaning as outlined in section 1 above). But the act of association itself was not the cause of the rise of the *madhhab*; rather, it was no more than an agency through which the doctrine found support in the social classes, and was transmitted from one generation to the next.

Thus the creation of educational institutions (the proto-*madrasa* and *madrasa*) that promoted the teaching of one school or another could hardly have been the cause of the rise of the *madhhabs*, since there must first have been a *madhhab* for it to be taught or promoted. The same is true of commentaries on the foundational texts of the early jurists (and not necessarily those of the eponyms). These commentaries started to appear around the very end of the third/ninth century and the beginning of the next and, like education, the commentaries constituted the media of authority construction but not its causes.

If education and commentaries were not the root causes of the unique institution (and concept) of doctrinal legal schools, then what was the real cause? It is often difficult to explain why a civilization adopts one cultural form or one institution rather than another. Islam certainly did not borrow the concept of schools from any cultural predecessor, since none is to be

[17] Christopher Melchert, *The Formation of the Sunni Schools of Law* (Leiden: E. J. Brill, 1997). The main reason behind this mistaken diagnosis is the definition of the *madhhab* as a personal school, which in our analysis represents merely a middle stage between the formation of the scholarly circles and the final emergence of doctrinal schools.

found in earlier civilizations. Thus, we can argue with confidence that the *madhhabs* were indigenous Islamic phenomena, having been produced out of the soil of Islamic civilization itself. That they were unknown to the Near Eastern cultures from which Islam inherited other features, coupled with the fact of their slow and gradual evolution within Islamic civilization, is demonstrable proof of their Islamic origins. The embryonic formation of the schools started sometime during the eighth decade after the Hijra (ca. 690 AH), taking the form of scholarly circles in which pious scholars debated religious issues and taught interested students. The knowledge and production of legal doctrine began in these circles – nowhere else. Due to their epistemic standing (i.e., their expertise and knowledge of the religious and legal values of the new religion), these scholars emerged as social leaders who commanded the respect of the populace. Once the Umayyads rose to power (as early as 41/661), the political leadership began to feel the need for a class of socially connected local leaders who could function as their link with the masses. Within three or four decades after the Umayyads had assumed power, and with the gradual abandonment by this dynasty of the egalitarian/tribal form of governance pursued by the early caliphs, this need was all the more obvious. The legal specialists, with their circles and social influence, were the perfect groups to be patronized and supported by the ruling power. We shall take up this theme in the next chapter.

The point, however, is that since law was from the beginning a matter of learning and knowledge, legal authority became epistemic rather than political, social or even religious. That epistemic authority is *the* defining feature of Islamic law need not be doubted.[18] In other words, a masterly knowledge of the law was the determinant of where legal authority resided; and it resided with the scholars, not with the political rulers or any other source. This is as much true of the last third of the first/seventh century as of the second/eighth century and thereafter. If a caliph actively participated in legal life – as ʿUmar II did – it was by virtue of his recognized personal knowledge of the law, not by virtue of his political office. Thus legal authority in Islam was personal and private; it was in the persons of the individual jurists (be they laymen or, on occasion, caliphs) that authority resided, and it was this epistemic competence that was later to be known as *ijtihād* – a cornerstone of Islamic law.

Devolving as it did upon the individual jurists who were active in the scholarly circles, legal authority never resided in the state, and this too was

18 On epistemic authority as the defining feature of Islamic law, see Hallaq, *Authority*.

a prime factor in the rise of the *madhhab*. Whereas law – as a legislated and executed system – was state-based in other imperial and complex civilizations, in Islam the ruling powers had virtually nothing to do with legal governance or with the production and promulgation of law. Therefore, in Islam, the need arose to anchor law in a system of authority that was not political, especially since the ruling political institution was, as we shall see in the next chapter, deemed highly suspect. The scholarly circles, which consisted of no more than groups of legal scholars and interested students, lacked the ability to produce a unified legal doctrine that would provide an axis of legal authority. For while every region, from Kūfa to Medina and from Fusṭāṭ to Damascus, possessed its own distinct, practice-based legal system, there was nevertheless a multiplicity of scholarly circles in each, and oftentimes the scholars within the same circle were not in total agreement.

The personal schools afforded the first step toward providing an axis of legal authority, since the application (in courts and *fatwās*) and the teaching of a single, unified doctrine – that is, the doctrine of the leading jurist around whom a personal school had formed – permitted a measure of doctrinal unity. Yet, the vast number of personal schools was only slightly more effective than the multiplicity of scholarly circles, so a polarizing axis of authority was still needed. The personal schools, forming around all the major scholars – including Ḥammād b. Abī Sulaymān, Ibn Shubruma (d. 144/761), Ibn Abī Laylā, Awzāʿī, Thawrī, Ibn Abī Sharīk al-Nakhaʿī (d. 177/793), Abū Ayyūb al-Sakhtiyānī (d. 131/748), Abū Ḥanīfa, Ḥasan b. Ṣāliḥ, Abū Yūsuf, Shaybānī, Mālik, Sufyān b. ʿUyayna (d. 198/814), ʿAbd Allāh b. al-Mubārak (d. during the 180s/800s), and Shāfiʿī, to name only a few who lived during the second/eighth century – were still very numerous. Furthermore, the personal schools did not guarantee a complete unity of doctrine. The leader's doctrine (which was little more than a body of legal opinions) was not always applied integrally, subjected, as it were, to the discretion or even reformulation of the jurist applying it. A case in point is that of Abū Yūsuf, presumably a member of the Ḥanafite personal school, who formulated his own doctrine and who in turn had his own following.

The second-/eighth-century community of jurists not only formulated law but also, as we saw in chapter 4, administered it in the name of the ruling dynasty. In other words, this community was – juristically speaking – largely independent, having the competence to steer a course that would fulfill its mission as it saw fit. Yet, while maintaining juristic (and largely judicial) independence, this community did serve as the ruler's link to the masses, aiding him in his bid to legitimacy. As long as the ruler benefited from this legitimizing agency, the legal community benefited from financial support and easily acquired independence, to boot.

Rallying around a single juristic doctrine was probably the only means for a personal school to acquire loyal followers and thus attract political/financial support. Such support was not limited to direct financial favors bestowed by the ruling elite, but extended to prestigious judicial appointments that guaranteed not only handsome pay but also political and social influence. These considerations alone – not to mention others – can explain the importance of such rallying around outstanding figures. The construction of the figure of an absolute *mujtahid* who represented the culmination of doctrinal developments within the school was a way to anchor law in a source of authority that constituted an alternative to the authority of the body politic. Whereas in other cultures the ruling dynasty promulgated the law, enforced it, and constituted the locus of legal authority, in Islam it was the doctrinal *madhhab* that produced law and afforded its axis of authority; in other words, legal authority resided in the collective, juristic doctrinal enterprise of the school, not in the body politic or in the doctrine of a single jurist.

4. SURVIVING AND DEFUNCT SCHOOLS

As we have seen, it was not until the first half of the fourth/tenth century that the doctrinal school was finally constructed, although further doctrinal developments continued to take place even after this period.[19] So the process of transition from personal schools to doctrinal *madhhabs* was a long one indeed, spanning the second half of the second/eighth century up to the end of the next, and in the case of personal schools that emerged during the third/ninth century, notably the Shāfiʿite and Ḥanbalite, the process continued well into the middle of the fourth/tenth. This is to say that the Ḥanafites and Mālikites had constructed their doctrinal *madhhabs* before all others.

In addition to the personal schools that formed around such second-/eighth-century figures as we enumerated in the previous section, nearly as many emerged during the next century. One of these was Ibrāhīm al-Muzanī, presumed to have been a student of Shāfiʿī but independent enough to have formulated his own brand of jurisprudence.[20] In fact, the doctrinal Shāfiʿite school that was fashioned by Ibn Surayj and his students

[19] On this continuing process of doctrinal development, see ibid., 57–165.
[20] Muḥyī al-Dīn al-Nawawī, *Tahdhīb al-Asmā' wal-Lughāt*, 2 vols. (Cairo: Idārat al-Ṭibāʿa al-Munīriyya, n.d.), I, 285.

in Baghdad was in effect largely a synthesis of Shāfiʿī's and Muzanī's differing versions of jurisprudence. Until Ibn Surayj rose to prominence, Muzanī seems to have had his own following, notable among whom was Abū al-Qāsim al-Anmāṭī (d. 288/900), who was finally claimed as a pure Shāfiʿite when the school was later transformed into a doctrinal *madhhab.* Like Muzanī, Ḥarmala (d. 243/857) was another of Shāfiʿī's students, said to have reached such a level of legal learning and accomplishment that he was credited with a personal school of his own.[21]

Another of Shāfiʿī's students around whom a personal school was formed was Ibn Ḥanbal, discussed in the previous chapter. There, we also mentioned Dāwūd b. Khalaf, known as al-Ẓāhirī after his literalist jurisprudential method. Yet another personal school seems to have formed around the jurist Ibrāhīm b. Khālid Abū Thawr (d. 240/854), whose followers included Manṣūr b. Ismāʿīl (d. 306/918) and Abū ʿUbayd b. Ḥarbawayh (d. 319/931). Like Muzanī, the latter seems to have been a loyal adherent of Abū Thawr's doctrine, but the later Shāfiʿites claimed him as a member of their school.[22]

To this list we must also add the very distinguished group of jurists known as the "Four Muḥammads," namely, Muḥammad b. Naṣr al-Marwazī (d. 294/906), Muḥammad b. Jarīr al-Ṭabarī (d. 310/922), Muḥammad Ibn Khuzayma al-Nīsābūrī (d. 311/923) and Muḥammad b. al-Mundhir al-Nīsābūrī (d. 318/930). Around these four there likewise formed personal schools, represented by students who applied their doctrines in courts over which they themselves presided as judges or in *fatwā*s that they issued as *muftī*s; furthermore, they taught their legal doctrines to students in scholarly circles. Interestingly, the Four Muḥammads were finally absorbed by the Shāfiʿite doctrinal school, as evidenced in notices accorded them in this school's biographical dictionaries. Later Shāfiʿism also laid claim to those opinions of theirs that "accorded" with this school's madhhabic doctrine.[23] This appropriation in effect constituted part of the process of building the *madhhab* as a doctrinal school.

Be that as it may, only four personal schools survived, a fact of paramount importance in the legal history of Islam. Whereas the Ḥanafite, Mālikite, Shāfiʿite and Ḥanbalite schools continued to flourish, the other personal schools either met with total failure or were absorbed by one or

[21] Jalāl al-Dīn al-Suyūṭī, *al-Radd ʿalā man Akhlada ilā al-Arḍ wa-Jahila anna al-Ijtihāda fī Kulli ʿAṣrin Farḍ*, ed. Khalīl al-Mays (Beirut: Dār al-Kutub al-ʿIlmiyya, 1983), 188.

[22] Subkī, *Ṭabaqāt*, II, 301–02.

[23] Ibid., II, 126 ff.

the other of the surviving schools, notably the Shāfiʿite. The question that poses itself then is: Why did these schools fail? Or, conversely, why did the four schools succeed?

The brief answer to these questions is that none of the personal schools, except the four just mentioned, managed to reach a level of doctrine-building that allowed it to transform itself into a doctrinal school. In other words, the doctrine of these failed personal schools remained limited to what amounted to a collection of legal opinions representing the individual doctrine of the leader. There was no process of authority construction that would produce an accretive doctrine and methodology and that would raise the figure of the leader to the status of an absolute *mujtahid* whose solutions were presumed to be the result of a direct confrontation with the revealed texts.

Still, this answer begs yet another question: Why did these schools fail to proceed to the stage of authority construction? Or, conversely, why was their growth stunted to the point where they finally came to a halt at the stage of personal schools? Again a brief answer to these questions is that none of these schools attracted high-caliber jurists who, with their juristic contributions, would augment the authority of the so-called founding imam and who would thereby construct, over generations, an accretive, substantive and methodological doctrine in his name. To explain the absence of such jurists in particular, and the failure of these schools in general, a number of factors must be considered.

First, and of paramount importance, is lack of political support. In the next chapter, we discuss the significance of the schools, both personal and doctrinal, for the rulers' political legitimacy. Constituting the link between the masses and the ruling elite, the legal scholars were supported by the latter through financial and other means. For example, in one recent study, it was convincingly argued that the success of the Ḥanafite personal school in Iraq was mainly due to the backing of the ʿAbbāsids, who used the Ḥanafite scholars to garner popular support. Another conclusion of this study is that in several locales where the Ḥanafites did not have this support, their school failed to flourish or even to recruit members. Anti-ʿAbbāsid Syria (a region loyal to the Umayyads) is a case in point.[24] Political support also explains the success of the Andalusian Mālikites who, around 200/815, not only received the unqualified support of the Spanish Umayyads, but

[24] See N. Tsafrir, "The Spread of the Hanafī School in the Western Regions of the ʿAbbāsid Caliphate up to the End of the Third Century AH" (Ph.D. dissertation, Princeton University, 1993).

also managed to displace the Awzāʿite personal school which had until then been dominant in that region. Support from the ruling elite was so crucial that the flourishing of a school in some areas can be entirely explained in such terms. Syria is again a case in point. Until 284/897, this province had no Shāfiʿites at all. But at that time, this school was introduced there by the Ṭūlūnids, who seized the province from the ʿAbbāsids in that year. It is clear then that political interference/support played a role in the career of schools.

Second, and also of central importance, was the failure to bring the doctrine of a personal school to the paradigm of what we have called (in the previous chapter) the Great Synthesis, namely, the synthesis between rationalism and traditionalism. This was obviously the main cause of the demise of the Ẓāhirite school, and possibly that of Abū Thawr.

Third, and closely connected with the Great Synthesis, was the alliance with what were perceived as non-mainstream theological movements. The failure of a school often resulted from continued adherence to such movements; success, on the other hand, meant allying the school with popular – or, at least, non-sectarian – theology. The early Ḥanafites not only rehabilitated their rationalist jurisprudence (as represented in Thaljī's contributions), but also ultimately dissociated themselves from the Muʿtazilites – who lost their bid for power in the Inquisition – and instead allied themselves with the mainstream theological doctrine of the Māturīdites. Furthermore, they also managed to garner significant legal support in Khurāsān and Transoxania by virtue of the relevance of their theological Murjiʾite doctrine to the new converts in these regions. This relevance stemmed from the Murjiʾite tenet that belief in Islam – and therefore full membership in the community– depended on mere confession, and did not require actual performance of religious duties or obligations. This tenet proved useful for the new converts who struggled to get rid of the *jizya* (a tax imposed on non-Muslims) that the Umayyads had continued to impose on them notwithstanding their conversion.[25] As a central tenet of Abū Ḥanīfa, Murjiʾism was embraced by the populations of Khurāsān and Transoxania and, together with it, the Ḥanafite school and its law.

On the other hand, the Shāfiʿites allied themselves with the even more mainstream theology of the Ashʿarites. Such alliances, in a society that was heavily engulfed by theological debate, were crucial for the success of

[25] Wilferd Madelung, "The Early Murjiʾa in Khurāsān and Transoxania and the Spread of Ḥanafism," *Der Islam*, 59, 1 (1982): 32–39, at 33.

a school. By the same token, swimming against the current of a mainstream or popular movement tended to marginalize a personal school, and marginalization in effect meant extinction. A case in point was the Jarīrite school of al-Ṭabarī, whose personal attacks on the Inquisition's hero, Ibn Ḥanbal, seem to have had adverse effects on his following. The animosity exhibited against it by Ibn Ḥanbal's zealous supporters must have been sufficient cause to deprive Jarīrism of any chance it may have had for success.[26]

Fourth, there was the absence of distinguishing juristic features that lent a personal school its distinct juristic identity (we must here stress yet again that the modern scholar's notion – that differences between and among the schools' doctrines were insignificant and pertained to details – is thoroughly flawed). It is possible that the school of Ibn al-Mundhir was too close to Shāfiʿite doctrine in terms of legal thought and juristic principles, so that, combined with its later origins, it could offer too little too late. The same can be said of Awzāʿī's personal school, which not only seems to have been heavily influenced by the Medinese doctrine, but also was unable in the long run to construct its own juristic identity. Thus, when the Spanish Umayyads adopted the Mālikite school, thereby displacing that of Awzāʿī, they were not, juristically speaking, straying too far. It is plausible to assume that the Umayyad preference for the Mālikites was prompted by their desire to retain the law as constructed by its original expounders, the Medinese, and not their Syrian imitators.

These are the four most identifiable factors that may account for the failure or success of a personal school. When each school is considered separately, a combination of one or more of these factors may explain its failure. Thus these factors can operate separately or aggregately. At times, a dialectic existed between these factors, one feeding the other. Thus, failure to participate in the Great Synthesis or alliance with a sectarian theological movement may have reduced a school's appeal to new members. Consequently, reduction in membership made a school less attractive for political support, since the ruling circles needed influence over large numbers of people in order to generate the political legitimacy they were seeking. For instance, it would have been inconceivable for the Jarīrites to receive any political support during the formation of their school (i.e., ca. 300/910–350/960), since the Baghdadian ruling elite (where Jarīrism began) knew well that such a move would arouse the wrath of the city's Ḥanbalites. By the same token, the latter managed to succeed without

[26] George Makdisi, "The Significance of the Schools of Law in Islamic Religious History," *International Journal of Middle East Studies*, 10 (1979): 1–8.

willing or formal political support, in that the ruling circles, in Baghdad and elsewhere, merely tolerated this school and in fact appointed some of its members as judges in an effort to appease it. The fact, however, remains that large or active membership (the latter being the case of the Ḥanbalites, the former, the Ḥanafites) did command the attention and interest of political power, from which support – willing or otherwise – was garnered for those schools. Furthermore, the fourth factor – i.e., lack of distinct juristic identity – may well have combined with any of the other factors. The Awzāʿite school is a case in point, as its undistinguished character, combined with withdrawal of crucial political support both in Andalusia (with the introduction of Mālikism) and Syria (with the introduction of Shāfiʿism), contributed to its eventual dissolution (although Awzāʿism did not disappear altogether from Syria until later).

5. DIFFUSION OF THE SCHOOLS

Our preceding discussion has touched on the regions into which some of the personal schools spread. Before we proceed, it is necessary to discuss the means by which a school could penetrate a city or a region, and these are mainly three: first, by gaining judicial appointment; second, by establishing a teaching circle or circles; and/or third, by engaging the local scholars in legal debates. These three were not mutually exclusive, since a scholar/judge might have been active on all three fronts. But it was often the case that a judge appointed by the central government was unable to penetrate the local jurists' circles, as happened with a number of Iraqian/Ḥanafite judges appointed to Egypt during the third/ninth century. Thus, the appointment of a personal school member to the bench in a city was not, in and by itself, an indication of that school's penetration into that city, although it frequently constituted one of the means for such penetration in the longer run. A more efficient means for the spread of a school was the success of a member in establishing a teaching circle, which meant that the school had a better chance of growing through the future activities of the students. Nonetheless, it must be emphasized, teaching and grooming students were not in themselves activities that led to the spread or success of a school, since the success or failure of pedagogy depended mainly on the four factors discussed in the previous section.

By the death of Abū Ḥanīfa in 150/767, his personal school had come to dominate the legal scene in Kūfa, and opponents such as Ibn Abī Laylā quickly withered away. Within less than two decades after the ʿAbbāsids had established their rule over Iraq, the Kūfan Ḥanafites received the full support of this dynasty, a fact that not only strengthened their judicial grip over this city, but also allowed them to export their brand of jurisprudence. In the early 160s/late 770s, the Ḥanafites arrived in Baghdad, the ʿAbbāsid capital, built in 145/762. There, they found legal circles mostly consisting of Medinese scholars – a number of whom were by then judges of the city. The Ḥanafite entrance to the city was also accompanied by Baṣran local scholars who seem to have added to the competition between and among the various groups. As befits a capital, Baghdad was represented by all the schools, first by the Mālikites and Ḥanafites, and, during the second half of the third/ninth century, also by the Shāfiʿites, Ḥanbalites and members of some soon-to-be-extinct schools.

But long before they penetrated the new capital, the Ḥanafites had begun to spread – though very slowly – into the cities adjacent to Kūfa. As early as 140/757 or thereabouts, Ḥanafite law was brought to Baṣra by the jurist and judge Zufar b. al-Hudhayl (d. 158/774), one of the four most distinguished of Abū Ḥanīfa's students (the three others having been Abū Yūsuf, Shaybānī and al-Ḥasan b. Ziyād).

In Wāsiṭ, a city located on the Tigris east of Kūfa, the Ḥanafites arrived during the 170s/790s, when their members began to be appointed as judges at the behest of the chief justice, Abū Yūsuf. It appears that the Medinese had until then been in control of this city's judiciary. But with the weakening of Ḥanafism during the second half of the third/ninth century – which was precipitated by the concurrent decline of the caliphate and Muʿtazilism, both of which supported the Ḥanafites and were supported by them – Wāsiṭ was to lose its Ḥanafite contingency in favor of the Mālikites and, later, the Shāfiʿites.

In Syria, however, the Ḥanafites failed to be even nominally represented, due to Syrian anti-ʿAbbāsid feelings, which were projected onto the Ḥanafites who allied themselves with this regime. But the failure of the Ḥanafites in Syria may also have to do with the strong presence, in the second/eighth century, of local legal circles headed by the Awzāʿite personal school. The latter's juristic loyalties, moreover, were not to the Iraqian jurists but rather to their opponents, the Medinese.[27]

The Ḥanafite presence in Egypt began when, for a brief period (164/780–167/783), Ismāʿīl b. Yasaʿ was appointed there as a judge by the caliph al-Mahdī. However, his Kūfan jurisprudence was rejected by the Egyptians, who finally managed to have him dismissed.[28] Two more

[27] Cf. Schacht, *Origins*, 288–89, who has a different view of Awzāʿī's legal doctrine.
[28] Kindī, *Akhbār*, 371–73.

Iraqians were appointed for relatively brief periods: Hāshim al-Bakrī spent eighteen months there between 194/809 and 196/811; Ibrāhīm b. al-Jarrāḥ, between 205/820 and 211/826.[29] But it was not until 246/860 that more permanent appointments of Ḥanafite judges were made. The first Ḥanafite judge to receive such an appointment was Bakkār b. Qutayba who served in this office between 246/860 and 270/883. Thereafter, and until the Ayyūbids rose to power in the sixth/twelfth century, the Ḥanafites continued to have little influence in that province, and much less so in North Africa.

Nowhere did the Ḥanafites enjoy as much success in diffusing their school as they did in the eastern provinces of Islam, although here again the extent of their success differed from one city to another. By the end of the third/ninth century, they were to be found active in most cities of Khurāsān, Fārs, Sijistān and Transoxania. In Iṣfahān, for instance, Ḥanafism was introduced, among others, by al-Ḥusayn b. Ḥafṣ (d. 212/827), al-Ḥusayn Abū Jaʿfar al-Maydānī (d. 212/827), and Zufar at the turn of the second/eighth century; and by the beginning of the next, the Ḥanafites had become established in that city. In Balkh, they seem to have been exceptionally influential, so much so that they virtually monopolized the office of judgeship from as early as 142/759 and for a long time thereafter.[30] By virtue of their popularity with the Sāmānids (who ruled Khurāsān and Transoxania around 280/893), the Ḥanafites gained significant strength in these regions. But their success was not matched in the Jibāl, a region lying between Iraq and Khurāsān, where they maintained a less active presence until the appearance of the Saljūqs in the fifth/eleventh century, when their school, in Iṣfahān as elsewhere in the Jibāl, was strengthened.[31]

Whereas Ḥanafism tended to spread in the eastern parts of the caliphate, the Mālikite school experienced growth in the west, first in Egypt and then in the Maghrib and Andalusia. With the death of Abū Muṣʿab al-Zuhrī in 242/857, the Mālikite school of Medina began to experience serious decline. No major scholars remained in it on either a permanent or long-term basis, while its juristic activity ceased to have a wide audience. A possible explanation for Medina's decline was the transfer of leading scholarship to Egypt which, by the turn of the second/eighth century,

[29] Ibid., 411–17, 427–33.
[30] Madelung, "Early Murjiʾa," 37–38.
[31] N. Tsafrir, "Beginnings of the Ḥanafī School in Iṣfahān," *Islamic Law and Society*, 5, 1 (1998): 1–21; Zayn al-Dīn Ibn Quṭlūbughā, *Tāj al-Tarājim* (Baghdad: Maktabat al-Muthannā, 1962), 61.

became the new center of Mālikism. This change in the Mālikite center is evidenced in the fact that nearly all students – from Baghdad to Andalusia – who were to rise to prominence in this school studied there with senior Mālikites.

Since the beginning, Baṣra had been under the influence of Medinese legal scholarship, and a number of its judges appear to have been either originally from Medina itself or students of Medinese jurists. But with the decline of Medina as the chief Mālikite center, the Baṣrans, like their Baghdadian and Andalusian schoolmates, looked to Egypt as the leading Mālikite center. During the first three or four decades of the third/ninth century, Baṣran Mālikism was headed by Ibn al-Muʿadhdhil (d. ca. 240/854), whose education was Egyptian, not Medinese. The spread of Mālikism to Baghdad originated with Ibn al-Muʿadhdhil's own students who became active in that city as jurists and judges. Most important of these were Yaʿqūb b. Shayba (d. 262/875), Ḥammād b. Isḥāq (d. 267/880), and his brother, the accomplished judge Ismāʿīl b. Isḥāq (d. 282/895). By the middle of the fourth/tenth century, however, the Mālikite school was waning in the ʿAbbāsid capital, and was on the verge of complete disappearance.

The two remaining major centers of Mālikism were Qayrawān and Muslim Iberia, especially Andalusia. Qayrawān's Mālikite school, like its Baghdadian counterpart, never gained significant strength throughout the entire early period, despite the presence among its members of such major figures as Saḥnūn. It is quite possible that Qayrawān's Mālikism failed to rise to a position of strength due to a lack of political support, by now a familiar feature that seems to explain the weakness of schools in many areas.

It is precisely the presence of such support that allowed Mālikism to dominate in Andalusia, and, as we have earlier mentioned, enabled it to oust the Awzāʿite school from that region permanently. However, Mālikism did not immediately receive the support of the ruling dynasty upon its introduction to that region. The initial spread of the school seems to have been associated with the name of Ziyād b. ʿAbd al-Raḥmān (d. ca. 200/815), and particularly that of Abū ʿAbd Allāh Ziyād b. Shabṭūn (d. 193/808 or 199/814), both of whom are reported to have been the first to introduce Mālik's *Muwaṭṭa*ʾ to that country. And it was ʿĪsā b. Dīnār (d. 212/827) who appears to have been the more active scholar in recruiting students and propagating Mālikite doctrine. But government support came only later, at the hands of Yaḥyā b. Yaḥyā al-Laythī (d. 234/849), who seems to have convinced Amīr ʿAbd al-Raḥmān II (r. 206/822–238/852) to adopt the school's doctrine as the official law of the Umayyad caliphate. From that point onward,

Mālikism became Andalusia's unrivaled legal school, and it continued to dominate until the Muslims were expelled from the Iberian peninsula in 898/1492.

The Shāfiʿite school lagged far behind in its ability to gain followers during the third/ninth century. Shāfiʿī appears to have cultivated a limited number of students in Egypt, where he died after having spent no more than six years there. Furthermore, there is no evidence that he had groomed any students prior to his arrival in that country. Thus, apart from the activity of a small circle of Egyptian scholars who must have transmitted (and worked out) his positive legal doctrine, there was little to speak of in terms of a Shāfiʿite school. It was not until three-quarters of a century after Shāfiʿī's death that the first Shāfiʿite judge emerged. The Jewish convert Muḥammad b. ʿUthmān Abū Zurʿa (d. 302/914) was appointed to the bench in 284/897; and it was at just about this time that Ibn Ṭūlūn also appointed him as chief justice in Syria, apparently combining the jurisdictions of both regions. But Shāfiʿism could neither oust Awzāʿism from Syria nor compete with the powerful Mālikites in Egypt. Most Syrians remained loyal (at least for another half a century) to the Awzāʿite school,[32] and the Mālikite competition in Egypt was accentuated by the infiltration of Ḥanafism, however weak the latter may have been. With the Fāṭimid takeover of Egypt in 297/909, the Shāfiʿite school declined. It was not until the coming of the Ayyūbids, in the sixth/twelfth century, that the school began to recover and indeed gain strength.[33]

But Shāfiʿism did not limit itself to Egypt, although its spread outside that country became evident only toward the end of the third/ninth century, around the time Abū Zurʿa received his two judicial appointments. One of the first names associated with the spread of Shāfiʿism in the east was Aḥmad b. Sayyār, an obscure figure, who "brought the books of Shāfiʿī to Marw," a city in Khurāsān.[34] It appears that a local Marwazī scholar, ʿAbdān b. Muḥammad (d. 293/905), read and became intensely interested in these books. When his request "to copy the books" was rejected by Ibn Sayyār, he apparently traveled to Egypt to acquire them

[32] Ismāʿīl b. ʿUmar Ibn Kathīr, *al-Bidāya wal-Nihāya*, 14 vols. (Beirut: Dār al-Kutub al-ʿIlmiyya, 1985–88), XI, 131; Subkī, *Ṭabaqāt*, II, 174, 214.

[33] On the spread of the Shāfiʿite school in general, see Heinz Halm, *Die Ausbreitung der šāfiʿitischen Rechtsschule von den Anfängen bis zum 8./14. Jahrhundert* (Wiesbaden: Dr. Ludwig Reichert Verlag, 1974).

[34] For the spread of Shāfiʿism as described in this and the next paragraph, see Subkī, *Ṭabaqāt*, II, 50, 52, 78–79, 321–22; Ibn Qāḍī Shuhba, *Ṭabaqāt*, I, 48, 71; Shams al-Dīn al-Dhahabī, *Tārīkh al-Islām*, ed. ʿUmar Tadmurī, 52 vols. (Beirut: Dār al-Kitāb al-ʿArabī, 1987–2000), XXII, 107.

by other means. There, he reportedly studied Shāfiʿī's doctrine with Muzanī (264/877) and al-Rabīʿ b. Sulaymān al-Murādī (d. 270/884), two of the most important students of the master. But instead of coming back to Marw with Shāfiʿī's books (ʿAbdān's original intention), he returned with Muzanī's *Mukhtaṣar*, a work that exhibits the latter's juristic independence despite the claim that it was an abridgment of Shāfiʿī's doctrine. Be that as it may, on his way to Marw from Egypt ʿAbdān is reported to have stayed in Syria and Iraq where he presumably was active in preaching what he had learned in Egypt. Given the chronological proximity of the deaths of Muzanī and Murādī, ʿAbdān and Ibn Sayyār must have been two of the first Shāfiʿite protagonists to operate outside Egypt. During the same period or slightly thereafter, other minor scholars who apparently studied with Muzanī and Murādī also became active in the Iranian world. Two such figures were Isḥāq b. Mūsā (d. ca. 290/902) and Yaʿqūb b. Isḥāq al-Nīsābūrī (d. 313/925 or 316/928), who "carried Shāfiʿī's *madhhab*" to Astrabādh and Isfarāʾīn, respectively.

However, the spread of Shāfiʿism to the east of Egypt was not achieved primarily by such scholars, but rather through the school's infiltration into Baghdad. The jurist responsible for the introduction of Shāfiʿī's and, especially, Muzanī's works to the capital city was the accomplished Abū al-Qāsim al-Anmāṭī (d. 288/900), a student of Muzanī himself as well as of Murādī. Anmāṭī was the teacher of such distinguished figures as Abū Saʿīd al-Iṣṭakhrī (d. 328/939), Abū ʿAlī b. Khayrān (d. 320/932), Manṣūr al-Tamīmī (d. before 320/932), and Ibn Surayj himself. But it was particularly the latter who established himself as the leader of Iraqian Shāfiʿism and who cultivated a large number of students. These in turn diffused Shāfiʿism (mostly as a compromise between Shāfiʿī and Muzanī's doctrines) into Iraq as well as to the east of it. Among these were Ibn Ḥaykawayh (d. 318/930), Abū Bakr al-Ṣayrafī (d. 330/942), Ibn al-Qāṣṣ al-Ṭabarī (d. 336/947), al-Qaffāl al-Shāshī (d. 336/947) and Ibrāhīm al-Marwazī (d. 340/951), to mention only a few.

These three schools were also present as pockets in various other parts of Islamdom. Shāfiʿism, for instance, made an ephemeral appearance in Andalusia; and so did the Ẓāhirite school, which soon became defunct. Ḥanafism was present in Qayrawān, but without any success. By the end of the third/ninth century, some Ḥanbalite circles (mostly theological in orientation) were active in the capital city, Baghdad, but the school as a legal entity was not to show any meaningful presence in that city or elsewhere until much later, perhaps as late as the second half of the fifth/eleventh century.

CHAPTER 8

Law and politics: caliphs, judges and jurists

Between the death of the Prophet and the first quarter of the second century of the Hijra (ca. 632–740 AD), Islam witnessed a major evolution in the relationship between the body politic and the law. Until the 80s/700s, the main representatives of the legal profession were the proto-*qāḍīs*, who, for all intents and purposes, were not only government employees and administrators of sorts but also laymen who – despite their experience in adjudication – had no particular legal training. As we saw in chapter 2, their appointments as *qāḍīs* were most often conjoined with the functions of tax-collectors, provincial secretaries of the treasury, police chiefs or story-tellers. In these capacities, they functioned as the provincial governor's assistants, if not – on rare occasions – as governors-cum-*qāḍīs*. In the near absence of a class of private, legal specialists at this time, these proto-*qāḍīs* constituted the bulk of what may be termed a legal profession, and as such they were an integral part of the ruling machine. During this phase, then, no noticeable distinction can be made between government[1] and law, since both functions resided in the same hands.

Yet, despite the formal inseparability of the proto-*qāḍī*'s office from that of government administration, the government did not always enjoy the prerogative of determining what law was applied. As shown in chapter 2, the proto-*qāḍīs* adjudicated cases on the basis of their *ra'y*, which was based in turn on either a *sunna māḍiya* (past exemplary actions, including those of the Prophet and the caliphs) or commonsense. They also increasingly resorted to the Quran. The caliphate was by no means a distinct or a comprehensive source of law. No edicts regulating law are known to have come down from caliphs, no constitutions, and certainly no legal codes of any kind. Even when no class of legal specialists had yet appeared, neither

[1] Here, I will avoid using the term "state" to refer to the caliphate as a ruling institution, since the term invokes modern connotations associated with the nation-state that is fundamentally different from its predecessors.

the caliphs nor their ministers or provincial governors made any effort to control or appropriate the province of the law. The legal role of the caliph was one of *occasional* legislative intervention, coming into play when called for or when special needs arose. The caliphal legislative role was thus minimal, even failing to match their role as sunnaic exemplars. In this latter role, some – but by no means all – caliphs were seen by the proto- and later *qāḍīs* as providing a good example to follow, but this was not borne out by royal edicts or high-handed policy. The occasional invocation – even application – of a caliph's *sunna* was an entirely private act, a free choice of a *qāḍī* or a scholar. On the other hand, caliphal orders enjoining a judge to issue a particular ruling were a rare occurrence. Thus the proto-*qāḍī* was principally a government administrator who seldom dabbled in law strictly so defined, but acted largely according to his own understanding of how disputes should be resolved – guided, as he was, by the force of social custom, Quranic values and the established ways of the forebears (*sunan māḍiya*).

The caliphs, on the other hand, saw themselves as equally subject to the force of these *sunan* and the then-dominant religious values. True, they were God's and the Messenger's deputies on earth, but they were distinguished from other world leaders by the fact that they acted within the consensual framework of a distinct and largely binding social and political fabric. Like their earlier predecessors – the Arab tribal leaders and even Muḥammad himself – they viewed themselves as a part not only of their communities but also, and primarily, of the social and political customs that had come down to them across the generations and from which they were unable to dissociate themselves, even if they wanted to. The proto-*qāḍīs*' relative judicial independence was therefore due to the fact that social, customary and evolving religious values governed all, and were no more known to, or incumbent upon, the caliph than his judges. If the judges queried the caliphs with regard to difficult cases, it was also true that the caliphs queried the judges. That knowledge of the law – or legal authority – was a two-way street in the early period is abundantly evident, and eloquent testimony to the fact that the caliph of Islam was never an exclusive source of law or even a distinct source at all. Rather, his legal role was minimal and partial, mostly enmeshed – and selectively at that – in the body of exemplary precedent that Muslims came to call *sunan* (but not Sunna, later to become the preserve of the Prophet alone).

The emergence, after the 80s/700s, of a class of private legal specialists signaled a new phase in Islamic history, one characterized by the spreading in Muslim societies of a new religious impulse, accompanied by an ascetic piety that became the hallmark of the learned religious elite in general and of the jurists (*fuqahā'*) and later mystics in particular. The importance of this piety in Muslim culture cannot be overemphasized, either at this early time or in the centuries to follow. If anything, its increasing force was to contribute significantly to later developments. Yet, even in this early period, ascetic piety took many forms, from dietary abstinence to abhorrence of indulgent lifestyles (with which the middle and later Umayyad caliphs were, with some exceptions, partly associated). Above all, this piety called for justice and equality before God – the very emblem of Islam itself.

By the end of the first century and the beginning of the second, it had become clear that a wedge existed between the ruling elite and the emerging religio-legal class. This wedge was to make itself evident with two concurrent developments, the first of which was the spread of the new religious ethic among the ranks of the legal specialists who increasingly insisted upon ideal human conduct driven by piety. In fact, it is nearly impossible to distinguish this ethic from the social category of legal scholars, since the latter's constitution was, as we have said, entirely defined by this ethic of piety, mild asceticism and knowledge of the law and religion. The second was the increasing power and institutionalization of the ruling elite, who began to depart from the egalitarian forms of tribal leadership the early caliphs had known, and according to which they had conducted themselves. Whereas the caliph ʿUmar I, for instance, led a life that many Arabs of his social class enjoyed, and mixed with his fellow believers as one of them, Umayyad caliphs lived in palaces, wielded coercive powers, and gradually but increasingly distanced themselves from the people they ruled. Add to this the intrigue of power relations and the realpolitik of running an empire.

The religious impulse that was permeated with ethical and idealistic values, and that was inspired and enriched by the proliferation of the religious narratives of the story-tellers, *akhbārī*s and traditionists, began to equate government and political power with vice, and as infested with corruption as the religious impulse of the pious was virtuous. This attitude originated sometime around the end of the first century, and was reflected in the multitude of accounts and biographical details speaking of appointment to the office of judgeship. As of this time, and continuing for nearly a millennium thereafter, the theme of judicial appointment as an adversity, even a calamity, for legists who receive it became a topos and a dominating detail of biographical narrative. Jurists are reported to have wept – sometimes together with family members – upon hearing the news of their appointment; others went into hiding, or preferred to be whipped or tortured rather than accept appointment. Just as Abū Qilāba al-Jarmī (d. 104/722 or 105/723) opted to flee Baṣra when he was appointed to judgeship, Abū Ḥanīfa was imprisoned and flogged for persisting in his refusal to serve in this capacity. Yet others resorted to ingenious arguments to escape the predicament. It is reported that in 106/724 the legist ʿAlī b. ʿAbd Allāh al-Muzanī claimed ignorance of the law when he was instructed by the governor to explain his refusal to accept the post he had been assigned. Realizing that his explanation did not do the trick, he continued to argue that if he turned out to be right, then it would be wrong to appoint an ignorant person to a judgeship; and if it turned out that he had lied as to his legal competence, then it would be no less wrong to appoint a liar to this noble office.[2]

Suspicion of political power and of those associated with it was so pervasive that the traditionists – and probably the story-tellers amongst them – managed to find a number of Prophetic traditions that condemned judges and rulers alike, placing both ranks in diametrical moral and eschatological opposition with the learned, pious jurists. On the Day of Judgment, one tradition pronounces, the judges will be lumped together with the sultans in Hellfire, while the pious jurists will join the prophets in Paradise. A less ominous tradition predicting the horrors of the Hereafter has two out of three judges slaughtered "without a knife," reserving a swifter, more merciful death for the chosen few.[3]

Yet, this profound suspicion of association with the political did not mean that the legists predominantly refused judgeships, or even that they did not desire them. In fact, by and large, they accepted appointment, and many junior legists must have viewed it as an accomplishment in their careers. On the other hand, the ruling elite could not dispense with the jurists, for it had become clear that legal authority, inasmuch as it was epistemically grounded, was largely divorced from political authority. Religion and, by definition, legal knowledge had now become the exclusive domain of the jurist, the private scholar. It is precisely because of this essentially epistemic quality that the ruling elite needed the legists to fulfill the empire's legal needs, despite its profound

[2] Shams al-Dīn al-Dhahabī, *Siyar Aʿlām al-Nubalāʾ*, ed. B. Maʿrūf and M. H. Sarḥān, 23 vols. (Beirut: Muʾassasat al-Risāla, 1986), IV, 534; Wakīʿ, *Akhbār*, I, 26, III, 25, 37, 130, 143, 146, 147, 153, 177, 184, and *passim*; Muḥammad Ibn Saʿd, *al-Ṭabaqāt al-Kubrā*, 8 vols. (Beirut: Dār Bayrūt lil-Ṭibāʿa wal-Nashr, 1985), VII, 183; Zaman, *Religion and Politics*, 78 ff.; also Ibn Khallikān, *Wafayāt*, II, 18, III, 201, 202.

[3] Al-Shaykh al-Niẓām, et al., *al-Fatāwā al-Hindiyya*, 6 vols. (repr.; Beirut: Dār Iḥyāʾ al-Turāth al-ʿArabī, 1400/1980), III, 310; Ibn Khallikān, *Wafayāt*, II, 18.

apprehensions that the legists' loyalties were not to the government but to their law and its requirements, which frequently conflicted with the views of the ruling class. But the fact remained that each side needed the other, and thus both learned how to cooperate – and cooperate they did.

The legists depended on royal and government patronage, the single most important contributor to their financial well-being. They were often paid handsome salaries when appointed to a judgeship, but they also received generous grants as private scholars. By the end of the Umayyad period, an average *qāḍī*'s salary was at least 150 *dirhams* a month, when the monthly income of a well-to-do tailor, for instance, did not reach 100 *dirhams*.[4] Shortly thereafter, and with the ascendancy of the ʿAbbāsids, remunerations for judicial appointments were steadily on the increase. During the late 130s/750s, an Egyptian judge could earn 30 *dīnārs* a month, equivalent to about 300 *dirhams*.[5] When Yaḥyā b. Saʿīd was appointed by the caliph al-Manṣūr (r. 136/754–158/775) as judge of Baghdad, the sources emphasize that his social and economic standing improved drastically.[6] By the end of the second/eighth century, a judge's salary was highly coveted. In 198/813, for instance, the judge of Egypt al-Faḍl b. Ghānim received 168 *dīnārs* a month, and a few years later, Ibn al-Munkadir was paid 4,000 *dirhams*, accompanied by a "starter" gift of 1,000 *dīnārs*.[7] The *qāḍīs*, however, were not alone in benefiting from government subsidy. The leading private scholars were no less dependent on the government's financial favors, and this, as we shall see, was for a good reason. The account relating how the ʿAbbāsid vizier Yaḥyā al-Barmakī bestowed on the distinguished jurist Sufyān al-Thawrī (d. 161/777) 1,000 *dirhams* every month is not untypical;[8] in fact, it accurately represents the benefits that accrued to the leading jurists from government circles.

On the other hand, the government was in dire need of legitimization, which it found in the circles of the legal profession. The legists served the rulers as an effective tool for reaching the masses, from whose ranks they emerged and whom they represented. It was one of the salient features of the pre-modern Islamic body politic (and probably those of Europe and Far Eastern dynasties) that it lacked control over the infrastructures of the

[4] For instance, cf. Kindī, *Akhbār*, 421 with Wakīʿ, *Akhbār*, III, 233.
[5] Wakīʿ, *Akhbār*, III, 235.
[6] Ibid., III, 242.
[7] Kindī, *Akhbār*, 421, 435.
[8] Ibn Khallikān, *Wafayāt*, III, 315.

civil populations it ruled. Jurists and judges emerged as the civic leaders who, though themselves products of the masses, found themselves, by the nature of their profession, involved in the day-to-day running of their affairs. As we saw in chapter 4, the judges were not only justices of the court, but the guardians and protectors of the disadvantaged, the supervisors of charitable trusts, the tax-collectors and the foremen of public works. They resolved disputes, both in the court and outside it, and established themselves as the intercessors between the populace and the rulers. Even outside the courtroom, jurists and judges felt responsibility toward the common man, and on their own often initiated action without any petition being made. For example, upon hearing that a man had been unjustly imprisoned, the famous Abū Ḥanīfa rushed to the authorities, pleading with them for his release, which they granted.[9] Similarly, when the Egyptians heard of the caliphal appointment of the reviled Abū Isḥāq b. al-Rashīd as their governor, their leaders turned to the judge Ibn al-Munkadir and asked him to intercede on their behalf by conveying, in writing, to the caliph their objections to the appointment. It is perhaps illustrative that Ibn al-Munkadir was to pay a heavy price shortly thereafter, for when the caliph, despite the petition, went ahead with the appointment, Ibn al-Rashīd, now governor, exacted revenge by dismissing him from his judgeship.[10]

Hence the religious scholars in general and the legists in particular were often called upon to express the will and aspirations of those belonging to the non-elite classes. They not only interceded on their behalf at the higher reaches of power, but also represented for the masses the ideal of piety, rectitude and fine education. Their very profession as Guardians of Religion, experts in religious law and exemplars of virtuous Muslim lifestyle made them not only the most genuine representatives of the masses but also the true "heirs of the Prophet," as a Prophetic *ḥadīth* came to attest.[11] When the caliph Hārūn al-Rashīd (r. 170/786–193/809) visited al-Raqqa, his trip coincided with the entry into the town of ʿAbd Allāh Ibn al-Mubārak, then one of the most distinguished and illustrious legal scholars of Islam.[12] It is reported that the latter attracted larger crowds than did the caliph, a sight which precipitated the comment – made by the

9 Ibid., III, 203–04.
10 Kindī, *Akhbār*, 440.
11 Abū ʿUmar Yūsuf Ibn ʿAbd al-Barr, *Jāmiʿ Bayān al-ʿIlm wa-Faḍlihi*, 2 vols. (Beirut: Dār al-Kutub al-ʿIlmiyya, n.d.), I, 34.
12 Shīrāzī, *Ṭabaqāt*, 94.

caliph's slave-wife who was present[13] – that "true kingship lies in the scholar's hands and hardly with Hārūn who gathers crowds around him by the force of police and palace guards."[14]

This anecdote, whether or not it is authentic, is both illustrative and representative of the locus of legitimacy and religious and moral authority in that era. A pious and erudite man could attract adulation by virtue of his piety and erudition, whereas a caliph could do so only by coercion. Thoroughly familiar with the ways of earlier caliphs, the likes of Abū Bakr, ʿUmar I and ʿUmar II, the later Umayyad and early ʿAbbāsid caliphs realized that brute power could not yield legitimacy, which they were striving to attain. Legitimacy lay in the preserve of religion, erudition, ascetic piety, moral rectitude and, in short, in the *persons* of those men who had profound knowledge of, and fashioned their lives after, the example of the Prophet and the exemplary forefathers.

It did not take long before the caliphs realized that inasmuch as the pious scholars needed their financial resources, they needed the scholars' cooperation, for the latter were the ruler's only means of securing legitimacy in the eyes of the populace. The growth of religious sentiment among the latter, and the enthusiastic support of the religious scholars, left the caliphs no option but to go the same way: namely, to endorse a religious law whose authority depended on the human ability to exercise hermeneutic. Those who perfected this exercise were the jurists, and it was they and their epistemological domain that set restrictions on the absolute powers of the rulers, be they caliphs, provincial governors or their agents. When the Persian secretary Ibn al-Muqaffaʿ (d. ca. 139/756) suggested to the ʿAbbāsid caliph that he, the caliph, should be the supreme legal authority, promulgating laws that would bind his judges, his suggestion was met with complete disregard.[15] For while his proposal insinuated that legal authority could have been appropriated by the caliph, the fact that nothing whatsoever came of it is a strong indication that the jurists' control over the law was, as before, irreversible. The legal specialists and the popular religious movement that had emerged by the 130s/750s were too well entrenched for any political power to expunge or even replace, for it is precisely this

[13] In fact, she was his *umm walad*, meaning a female slave who had borne the caliph's child. Legally and socially, *umm walad*s enjoyed special status, above and beyond that of other slaves. In caliphal courts, they at times were as powerful as the caliphs' immediate family members and advisors.

[14] Ibn Khallikān, *Wafayāt*, II, 16.

[15] A fine analysis of this proposal may be found in Zaman, *Religion and Politics*, 82–85. See also S. D. Goitein, "A Turning Point in the History of the Islamic State," *Islamic Culture*, 23 (1949): 120–35.

movement and its representatives that gave rise to the wedge between political power and religious authority.

Later epistles and treatises written by way of advice to the caliphs confirm the ascendancy of religious law as represented by the jurists and by their social and hermeneutical authority. No longer could anyone propose a caliphal appropriation of legal power. In the letter of ʿAnbarī (d. 168/785) to the caliph al-Mahdī and in Abū Yūsuf's (182/798) treatise to Hārūn al-Rashīd, the subservience of the caliph to the religious law and to the Sunna is a foregone conclusion.[16] The caliph and the entire political hierarchy that he commanded were subject to the law of God, like anyone else. No exceptions could be made.

Yet, ʿAnbarī and Abū Yūsuf did not conceive of themselves as adversaries of the caliphs. Their writings clearly exhibit the cooperation that the jurists were willing to extend to the rulers, for both were financially dependent on the caliphs, although both also hailed from a background entirely defined by religious law and religious morality. This cooperation, coupled with the realization that rulers too, not too long ago, were counted among the ranks of jurists, justified ʿAnbarī and Abū Yūsuf in their decision to treat the caliphs as peers of legists and judges. Their writings call on the caliphs to act as guides to their judges when faced with hard cases, a measure not only of the role that the legal scholars wanted to assign to caliphs as religious leaders but also of the latter's need to portray themselves as legitimate rulers standing in protection of the supreme law of God. It is clear then that in the legal sphere the caliph never acted with, or thought himself to embody, an authority superior to that of the jurists, be they judges appointed by him or private legal scholars. As M. Q. Zaman aptly put it:

> The caliph's participation in resolving legal questions gives him a religious authority akin to that of the [legal] scholars, not one over and above or against theirs; and it is in conjunction with the ʿulamāʾ that the caliph acts, even when he acts only as an *ʿālim.* What emerges . . . is not a struggle over religious authority, with the caliphs and scholars as antagonists, but rather the effort, on the part of the ʿAbbasid caliphs, to lay claim to the sort of competence the ʿulamāʾ were known to possess. This effort was not meant as a challenge to the ʿulamāʾ. It signified rather a recognition of their religious authority and an expression of the caliphal intent to act as patrons themselves. What is more, it signified the assertion of a public commitment to those fundamental sources of authority on which the ʿulamāʾ's expertise, and a slowly evolving Sunnism, were based.[17]

[16] Zaman, *Religion and Politics*, 85–100.
[17] Ibid., 105.

However, like all senior jurists as well as the caliphs themselves, ʿAnbarī and Abū Yūsuf knew very well that the caliphs of their time were not equipped with the legal erudition necessary to discourse on complex matters of law. Hence the added advice – already duly observed in practice – that caliphs should surround themselves with competent jurists who would assist them in addressing such difficult legal matters. This suggestion was the solution to caliphal legitimacy, and the caliphs generally heeded this advice. Thus, while the earliest caliphs could acquire legitimacy by virtue of their own knowledge of the law, it later became necessary to supplement the caliphal office with jurists who made up for the sovereign's comparative ignorance – another way of saying that the jurists constituted the legitimacy that the caliphs desperately needed.

Our sources are replete with references to the effect that caliphs "sat" in the company of distinguished jurists. There they not only discussed with them matters of religion, law and literature, but also listened to their arguments and scholarly disputations.[18] Almost every caliph of the second, third and fourth centuries was known to have befriended the *fuqahāʾ*, from Abū Jaʿfar al-Manṣūr and Hārūn al-Rashīd down to al-Maʾmūn, al-Muʿtazz (r. 252/866–255/868), and the Fāṭimid al-Muʿizz (341/953–365/975).[19] Provincial governors took care to do the same. The biographer and historian Kindī, who wrote sometime between 320/932 and 350/960, speaks of the Egyptian governors' regular practice of holding assemblies (*majālis*) of the jurists, a practice that seems to have continued uninterrupted between the middle of the second/eighth century down to Kindī's time.[20]

The privileges and favors the jurists acquired not only brought them easy access to the royal court and to the circles of the political elite,[21] but also rendered them highly influential in government policy as it affected legal matters, and perhaps in other matters of state. From the middle of the second/eighth century, almost all major judicial appointments were made at the recommendation of the chief justice at the royal court or the assembly of jurists gathered by the caliph, or both. And when the provincial governor wished to find a qualified judge, he too sought the advice of

[18] Later to become a specialized field on its own, generating much writing and theory. See Wael Hallaq, "A Tenth–Eleventh Century Treatise on Juridical Dialectic," *The Muslim World*, 77, 2–3 (1987): 189–227.

[19] Wakīʿ, *Akhbār*, III, 158, 174, 247, 265 and *passim*; Ibn Khallikān, *Wafayāt*, II, 321, 322; III, 204, 206, 247, 258, 389.

[20] Kindī, *Akhbār*, 388.

[21] In addition to the sources cited in nn. 19–20, above, see al-Khaṭīb al-Baghdādī, *Tārīkh Baghdād*, 14 vols. (Cairo: Maṭbaʿat al-Saʿāda, 1931), IX, 66.

jurists. Even Ibn Idrīs al-Shāfiʿī, whose ties to the ruling circles were tenuous, was consulted by Egypt's governor. One of his recommendations to the latter is said to have led to the appointment of Isḥāq b. al-Furāt as judge of Fusṭāṭ.[22]

At times, however, the jurists' influence in legal and political matters was immeasurable, as attested by the career of Yaḥyā b. Aktham b. Ṣayfī (d. 242/856). One biographical account portrays him as a highly learned and reputable scholar and jurist who "made himself equally accessible" to both the common folk and high society. He particularly excelled in knowledge of the law, and was so revered by the caliph al-Maʾmūn that he "dominated the caliph." No one could come closer to al-Maʾmūn than he did, so much so that not only was he appointed chief justice of the empire but also no vizier could act without consulting him first, even – we understand – in political matters. Only one other person, the account continues, was known to influence al-Maʾmūn as deeply, namely, Ibn Abī Dāwūd who, not surprisingly, was another jurist and judge who became well known for presiding over the infamous Miḥna.[23]

Although keeping company with jurists and assigning them positions of power were salient features of the caliphal bid to acquire legitimacy, the involvement of the caliphs in legal and religious life took many other, different forms. When the caliph went on pilgrimage, he did so together with the distinguished legal scholars who staffed his court, and when a leading jurist died, the funeral prayer (*ṣalāt al-janāza*) was performed by the caliph himself. Likewise, it was normally the distinguished jurists who performed this prayer when a caliph died. Moreover, the caliphs continued to display an interest in religious learning in an attempt to maintain the image of erudition for which some early caliphs were known. Thus, they dabbled in legal matters and studied and memorized *ḥadīth* that were usually effective as tools of legitimization when cited in courtly audiences.[24]

That the caliphs strove to acquire legitimacy through religious and juristic channels is therefore abundantly obvious. But this cannot mask the fact that there always remained a point of friction between worldly, secular power and religious law. This relationship between the two was constantly negotiated, and it was never devoid of sporadic challenges mounted by political forces against the law and its representatives. For

22 Kindī, *Akhbār*, 393.
23 Ibn Khallikān, *Wafayāt*, III, 277 ff.
24 Baghdādī, *Tārīkh*, IX, 33, 35–36; Zaman, *Religion and Politics*, 120–27.

instance, in 135/752, a soldier defamed the character of a man who brought his case before the judge of Fusṭāṭ, Khayr b. Nuʿaym. Upon the testimony of a single witness, the judge imprisoned the soldier until the plaintiff produced other witnesses. But the Egyptian governor, ʿAbd Allāh b. Yazīd, released the soldier before the case was resolved, thus interfering in the judicial process. On hearing the news of the soldier's release, Khayr resigned his post in protest and persisted in his refusal to resume his function despite the pleas of the governor. Khayr made the re-arrest of the soldier a condition for his return to the post. The governor refused the condition and soon appointed another judge in lieu of Khayr, apparently absolving the soldier of all liability once and for all.[25] Similarly, in 89/707, the court scribe of Egypt's governor was convicted by the *qāḍī* ʿImrān b. ʿAbd Allāh al-Ḥasanī on a charge of drinking wine. The governor accepted the verdict in principle, but refused to allow the court to mete out punishment. Like Khayr, al-Ḥasanī resigned in protest,[26] and the scribe apparently was left unpunished. A more striking case is one that reportedly occurred sometime during the tenure of the judge Abū Khuzayma al-Ruʿaynī (144/761–154/770), who was asked by the Egyptian governor to divorce a woman on the grounds that her husband was incompatible (*ghayr kafuʾ*)[27] with her status, a request that al-Ruʿaynī rejected. The governor nonetheless went ahead and dissolved the marriage himself without the judge's consent.[28]

Although most such violations seem to have occurred at the provincial and periphery courts, the caliphs themselves also appear, on rare occasions, to have interfered in the judiciary and the judicial process. Fusṭāṭ's judge, ʿAbd al-Raḥmān al-ʿUmarī, was known for his corruption and unjust conduct, which caused a number of the city's learned scholars to travel to Baghdad in order to complain about him to the caliph Hārūn al-Rashīd. Despite the serious accusations, which seem to have been well founded,[29] Hārūn refused to dismiss him, on the ground (or pretext) that ʿUmarī was a descendant of caliph ʿUmar I.[30] Similarly, the animosity that a group of people harbored toward the Baghdadian judge Muḥammad b. ʿAbd Allāh al-Makhzūmī drove them to take action against him. They argued before

[25] Kindī, *Akhbār*, 356; Wakīʿ, *Akhbār*, III, 232.
[26] Kindī, *Akhbār*, 328.
[27] A legal requirement, compatibility (*kafāʾa*) means that there cannot be a significant gap between husband and wife in respect of lineage, religion, freedom or economic status. Thus, a marriage of a tailor to a merchant's daughter may be invalidated on grounds of economic disparity. See Ibn Naqīb al-Miṣrī, *ʿUmdat al-Sālik*, 523–24.
[28] Kindī, *Akhbār*, 367.
[29] For ʿUmarī's eventful career as a corrupt judge, see ibid., 394–411.
[30] Ibid., 410–11.

the caliph al-Maʾmūn that Makhzūmī had fought on the side of his brother al-Amīn when the latter was a contender for the throne against al-Maʾmūn. Although the caliph does not seem to have been convinced of the accusation, and despite his initial, adamant reluctance to remove the judge, he finally bowed to their wishes. In what seems to have been a diplomatic move, the caliph sent an emissary to persuade Makhzūmī to submit his resignation. Makhzūmī obliged the caliph and received a generous monetary reward as recompense.[31]

If these anecdotes illustrate caliphal abuses of the law, they are still exceptions to an overwhelming pattern, displayed in the sources, of caliphal reluctance to overstep their limits in judicial intervention. Thus, when the caliph Abū Jaʿfar al-Manṣūr (r. 136/754–158/775) wrote to his Baṣran judge, Sawwār, with regard to a case, the latter treated the caliph's request (the details of which we do not know) as legally unwarranted and thus dismissed it. Offended by this verdict, Manṣūr resorted to threats, but never acted upon them, for an advisor or a confidant of his is reported to have told him: "O Commander of the Faithful, Sawwār's justice is, after all, an extension of yours."[32] The implication of this statement is that a judge's just and fair decisions are ultimately attributed to the caliph who is deemed the highest authority commanding good and forbidding evil.

That the caliphal office was thought to uphold the highest standards of justice according to the holy law was undeniable, and the caliphs themselves felt such responsibility, generally conducting themselves in accordance with these expectations. Sawwār's career provides an illustration of this principle as well. When Baṣra's chief of police ʿUqba b. Sālim appropriated a pearl belonging to a man, the latter's wife brought a complaint to Sawwār's court. The judge sent a messenger to ʿUqba to enquire into the facts, but the latter, instead of cooperating, insulted the messenger "most severely." After another court assistant met with the same reception, Sawwār sent ʿUqba a letter carrying a stern warning, threatening him with severe punishment if he did not restore the pearl to its lawful owner. The letter apparently was read to ʿUqba in the presence of counselors who advised him to comply immediately with the *qāḍī*'s request. The reason given was that Sawwār was not only a powerful man but also, and perhaps more importantly, because he was "the *qāḍī* of the Commander of the Faithful."[33] In as much as the law in and of itself possessed authority – which

[31] Wakīʿ, *Akhbār*, III, 271–72.
[32] Ibid., II, 60.
[33] Ibid., II, 59.

would only increase after Sawwār's time – the caliph and his office were seen not only as another locus of the holy law, but also as its upholder and enforcer.

The overwhelming body of evidence at our disposal compels us to conclude that, as a rule, the caliphs and their provincial representatives upheld court decisions and normally did not intervene in the judicial process. (This is borne out by the fact that the sources record the unusual, those events worthy of note, because they stood out from the rest. Biographers and historians were not interested in recording the day-to-day routine of the judiciary, and if we know something about this routine, it is because it often creeps into those relatively few accounts of an unusual nature. Thus, whatever caliphal or governmental encroachment on the judiciary happened to be recorded in the historical annals of Islam, they were likely to have been exceptional cases and, therefore, statistically out of proportion to the – probably hundreds of thousands of – cases that went unnoticed due to the fact that they were "usual cases" in which law and the judicial process took their normal course.)

However, when caliphs or their subordinates became involved in the judicial process – however rarely – it was often the case that they did so within the standard, acceptable legal channels. One example must suffice here. In what seems to have been a problematic case of *waqf* in Fusṭāṭ, a number of consecutive judges reversed the rules of their predecessor regarding the entitlement to benefits on the part of the children of the *waqf*-founder's daughters. Early in the third/ninth century, Hārūn b. ʿAbd Allāh had ruled against their inclusion as beneficiaries, but his successor, Muḥammad b. Abī al-Layth reversed his ruling. When al-Ḥārith b. Miskīn was appointed as judge in 237/851, he in turn reversed the latter's decision, depriving the daughters' children of any benefits. One of the claimants to these benefits, Isḥāq Ibn al-Sāʾiḥ, traveled to Baghdad and presented his case against Ḥārith's ruling to the caliph al-Mutawakkil. Following his habitual practice, the caliph referred the case to his assembly of jurists. Kūfans to a man, and therefore basing themselves on Ḥanafite principles, the jurists ruled that Ḥārith's decision was invalid. Ḥārith, however, had ruled on the case according to Medinan Mālikite principles. On hearing of the reversal of his ruling, Ḥārith – in typical fashion – resigned his post, for he seems to have regarded the reversal as an unjustified judicial intervention (and rightly so, since a *qāḍī*'s decision is irrevocable during his tenure). His successor, Bakkār b. Qutayba, was a Ḥanafite and as such ruled – reportedly with great reluctance – in favor of the daughters' male line.[34] It is not clear whether or not the caliph had any personal stake in the dispute, but it remains true that his judicial intervention was effected by "legal" means, since, theoretically, the caliph is empowered to determine jurisdiction and can thus specify under which doctrine a judge should decide cases.

Our sources reveal that the caliphs and their subordinates generally did comply with the law, if for no other reason than in order to maintain their political legitimacy. Yet, it appears reasonable to assume that their compliance stemmed from their acceptance of religious law as the supreme regulatory force in both society and empire, coupled with the conviction that they were in no way rivals of the religious legal profession. Instances of judges deciding in favor of persons who litigated against caliphs and governors are well attested in the literature, with the latter accepting and submitting to such verdicts.[35] Illustrative is the case of a debtor who died leaving behind small children during the judgeship of the aforementioned Bakkār b. Qutayba. The creditor was none other than the governor of Egypt, Ibn Ṭūlūn, who deployed his tax-collector to petition the judge for the sale of the debtor's house in order to repay the debt. Bakkār demanded proof of the existence of the debt, a demand that the governor met. When asked again to permit the sale of the house, the judge imposed a second requirement, namely, that Ibn Ṭūlūn had to take the oath that he was entitled to the value of the debt. This Ibn Ṭūlūn did too. Only then did Bakkār decree that the house could be sold.[36] Likewise, when the caliph Hārūn wished to buy a slave-girl from a man who refused to sell her due to a legal predicament in which he found himself, the jurist and judge Abū Yūsuf was asked to intervene. He is reported to have found a way out, and to have convinced the man to sell the slave to the caliph.[37] These accounts suggest that even the highest political and military offices in the land found it necessary to resort to the law and to submit to its (sometimes lengthy) procedures, even when they easily could have accomplished their ends through sheer coercion. That there are nearly as many accounts attesting to this compliance as there are those portraying encroachment by the political authorities is, once again, deceptive, since lack of compliance

[34] Kindī, *Akhbār*, 474–75.
[35] See, e.g., Ibn Khallikān, *Wafayāt*, III, 392; Ibn ʿAbd Rabbih, *al-ʿIqd al-Farīd*, ed. Muḥammad al-ʿAryān, 8 vols. (Cairo: Maṭbaʿat al-Istiqāma, 1953), I, 38–48.
[36] ʿAsqalānī, *Rafʿ al-Iṣr*, printed with Kindī, *Akhbār*, 508.
[37] Ibn Khallikān, *Wafayāt*, III, 392.

was, as we have stated, more worthy of being recorded by historians and biographers than was compliance itself.

The relative infrequency of the rulers' encroachment on the legal sphere appears to follow a particular pattern, namely, that such infringements were usually associated with cases in which the rulers' own interests were involved. Although this in no way means that encroachment occurred whenever such interests were present, it does suggest that whenever rulers staked their interest in the judicial process, they had to weigh their overall gains and losses. To have accomplished their ends through coercion would have meant that their legitimacy had failed the test. On the other hand, total compliance with the law at times meant that their quest for material gain or will to power would be frustrated. It was this equation that they attempted to work out and balance carefully, at times succeeding but at others not. The post-formative centuries of Islamic history suggest that rulers generally preferred to maintain an equation in favor of compliance with the religious law, since compliance was the means by which the ruling elite could garner the sympathies, or at least tacit approval, of the populace.

This tendency toward compliance holds true despite the events of the Miḥna, which in fact increased the level of compliance after its disastrous failure. The Inquisition began in 218/833, toward the end of the caliph al-Maʾmūn's reign, and came to an end in 234/848, some fifteen years later. Its main hallmark was the caliphal will to impose on all religious scholars and employees of the government the Muʿtazilite creed that the Quran was the created word of God, and that it was not coeternal. Many jurists, judges and jurisconsults, among others, were imprisoned, even tortured, for their refusal to subscribe to this creed. Moreover, no one who refused the doctrine of createdness could be deemed a qualified court witness. Yet, it was a judge, Ibn Abī Dāwūd, who carried out the caliphal wish. That there were legists who supported the doctrine and many others who did not suggests that the caliphs of the Miḥna did not intend to challenge the *legal* authority of the religious scholars. In any event, the relatively quick demise of the Miḥna demonstrated not only its extraordinary and exceptional nature, but also the inability of the powers-that-be to manipulate the religious establishment and its traditionalist character. Traditionalism was restored, but now with a greater force. We saw earlier that traditionalism was on the rise, but the Miḥna hastened its upsurge and made it all the more compelling. If the caliphs were not the legists' challengers before the Miḥna, they were even less so after it. Legal authority and power were and remained the lot of the private legal specialists, and the caliphs and their subordinates remained careful in balancing their will-to-power with the need for legitimacy – and this they could obtain mainly, if not only, through compliance with the religious law and requirements of the jurists. Whereas the jurists, on the whole, never compromised their law (although they had to skate on thin ice when dealing with political power), the caliphs had to account for the law and its demands, observing it more often than not. On balance, if there was any pre-modern legal and political culture that maintained the principle of the rule of law so well, it was the culture of Islam.[38]

[38] For more on this theme and its implications for both the modern and pre-modern periods, see Wael Hallaq, "'Muslim Rage' and Islamic Law," *Hastings Law Journal*, 54 (August 2003): 1–17.

Conclusion

With the massive migrations during the centuries preceding the rise of Islam, many large tribal federations from south Arabia had finally come to settle in southern Iraq and Syria, where they established themselves as powerful vassal kingdoms of the Sasanid and Byzantine empires. Despite their intermittent function as protectors of the imperial powers against tribal penetration from the south, these flourishing kingdoms constituted significant links between the Peninsular Arabs and the Fertile Crescent. Migration of the southern Arabs to the north – and much less frequently from the north back to the south, south-west and south-east – continued incessantly, and with it the shifting of demographic boundaries worked in favor of an increasing proportion of Arabs settling in the Fertile Crescent. This constant demographic movement and penetration was supported by trade and commerce that served the interests of both the tribal and sedentary Arabs of the south and of those societies in the Fertile Crescent, if not of the imperial powers that indirectly ruled the entire northern regions. Vibrant religious movements and missionaries further encouraged the otherwise intensive contacts between the Peninsula and the north. Yet, it was mainly trade – whether on a massive or more modest scale – that exposed the Hejaz, the birthplace of Islam, to the cultures of the north, thus making the Peninsula a more or less integral part of the all-pervasive Near Eastern culture. The ancient legal and cultural institutions of Mesopotamia and Syria (which at the time included the southern borders of today's Jordan), were mostly Semitic, though possessing a Greek and Roman veneer, and were known to the Arabs of the Peninsula, especially to those populations of the commercial and agricultural centers of the Hejaz.[1]

[1] On the continuity of penal law from antiquity to Islam, see Walter Young's remarkable thesis "*Zinā, Qadhf* and *Sariqa*: Exploring the Origins of Islamic Penal Law and its Evolution in Relation to Qur'ānic Rulings" (MA thesis, McGill University, in progress).

Tribal societies were not uniform throughout Arabia. While the eastern and central parts of the Peninsula were largely nomadic and did preserve the ancient tribal ties and customary laws, regions of western and south-western Arabia were often only nominally tribal. It was often the case that nomadic tribes would finally settle on the fringes of sedentary communities, and would maintain their tribal affiliation and even genealogies. But in all other respects, they would be full participants in the sedentary lives of these communities. To argue that Arabia was predominantly nomadic because our sources continued to transmit tribal genealogies is therefore to ignore the more recent evidence concerning a significant movement toward tribal settlement. Yet, this is not to say that, once settled, the tribes of Arabia (even those of the western and south-western regions) abandoned their laws and customs. The tribal structure no doubt continued to operate, as evidenced by the fact that it represented one of the major challenges that the new religion of Islam attempted to combat.

Muḥammad's initial mission was to propound a form of monotheism that seems to have been largely in line with a version of Ḥanīfism, a Meccan sect that had adopted Abraham as its strictly monotheistic Prophet. Muḥammad's call to the new religion was at the outset largely preoccupied with eschatological themes – law as a regulative system being largely absent at this early stage. In fact, it was not until a few years after his arrival in Medina, and only when he had secured for himself an unshakable position in that city, that he began to entertain the possibility of defining his religion in terms of law. It was his encounter with the relatively powerful Jewish tribes, and in particular their reluctance to acknowledge his mission as equally legitimate to their own religion, that prompted him to escalate the challenge: If Judaism and, for that matter, Christianity could and did possess laws, then so could Islam. The logic was simple: God created religious communities, each with its own law, and since Islam was undoubtedly one such community, then it had to have its own law. This transformation marks the beginning of an Islamic legal conception, but obviously not yet of law as a legal system. In fact, Muḥammad could not have thought of law in such developed terms, since in the world in which he lived there was no religious law that was at once the law of the body politic. This was to be one of Islam's greatest innovations.

Preserved within the most sacred entity in Islam – namely, the Quran – this legal conception was not to be forgotten. On the contrary, it was intensely promoted by the succeeding caliphs, who declared themselves both Muḥammad's and God's deputies on earth, seeing their authority as an extension of both Prophetic and Quranic authority. Yet, despite the importance of the Quran and the person of the Prophet, the Arab tribal values of consensus and collective model conduct could not be forgotten or even minimized. Good conduct worthy of being emulated was not only dictated by the Quran, but also, and to an even greater extent, by notions embedded in the *sunan*, the good example of the predecessors, both as collectivities and individuals. The time-honored communal and tribal practices of the Arabs constituted a source of these *sunan*, but so did the examples of Abraham, Ishmael and Muḥammad himself, among many others. As leaders of the Muslim community (Umma), Abū Bakr and ʿUmar I, the first two caliphs, possessed their own *sunan*, also to be emulated and followed as a matter of course. But with these two caliphs, as well as with their colleagues who came to be known as the Companions of the Prophet, the authority they acquired as *sunan*-bearers was not exclusively "secular," as had been the case before and during Muḥammad's early career. Now, the authority they enjoyed was both tribal and religious, in the sense that the model conduct they provided was due not only to the fact of their charismatic and influential leadership, but also because their conduct was viewed as having been in line with the principles of the new religion – principles that they absorbed by virtue of their intimate knowledge of what the Prophet and his religion were all about.

The propagation of Quran teaching throughout the Muslim garrison towns not only encouraged the spread of the ethical values of the new religion but also imbued the *sunan* with a religious element. To this process of Islamicization, the story-tellers, teachers and preachers contributed much through their heavily layered religious narratives, especially their stories that recounted the Prophet's biography (*sīra*). The story-tellers, from amongst whom part of the traditionist movement was later to emerge, promoted a Prophetic biography that, within a few decades after the Prophet's death, led to raising his *sunna*ic model to the forefront of the *sunan*, thereby elevating his status above and beyond that of any other. But such elevation in Prophetic status did not mean the obliteration of other *sunan*, for the simple reason that Prophetic Sunna was not seen at the time as necessarily distinct or independent from the other recognized *sunan* of the Companions. The *sunan* of the garrison towns – which provided the basis of conduct and, therefore, of law – were thus primarily modeled after, or derived from, the recognized conduct of the leading elite, the Companions of the Prophet who mostly (if not exclusively) were Hejazians and who were entrusted by the Medinan leadership with building the new Muslim societies in the recently conquered lands. The Companions' conduct was seen to reflect the best understanding of what the Prophet and his religion were supposed to achieve, and thus their *sunan* were, at least conceptually, the embodiment of the Prophetic model. This explains not only why Companion authority persisted for so long as constitutive of the *sunan*, but also why, when the Prophet's authority was finally fully deified, Companion narrative was readily transformed into Prophetic Sunna (in what has been called by modern scholarship back-projection of Prophetic *ḥadīth*). Broadly speaking, this transformation was far less substantive than one having to do with the substitution in the locus of authority – namely, from Companions, caliphs and others to a Prophetic axis. This little-understood *organic* connection between Companion and Prophetic narratives is essential for understanding the dynamics of religio-legal transformation from the former to the latter, a transformation that began during the second half of the first/seventh century, and culminated in the middle of the third/ninth century.

Yet, long before Prophetic authority began to be distinguished from that of the *sunan*, the Quranic legal spirit, if not the letter, had asserted itself from the beginning. True, the proto-*qāḍī*s appointed by military commanders held a variety of non-legal, administrative functions, but within the narrow confines of their judicial duties as judges and arbiters they seem to have applied two sets of law – one tribal, the other Quranic. This is not to say, however, that the two were always distinct, for the Quran, innovative as it was, equally provided tacit sanction of many of the preexisting customs and unwritten laws of Arabia; and it did so as much as it was an innovation. The all-important penal laws of the tribal Arabs, for instance, remained largely intact, based as they were on the principles of retaliation and blood-money (to which the Quran would add the desirable conduct of forgiveness).

The strictly legal and judicial functions of the proto-*qāḍī*s for long continued to be narrow in scope, a fact explained by the nature of the population they were appointed to serve. It is remarkable that the Muslim conquests were by no means systematic, but rather geared toward centers. The early Muslims managed to conquer vast lands by subduing the main populations in large cities and towns, and by settling in military garrisons outside some of the conquered cities. These garrisons were later to develop into major urban centers, with complex social forms, but during the first decades of the conquests they maintained basic tribal structures, since the great majority of Muslim soldiers came – with their families and clans – from the various tribes of Arabia. Whatever problems and disputes arose amongst them were, expectedly, of a tribal nature. The work of the proto-judges was thus limited to disputes over booty distribution, to inheritance of such booty rights by the families of deceased soldiers, to blood feuds, to personal injuries, and to such matters as might be expected to arise among a newly settled tribal population. It is also remarkable that the Muslims did not impose their customs and laws on the conquered populations, but only on themselves. Nor did they interfere in any manner with the laws that governed these populations. This policy of segregation allowed the new Muslims to develop their own regulations and rudimentary laws on the basis of their own needs and what they knew best. In other words, they were guided by what was of paramount importance to them, namely, their own venerable customary laws reflecting an amalgam of tribal values and commercial and other practices that represented a regional variation of the largely Semitic culture of the Near East. Permeating all this, no doubt, was the Quranic spirit that was increasingly, but only partially, altering these preexisting laws and customs.

Medina, on the other hand, was obviously not a garrison town, but it still developed, legally and juristically speaking, along the same lines as Kūfa and other such centers. This phenomenon cannot, for one thing, be attributed to its role as capital of the new empire, since within four decades after the Hijra it had lost its geo-political importance – a fact bearing much significance. That Medina did become a prominent legal center and one that fundamentally affected the later development of Islamic law, bespeaks the similarities in social structures that existed between it and the garrison towns, structures that ultimately generated what came to be the legal norms of Islam. Of course it might be argued that the garrison towns, despite their segregation from the conquered populations, constructed their law through borrowings from the surrounding legal cultures (as some scholars would have it), and that Medinan law must have been subject to the same influences. This possibility, however, is highly improbable, not only because Medina was too remote from the conquered populations, but also because its own developed institutions and customs possessed a certain tenacity that precluded other laws and legal conceptions from being allowed to supplant its own traditions. Evidence of this can be seen in an array of commercial and other practices that were known to have existed there before Islam emerged and which persisted and survived into what later came to be Islamic law. Therefore, an eminently plausible explanation for the genetic similarities between Medinan and garrison laws is the fact that what the southern Arabs brought with them to the conquered territories was a version of the Near Eastern legal tradition that was, *ipso facto*, neither alien to nor even moderately different from the indigenous legal traditions of the conquered populations themselves.

The increasing legal specialization of the proto-*qāḍīs*' functions toward the end of the first/seventh century was not, therefore, a function of borrowing from other legal traditions but rather a reflection of the growing complexity of societal structures among the conquering Muslim populations in the garrison towns. The more entrenched these populations became in these towns, the more complicated these structures became, and with this grew the need to invoke the legal traditions that were known to them from the Hejaz. That the legal traditions of these garrison towns came to differ in detail (but not substantially) from those of Medina must be seen as a regional elaboration and modification of the same original laws that the Arabs upheld in their early days in the Peninsula in general and in the Hejaz in particular.[2] For despite the legal significance and ramifications of such difference in detail, the fact remains that their source and make-up were genetically identical.

The increasing legal specialization of the proto-*qāḍīs* also signified an enlargement of the body of law with which they had to work, for, after all, this enlargement appears to have precipitated the need for further specialization and the attendant abandonment of other administrative and financial functions. This new reality forced the proto-*qāḍīs*, who were now emerging as *qāḍīs* proper, to deal with questions of law as a technical discipline. Here, they exercised their considered opinion (*raʾy*), but not without due reliance on what they conceived to have been the model conduct, the *sunan*, of the forebears. *Raʾy*, therefore, was an extension of, and based upon, *ʿilm*, the knowledge of precedent. And as we have seen, the *sunan*, the corpus of model precedent, were not, even during the first decades after the Prophet's death, entirely "secular," but imbued with religious elements derived from the assumption that good conduct must now be in line with either the Quranic spirit, a Companion's behavior, or the conduct of any other personality associated with the emerging ethic of the new religion. Here, the Prophet and his immediate colleagues, especially the earliest caliphs, no doubt stood foremost.

Thus, if the *sunan* had begun to acquire religious significance as early as the reign of ʿUmar I (if not that of Abū Bakr or even during the later career of the Prophet himself), then the origins of Islamic law – as a *religious* system – cannot be rigidly defined as exclusively limited to its *direct* (and

[2] See now Z. Maghen, "Dead Tradition: Joseph Schacht and the Origins of 'Popular Practice'," *Islamic Law and Society*, 10, 3 (2003): 276–347; P. Hennigan, "The Birth of a Legal Institution: The Formation of the *Waqf* in Third Century AH Ḥanafī Legal Discourse" (Ph.D. dissertation, Cornell University, 1999). I thank David Powers for drawing my attention to Maghen's article before it was published; and to the information that Hennigan's thesis will be soon published in the form of a book.

formal) association with the Prophet. For one thing, as we saw in chapter 5, Prophetic authority was substantively intermeshed with the authority of other *sunan*, including those of the Companions, which contributed much to the early formation of law. Second, Islam, however it was understood by the early followers, was not only that construction portrayed in the Quran and Prophetic *ḥadīth*, as many modern scholars and modern Muslims seem to assume. Obviously, even the Quranic provisions did not mean the same thing to all Muslims of the earliest generations. The meaning of Islam, particularly during the first century, was no doubt constantly evolving, undergoing significant and dramatic changes – a fact that, in this respect, distinguished the first/seventh century from later periods during which legal change took on a more steady pattern. That the conception of Muslims living, say, during the 50s/670s, was not based on a definitive Prophetic, Muḥammadan authority does not make their belief or conduct less Islamic than, for example, those who flourished three or five centuries thereafter. We must therefore be wary of the fallacy (dominating much of modern scholarship) that law began to be *Islamic* only when Prophetic authority, *as formally exemplified by ḥadīth*, came into being. The rise of this authority in no way signaled the rise of Islamic values, but rather constituted a continuing evolution of earlier conceptions of "Islam" as well as of forms of authority-statements. To search for the "origins" of Islamic law in the long process of *ḥadīth* evolution – as some prominent modern scholars have done – is therefore to miss the point altogether. In the present work, the pre-*ḥadīth* forms of Islam (including *sunan*, *ʿilm* and *raʾy*) are as valid as those that emerged later. And it is precisely this conception that made it incumbent to exclude from our survey any extended discussion about dating the appearance of Prophetic *ḥadīth* as a yardstick by which to date the rise of Islamic legal norms. Rather, the rise of *ḥadīth* is seen here as an index of the evolution of a particular *form of authority* (namely, Prophetic), not as the emergence of an unprecedented Islamic content of the law. For, in addition to the clearly religious character of the first-/seventh-century *sunan*, Islamic law was, substantively and doctrinally speaking, already formed when Prophetic *ḥadīth* – as an independent source – appeared on the scene. That this *ḥadīth* replaced the *sunan* during the second/eighth and third/ninth centuries was largely a matter of rationalization and authorization, but hardly one of content or substance.

Furthermore, it is important to realize that the rise of *ḥadīth* was a process through which the Prophetic model was historically documented. In other words, *ḥadīth* represented the documentation of Prophetic praxis but did not exclusively embody Prophetic authority. This is a fact of paramount importance, as evidenced in early Medinese jurisprudence. For the jurists of Medina, authority resided in their own legal practice, which they saw as possessing authority by virtue of the fact that it had been the continuous practice of the "people of Medina" since the time of the Prophet, sanctioned and reaffirmed by the practices of his Companions and their Successors. They rejected any *ḥadīth* that contradicted such "well-known" practices, however credible this *ḥadīth* may have been in the view of others. Until such time as *ḥadīth* achieved its dramatic victory against what we have called practice-based *sunna*, this latter continued to be the source of legal authority. When *ḥadīth* finally proved itself as the highest form by which exemplary Prophetic biography could be documented, and, more importantly, when it gained near-universal acceptance, the practice-based *sunna* as foundational authority was largely – but not entirely – abandoned.

The difference between practice-based *sunna* and *ḥadīth* is that the majority of the former was Prophetic authority mediated by the practices of the Companions (and to some extent of the Successors), whereas the latter conveyed Prophetic authority through a documented chain of transmitters who were just that: transmitters. With the passage of time, the status of these transmitters – including the Companions – was gradually to become equal. In practice-based *sunna*, on the other hand, the idea of viewing Companion practice and authority as possessing a less than paramount status (after the Prophet, of course) was unthinkable. More unthinkable was the idea that the Companions are no more than narrators or transmitters of *ḥadīth*. But this is not to say that their authority stood independent from any other; on the contrary, theirs was a derivative authority, and the Prophetic model was tacitly its source. They were bestowed with such elevated authority not only because of their *knowledge* of what the Prophet had said and done, but also because they acted on, and lived by, that knowledge. *Ḥadīth* or not, first-/seventh-and second-/eighth-century practice-based *sunna* was therefore imbued with Prophetic authority, but mediated through the discursive practice of the first generation of Muslims.

It is obvious that the Companions' generation operated within the contours of its own culture, but this cannot mean that all their solutions to the newly arising problems were based on an exclusively Prophetic precedent. Yet there is little doubt that their practices were in line with the *sunan māḍiya*, the established ways of the forebears, be they Islamic or pre-Islamic. The emerging Prophetic authority was to claim both forms of the *sunan*: whatever pre-Islamic values the Quran and the Prophet did not shun became part of these recognized *sunan*, for, after all, they reflected the venerated traditions that defined the world of early Muslims. And since the practices of the first (and, for that matter, the second) generation were deemed to fall within the recognized *sunan*, they were in turn attributed to the Prophet and thus represented a part of the model Prophetic conduct, to be emulated and followed. This, in short, is the process through which Muḥammad acquired Prophetic authority, a process that began in the Quran itself (which enjoined believers to take their Prophet as a model) and continued to gain support by the operation of the time-honored *sunan māḍiya* that Prophetic authority gradually came to shape and define.

The activities of the Quran teachers, preachers and story-tellers contributed, from the very beginning, to the evolution of this Prophetic authority. The more knowledge one possessed of the Quran and the Prophetic *sīra*, the more authority one gained to speak of what "true" religion was. From the circles of these teachers, preachers and story-tellers there emerged, within a few decades after the Prophet's death, a new generation of young, pious men who focused their attention on the study of the Quranic text and/or *sunan māḍiya*, including the all-important Prophetic, Companion and caliphal *sunan*. At a mature age (during and after the 80s/700s), this generation had already produced an epistemic oral tradition that encompassed many facets of Quranic exegesis and religious narratives of *sunan māḍiya*. Those amongst them who focused their attention on legal subject matter – e.g., Quranic inheritance, family law, ritual and pecuniary and commercial transactions – were the legal specialists who began to teach these relatively specialized subjects to the ever-increasing circles of students. Their specialized knowledge of these subjects bestowed on them what we have called epistemic authority, namely, the recognized ability to declare what was permissible or impermissible, or, in other words, what the law was. The Quran and the *sunan* – including those of the Prophet, caliphs and Companions – became the subject matter for what came technically to be known as ijtihādic activity, a hermeneutical apparatus that defined what law might be derived from that subject matter. The increasing specialization of the law meant a commensurate specialization in, and refinement of, technical legal thought, which in turn meant that law can no longer be defined by, or limited to the reproduction of, the subject matter of the Quran or the *sunan*. These latter, in other words, became the substrate of an intellectual and technical super-structure that was the law. Individual ijtihādic activity was the emblem of legal development as embodied in the emergence of the circles of legal specialists, an activity that was to endure and flourish for over a millennium as perhaps the most fundamental feature of that culture.

The individual ijtihādic activity of the next generation of legal specialists – those who flourished after the second or third decade of the second/eighth century – involved the development of more conscious legal methodology and principles of positive law, albeit still somewhat rudimentary. Each recognized *mujtahid* not only established such methodology and principles, but also gathered around him students who would recognize his doctrine as a particular brand of jurisprudence. This development marked the beginning of the personal schools that were to persist well into the beginning of the next century. The hallmark of these schools was then the individual doctrine of the leading jurist and teacher, the *mujtahid*. The distinctiveness of each personal doctrine was, as we have said, to be found in the particular set of positive legal principles that he elaborated. But his doctrine was not to remain intact. His students and their own students elaborated and expanded his doctrine, and in doing so drew on the doctrines of other leading jurists who did not always share the same juristic premises as their principal teacher. Thus, a student – or the student of a student – of Shāfiʿī may have drawn primarily on the latter's doctrine, but he may well have incorporated into his (what were later deemed) Shāfiʿite solutions a heavy element from (what, again, was later considered to be) Ḥanafite law. The personal schools were thus also characterized by the absence of exclusive loyalty to one doctrine, and this lay at the heart of a fundamental development in the nature of schools. The cumulative build-up of legal doctrine gave rise to the doctrinal school, which emerged as significantly different from its personal predecessor. But once the cumulative legal doctrine of the school took shape, loyalty to it became one of its defining features. And though this loyalty was to a collective doctrine, it was different from the eclectic loyalty of the personal schools. For, unlike the latter, the doctrinal schools commanded loyalty, not to the person or even positive law of a teacher or master-jurist (the so-called eponym), but to what came to be recognized as his *consciously constructed methodology and principles of positive law* – methodology and principles that in reality were the product of an effort extending over generations of juristic and jurisprudential output. Constructing the eponyms as the final authorities who, as absolute *mujtahids*, single-handedly elaborated the law of the doctrinal schools was precisely the accomplishment that defined these schools, which in turn shaped – in the most fundamental ways – the entire remaining history of Islamic law.

But the doctrinal schools could not have been fully formed without a methodology of law (*uṣūl al-fiqh*; to be distinguished from the abovementioned "principles of positive law"), for it was this very methodology that presumably lay at the core of the constructed image of the founding master-jurist, the absolute *mujtahid*. Nor could this methodology itself have arisen without the creation of a synthesis between the opposing forces of rationalism and traditionalism, a synthesis that gave Sunnite Islam its defining features. The doctrinal schools were therefore the last major stage of development that in turn gave Islamic law its final form (without this implying that Islamic law did not later experience internal and piecemeal change within its established boundaries).

The uniqueness of the doctrinal schools in world legal cultures – and they are unique – must prompt at least two important observations: First, if other cultures did possess law and legal systems without having to construct for themselves doctrinal schools, then these schools in Islam must have had a purpose other than providing a positive law, a legal philosophy or a legal system. And second, if they were not necessary for fulfilling such purposes, then they must have evolved for another reason. But what was this reason?

Unlike other world legal cultures, however "complex," Islamic law was never a state mechanism (to use "state" anachronistically). To put it differently, Islamic law did not emerge out of the machinery of the body-politic, but rather arose as a private enterprise initiated and developed by pious men who embarked on the study and elaboration of law as a religious activity. Never could the Islamic ruling elite, the body politic, determine what the law was. This significant fact clearly means that, whereas in other legal cultures the body politic was the source of legal authority and power, in Islam this body was largely, if not totally, absent from the legal scene. The rise of doctrinal schools was the compensation, the alternative solution. The lack of governmental legal authority and power were made up for by the evolution and full emergence of the *madhhab*, an entity which came to possess even greater legal authority than that produced in other cultures by the body politic. If the body politic commanded obedience because it possessed political and coercive powers, the *madhhab* commanded a more evincive form of obedience because it spoke on behalf of God through his absolute *mujtahids*, those who *knew best* what God might have in mind as to what Muslims should or should not do. This epistemic ijtihādic feature, we have already said, not only shaped and defined Islamic law throughout twelve centuries of its history, but also replaced the legal authority of the body politic, which was (and remains more so today) suspected of harboring every kind of vice.

But to say that legal authority remained in the hands of jurists because the body politic was morally suspect is to commit an error in causality.

This tenet of political moral corruption was the by-product, rather than the cause, of lodging legal authority in the jurists' domain. It was, in other words, part of the jurists' discursive strategy in their bid to augment their own legal powers. They were the ones who spoke on behalf of the law, not the body politic; and it is they to whom we listen when we study Islamic law. As part of their exclusive construction of the image of legal Islam, they possessed the power to control knowledge, and it is this knowledge that will continue to influence our understanding as well as our own constructions of them and of the silent – nay, absent – legal authority of the body politic.

This is not to say that the ruling elite did not have an important role to play (nevertheless, we must continue to insist that its role in *determining the law* was virtually nonexistent). We have seen, for instance, that the success or failure of personal and doctrinal schools had much to do with the material and political support that this elite elected to give or withhold. The legists constituted the linkage between this elite and the masses, providing an efficient instrument to the ruling elite for gaining political control and legitimacy. Thus, inasmuch as the legists depended on the financial favors of those holding political power, the latter depended on the legists for accomplishing their own interests. This symbiosis defined the dynamics of the relationship between the two groups: the more the political elite complied with the imperatives of the law, the more legitimizing support it received from the legists; and the more these latter cooperated with the former, the more material and political support they received. Law as a substantive doctrine aside, the interplay between the legal and the political remained within the province of the judiciary and of financial/political interests. The dire need for political legitimacy imposed on the ruling powers the imperative of compliance with the law, and if they manipulated their way out of such compliance – which they at times did – it was an act that could not have been so significant as to deprive them of the mantle of legally approved political legitimacy. It was this reality – which made the approval of the men of law indispensable to the acts of politics – that gave formative Islam what we call today the rule of law. The dismantling of Islamic law and the religious legal institutions during the nineteenth and early twentieth centuries automatically meant the decimation of whatever rule of law there was in that traditional society. The dynamics that governed the relationship between the madhhabic jurists and political power disappeared with the wiping out of the class of legal professionals who mediated another relationship between the masses and what has now become the all-powerful nation-state of modernity. The rise of modern dictatorships in the wake of the colonial experiences of the Muslim world is merely one tragic result of the process in which modernity wreaked violence on venerated traditional cultures.

Glossary of key terms

āḥād: solitary *ḥadīth*s transmitted through fewer channels than *mutawātir*; as such, the knowledge of their contents is probable; see *tawātur*.

ʿahd: a royal decree of judicial appointment; see also *kitāb*.

ahl al-ḥadīth: the traditionalists, those who held that the law must rest squarely on the Quran and Prophetic *ḥadīth*.

ahl al-raʾy: the rationalists, those who held that the law may be derived through human reason as guided by social and worldly experience.

akhbārī: one who collected reports of ancient events and recorded genealogies and poetry; see also *quṣṣās*.

amīn al-ḥukm (pl. *umanāʾ al-ḥukm*): trustee of the court who was in charge of the safekeeping of records, of confidential information and documents, and of property and cash.

aṣḥāb (sing. *ṣāḥib*): associates, colleagues or students; scholars who study and debate with each other, or students of a master; followers of a leading jurist without having studied under him or even having known him in person.

aṣḥāb al-masāʾil (sg. *ṣāḥib al-masāʾil*): court examiners who investigated the character of witnesses.

dīnār: a gold coin, equivalent to ten or twelve *dirham*s (q.v.).

dirham: a silver coin; see *dīnār*.

dīwān (*al-qāḍī*): the court register in which the scribe recorded minutes of court sessions, judgments and a variety of documents, such as contracts, pledges and acknowledgments; see also *maḥḍar*, *sijill*.

faqīh (pl. *fuqahāʾ*): an expert in the law.

fatwā: a legal opinion issued by a *muftī* (q.v.); although formally non-binding, judges adhered to *fatwā*s routinely.

ḥadīth: Prophetic traditions; reports of what the Prophet had said, done or tacitly approved; see also *sunan*, Sunna.

ḥakam (pl. *ḥukkām*): pre-Islamic arbiter whose decision, although non-binding, was usually accepted by the two parties.

ḥalaqa (or *ḥalqa*; pl. *ḥalaqāt*): scholarly or teaching circle.

Ḥanīf: pre-Islamic monotheistic religion that formed around the figure of Abraham.

ijmāʿ: consensus of the scholars of a particular region as embodying their sunnaic practice, by definition exemplary; in later theory, consensus of the *mujtahids* (q.v.) – as representatives of the community of Muslims – on a legal matter.

ijtihād: a process of legal reasoning and hermeneutics through which the jurist-*mujtahid* derives or rationalizes law on the basis of the Quran and the Sunna; during the early period, the exercise of one's discretionary opinion (*ra'y*) on the basis of *'ilm* (q.v.).

ikhtilāf: juristic disagreement; the science of juristic disagreement (also *'ilm al-khilāf*).

'illa (lit., cause): see *ratio legis*.

'ilm: knowledge of precedent, consisting, in the early period, of *sunan* (q.v.), but later of the Quran and Prophetic Sunna.

imam: generally, prayer leader; in the doctrinal schools, the eponym or master-jurist who is presumed to have constructed the methodological foundations and the positive and theoretical principles of the *madhhab* (q.v.).

istiḥsān: juristic preference based, in the early period, upon practical considerations, and later, on a particularized textual *ratio legis* (q.v.).

istiṣlāḥ: legal reasoning dictated by considerations of public interest that are, in turn, grounded in universal legal principles.

jilwāz: court sheriff or bailiff.

kātib: court scribe.

khilāf: see *ikhtilāf*.

kitāb: generally, an epistle; juridically, a written instrument sent by one judge to another demanding the enforcement of a decision or a right; also, a letter of judicial appointment; see also *'ahd*.

madhhab: legal opinion or legal doctrine espoused by a jurist; after the third/ninth century, it also referred to a doctrinal school.

madhhab-opinion: a legal opinion held to be the most authoritative by a doctrinal school.

madrasa: law college.

majlis al-qāḍā': the place where the activity of *qaḍā'*, performed by the judge, takes place. By extension, it is any place where the judge sits to adjudicate cases.

maḥḍar (pl. *maḥāḍir*): records made by the court's scribe and signed by the judge, containing a summary of actions and claims adduced by litigating parties; also, records of statements made by court witnesses to the effect that a certain action, such as a sale or a pledge, had taken place; see also *dīwān*.

mansūkh (lit. abrogated): see *naskh*.

maṣlaḥa: public interest; see *istiṣlāḥ*.

mawlā: non-Arab convert to Islam who entered into legal patron–client relations that created an artificial kinship with the Arabs.

maẓālim: extra-judicial tribunals held by the ruler but usually presided over by *qāḍīs*.

Miḥna: the Inquisition, pursued by the caliphs and rationalists between 218/833 and 234/848; it revolved around the issue of whether or not the Quran was created.

muftī: jurisprudent who issues *fatwās* (q.v.); see also *mujtahid*.

mujtahid: often interchangeable with *muftī*, one who is competent to reason from the revealed texts, fashion new rules or justify and rationalize preexistent law; see also *ijtihād*.

mukharrijūn (sg. *mukharrij*): leading jurists who contributed to the formation of doctrinal schools; also independent and semi-independent *mujtahids* (q.v.) whose legal doctrine, or a part thereof, was appropriated by the doctrinal schools; see also *takhrīj*.

munādī: court official whose task, *inter alia*, was to call publicly on defendants or witnesses to appear before the court.

muqallid: a jurist or layman who follows a *mujtahid* (q.v.).

mushāwar: a jurist advising the court in Andalusia and the Maghrib.

mutawātir: see *tawātur*.

muwaththiq: private notary who drafted legal formulae; syn. *shurūṭī*.

nā'ib: judge's deputy.

naskh: abrogation.

naṣṣ: unambiguous language of the Quran; language capable of yielding only one meaning.

qaḍā': judgeship, the entire range of the judge's judicial activities.

qāḍī al-quḍāt: chief justice.

qāṣṣ: see *quṣṣāṣ*.

qimaṭr: a bookcase in which court documents are preserved; a court register in which documents are recorded.

qiyās: a collective name for a variety of legal arguments including, *inter alia*, analogy, *argumentum a fortiori*, *reductio ad absurdum*, or deductive arguments; see also *ratio legis*.

quṣṣāṣ (sg. *qāṣṣ*): story-tellers.

ratio legis: "cause" or "factor" occasioning – in analogical *qiyās* (q.v.) – a rule in the original case; the presence of the same *ratio* in the new case requires the transfer of the rule from the original case to the new.

ra'y: discretionary opinion or reasoning based on precedent (*'ilm*, q.v.) or, at times, on subjective considerations.

ṣāḥib al-masā'il: see *aṣḥāb al-masā'il*.

shāhid (pl. *shuhūd*): witness.

Sharī'a: Islamic law, including legal doctrine and the judiciary.

shurūṭī: private notary who drafted legal formulae; syn. *muwaththiq*.

sijill (pl. *sijillāt*): witnessed record of the contents of *maḥḍar* (*q.v.*), together with the judge's decision on each case.

sīra: the Prophet's biography.

siyāsa shar'iyya: law legislated and administered by the ruler.

sunan (sg. *sunna*): exemplary conduct of both groups and individuals that, over time, became a model to be emulated and followed by others.

sunna: see *sunan*.

Sunna: the Prophet's conduct that had been established as a model for others to follow; this conduct may be expressed in the Prophet's own practices, his utterances or his tacit approval of events or pronouncements made in his presence; with the passage of time it became, after the Quran, the second source of Islamic law.

sunna māḍiya (pl. *sunan māḍiya*): established, continuous practice that had become a model to follow.

sunnaic practice: continuous practice based upon the *sunan* (q.v.).

tābūt al-ḥukm (also *tābūt al-quḍāt*): security box in which the judge kept cash and other valuables.

takhrīj: legal reasoning (*ijtihād*, q.v.) derived from, and based upon, earlier, authoritative law; see also *mukharrijūn*.

taqlīd: following the authority of a *mujtahid* (q.v.) or of one's school, with or without the ability to practice *ijtihād*.

tawātur: recurrent Prophetic traditions, transmitted through so many channels and by so many people that collusion upon forgery is inconceivable; as such, their contents are known with certainty.

traditionalist: a proponent of the view that law must squarely rest on the revealed sources.

tradition(al)ist: a legist who is both a traditionist and a traditionalist.

traditionist: a specialist in *ḥadīth* collection, transmission and authentication.

umanāʾ al-ḥukm: see *amīn al-ḥukm*.

Umma: the Muslim community.

uṣūl al-fiqh: legal theory that laid down the principles of linguistic–legal interpretation, theory of abrogation (*naskh*), consensus and juristic reasoning, among others.

waqf (pl. *awqāf*): a perpetual charitable trust or endowment for the benefit of family members or the public at large.

zakāt: alms-tax.

Short biographies

ʿAbd Allāh b. Nawfal: proto-judge in Medina during the late 60s/680s.
ʿAbd Allāh al-ʿUmarī: see ʿUmarī.
ʿAbd Allāh b. ʿUtba (d. 98/716): Medinan legal specialist.
ʿAbd al-Malik: Umayyad caliph (r. 65/685–86/705).
Abū Ayyūb al-Sakhtiyānī (d. 131/748): Baṣran jurist.
Abū Bakr (d. 13/634): the Prophet's Companion and the first caliph of Islam.
Abū Ḥanīfa (d. 150/767): leading Kūfan jurist and eponym of the Ḥanafite legal school.
Abū Hurayra: Companion of the Prophet.
Abū Ṭāhir Muḥammad b. Aḥmad: judge in Ikhshīdid Egypt around 348/959.
Abū Thawr, Ibrāhīm b. Khālid (d. 240/854): leading Iraqian jurist and founder of an extinct legal school.
Abū Yūsuf, Yaʿqūb (d. 182/798): leading Kūfan jurist, first chief justice in Islam and co-founder of the Ḥanafite legal school.
Abū Zurʿa, Muḥammad b. ʿUthmān (d. 302/914): Shāfiʿite scholar, appointed in 284/897 as chief justice of both Syria and Egypt.
ʿAdī b. Arṭa'a: Baṣran judge appointed by ʿUmar II (r. 99/717–101/720).
ʿAlī b. Abī Ṭālib (d. 40/661): cousin of the Prophet and fourth caliph of Islam.
Amīn: ʿAbbāsid caliph, the son of Hārūn al-Rashīd (r. 193/809–198/813).
ʿĀmir al-Shaʿbī: see Shaʿbī.
ʿAmr b. Dīnār (d. 126/743): Meccan legal specialist.
Anas b. Mālik: Companion of the Prophet.
ʿAnbarī, ʿUbayd Allāh b. al-Ḥasan: judge of Baṣra between 156/772 and 166/782.
Anmāṭī, Abū al-Qāsim (d. 288/900): leading Shāfiʿite jurist.
Anṣārī, Abū Bakr b. Ḥazm: judge of Medina in and after 94/712.
ʿAṭāʾ b. Abī Rabāḥ (d. 105/723): Meccan/Medinan legal specialist.
Athram, Abū Bakr (d. 261/874): student of Aḥmad b. Ḥanbal.
ʿAṭṭāf b. Ghazwān: *maẓālim* judge in Fusṭāṭ between 211/826 and 212/827.
Awzāʿī (d. 157/773): leading Syrian jurist and founder of the Awzāʿian legal school.
Azdī: see ʿIyāḍ.
Bakkār b. Qutayba: Kūfan Ḥanafite judge serving in Egypt between 246/860 and 270/883, when he died.
Baṣrī, al-Ḥasan (d. 110/728): Baṣran intellectual and proto-theologian.

Burnī, Aḥmad b. ʿĪsā: judge appointed to the east side of Baghdad around 170/786.
Dāwūd b. Khalaf al-Ẓāhirī (d. 270/883): leading Baghdadian jurist and eponym of the Ẓāhirite legal school, later extinct.
Faḍāla b. ʿUbayd al-Anṣārī: proto-*qāḍī* and governor of Syria in or around 38/658.
Faḍl b. Ghānim: judge of Fusṭāṭ between 198/813 and 199/814.
Fārisī, Abū Bakr (fl. ca. 350/960): leading Shāfiʿite jurist and student of Ibn Surayj.
Ghawth b. Sulaymān: appointed twice as judge in Egypt between 135/752 and 144/761.
Ḥabīb b. Thābit (d. 119/737): weak traditionist.
Hādī: ʿAbbāsid caliph (r. 169/785–170/786).
Ḥammād b. Isḥāq (d. 267/880): leading Mālikite jurist and judge in Baghdad.
Ḥammād b. Abī Sulaymān (d. 120/737): distinguished Kūfan jurist.
Ḥarbī, Ibrāhīm b. Isḥāq (d. 285/898): follower of Ibn Ḥanbal and a proto-Ḥanbalite.
Ḥārith b. Miskīn: judge in Egypt between 237/851 and 245/859.
Ḥārithī, Khālid b. Ḥusayn: Baṣran judge between 158/774 and 169/785.
Ḥarmala (d. 243/857): student of Shāfiʿī and a leading jurist whose own nascent school did not survive.
Hārūn b. ʿAbd Allāh: judge in Egypt between 216/831 and 226/840.
Hārūn al-Rashīd: ʿAbbāsid caliph (r. 170/786–193/809).
Ḥasan b. Ziyād (d. 204/819): leading Kūfan jurist, judge and traditionist, and Abū Ḥanīfa's student.
Hāshim al-Bakrī: Iraqian Ḥanafite judge appointed in Egypt between 194/809 and 196/811.
Ḥazmī, ʿAbd Allāh b. Ṭāhir: judge in Egypt between 169/785 and 174/790.
Ibn ʿAbbād, Muḥammad: *maẓālim* judge in Egypt between 215/830 and 216/831.
Ibn ʿAbbās: Companion of the Prophet.
Ibn ʿAbd al-Ḥakam, ʿAbd Allāh (d. 214/829): Egyptian judge and witness examiner.
Ibn Abī Dāwūd (d. 240/854): chief justice and chief inquisitor during the Miḥna.
Ibn Abī Laylā (d. 148/765): distinguished Kūfan judge and jurist.
Ibn Burayda, ʿAbd Allāh: judge in Khurāsān (probably early second/eighth century).
Ibn al-Furāt, Isḥāq: judge in Egypt between 184/800 and 185/801.
Ibn Ḥafṣ, Ḥusayn (d. 212/827): Hanafite jurist who operated in Iṣfahān.
Ibn Ḥanbal, Aḥmad (d. 241/855): distinguished traditionist and traditionalist, and the eponym of the Ḥanbalite school of law.
Ibn Ḥarbawayh, Abū ʿUbayd (d. 319/931): leading Thawrian jurist. See Abū Thawr.
Ibn Ḥaykawayh (d. 318/930): Shāfiʿite jurist and student of Ibn Surayj.
Ibn Ḥujayra, ʿAbd al-Raḥmān: Egyptian judge between 70/689 or 71/690 and 83/702, when he died.
Ibn Jarrāḥ, Ibrāhīm: Ḥanafite judge, served in Egypt between 205/820 and 211/826.
Ibn Jubayr, Saʿīd: judge in Kūfa after 105/723.
Ibn Khadīj, ʿAbd al-Raḥmān: judge serving in Egypt for six months during 86/705–87/706.

Ibn Khayrān, Abū ʿAlī (d. 320/932): Shāfiʿite jurist and student of Anmāṭī.
Ibn Masʿūd (d. 32/652): Companion of the Prophet.
Ibn Maymūn, Yaḥyā: judge serving in Egypt between 105/723 and 115/733.
Ibn al-Muʿadhdhil (d. ca. 240/854): leading Mālikite jurist in Baṣra.
Ibn al-Mubārak, ʿAbd Allāh (d. ca. 185/801): leading Khurāsānian, and later Iraqian, jurist, and student of Sufyān al-Thawrī and Mālik.
Ibn al-Munkadir, ʿĪsā: judge of Fusṭāṭ between 212/827 and 214/829.
Ibn al-Muqaffaʿ (d. ca. 139/756): Persian secretary during the first years of the ʿAbbāsids.
Ibn al-Qāsim, Abū ʿAbd Allāh (d. 191/806): leading Medinan jurist and student of Mālik.
Ibn al-Qāṣṣ al-Ṭabarī (d. 336/947): leading Shāfiʿite jurist and student of Ibn Surayj.
Ibn Ṣayfī, Yaḥyā b. Aktham (d. 242/856): Shāfiʿite jurist and confidant of the caliph Ma'mūn.
Ibn Shabṭūn, Abū ʿAbd Allāh (d. 193/808 or 199/814): Medinan Mālikite jurist who, among others, introduced Mālikism to Andalusia.
Ibn Shayba, Yaʿqūb (d. 262/875): leading Mālikite jurist in Baṣra and later in Baghdad.
Ibn Shubruma: Kūfan judge during the 130s/750s.
Ibn Surayj, Abū al-ʿAbbās (d. 306/918): Baghdadian Shāfiʿite jurist, one of the most important contributors to the formation of Shāfiʿism.
Ibn ʿUmar, ʿAbd Allāh (d. 73/692 or 74/693): Companion of the Prophet and Medinan authority.
Ibn ʿUtba, ʿAbd Allāh: judge serving in Kūfa around 95/713.
Ibn ʿUyayna: see Sufyān.
Ibn Yasār, Abū ʿAbd Allāh Muslim (d. ca. 110/728): leading Baṣran legal specialist.
Ibn Yasār, Sulaymān: see Sulaymān.
Ibrāhīm b. Isḥāq: judge of Fusṭāṭ between 204/819 and 205/820, when he died.
ʿIkrima (d. 107/725 or 115/733): Meccan legal specialist.
ʿImrān b. ʿAbd Allāh al-Ḥasanī: appointed as judge of Fusṭāṭ in 86/705.
ʿĪsā b. Dīnār (d. 212/827): leading Mālikite jurist who introduced Mālikism to Andalusia.
Isḥāq b. Mūsā (d. ca. 290/902): Egyptian Shāfiʿite scholar who introduced Shāfiʿism to Astrabādh.
Ismāʿīl b. Isḥāq: appointed as judge to the west side of Baghdad around 170/786.
Ismāʿīl b. Isḥāq (d. 282/895): distinguished Mālikite judge and jurist in Baghdad.
Ismāʿīl b. Yasaʿ: Iraqian Ḥanafite judge serving in Egypt between 164/780 and 167/783.
Iṣṭakhrī, Abū Saʿīd (d. 328/939): Shāfiʿite jurist and student of Anmāṭī.
ʿIyāḍ al-Azdī: judge in Egypt around 98/716.
Iyās b. Muʿāwiya: judge of Baṣra (d. 122/739).
Jayshānī, ʿAbd al-Raḥmān: judge and tax-collector in Fusṭāṭ during the 130s/750s.
Kaʿb b. Suwar al-Azdī: proto-*qāḍī* of Baṣra in around 14/635.
Khallāl, Abū Bakr (d. 311/923): one of the chief founders of the Ḥanbalite legal school.

Khārija b. Zayd (d. 99/717): distinguished Medinan jurist.
Khayr b. Nuʿaym: judge and story-teller serving twice in Egypt, first between 120/737 and 127/744, and second between 133/750 and 135/752.
Khuwārizmī, Muḥammad: Iraqian copyist, appointed as a judge in Egypt in 205/820.
Khuzayma b. Ibrāhīm: served as judge in Egypt around 135/752.
Lahīʿa b. ʿĪsā: judge serving twice in Egypt, first between 196/811 and 198/813, and second between 199/814 and 204/819.
Laythī, Yaḥyā b. Yaḥyā (d. 234/849): Medinan Mālikite jurist who, among others, introduced Mālikism to Andalusia.
Mahdī: the third ʿAbbāsid caliph (r. 158/775–169/785).
Makḥūl, Abū ʿAbd Allāh (d. 113/731 or 118/736): Syrian legal specialist.
Makhzūmī, Muḥammad b. ʿAbd Allāh: judge in Baghdad during Maʾmūn's reign.
Mālik b. Anas (d. 179/795): leading Medinan jurist and eponym of the Mālikite school of law.
Maʾmūn: ʿAbbāsid caliph between 198/813 and 218/833, and son of caliph Hārūn al-Rashīd.
Manṣūr, Abū Jaʿfar: the second ʿAbbāsid caliph (r. 136/754–158/775).
Manṣūr b. Ismāʿīl (d. 306/918): leading Thawrian jurist. See Abū Thawr.
Marwān: Umayyad caliph (r. 64/683–65/684).
Marwazī, Muḥammad b. Naṣr (d. 294/906): prominent Baghdadian/Samarqandian jurist and traditionist.
Maydanī, Ḥusayn Abū Jaʿfar (d. 212/827): Ḥanafite jurist in Iṣfahān.
Maymūnī, ʿAbd Allāh (d. 274/887): student of Aḥmad b. Ḥanbal.
Muʿādh b. Jabal: governor/commander/proto-*qāḍī* of Yemen during the Prophet's lifetime.
Muʿāwiya b. Abī Sufyān: the first Umayyad caliph (r. 41/661–60/680).
Mufaḍḍal b. Faḍāla: appointed judge of Fusṭāṭ twice, first between 168/784 and 169/785, and second between 174/790 and 177/793.
Muḥammad b. Abī al-Layth: judge in Fusṭāṭ between 226/840 and 235/849.
Muḥammad b. Sīrīn (d. 110/728): Kūfan legal specialist.
Muḥammad b. Yūsuf: judge of Baghdad around 301/913.
Mujāhid b. Jabr (d. between 100/718 and 104/722): Meccan legal specialist.
Murādī, ʿĀbis b. Saʿīd: proto-*qāḍī* of Fusṭāṭ around 65/684.
Murādī, al-Rabīʿ b. Sulaymān (d. 270/884): leading Shāfiʿite jurist in Egypt.
Muslim b. Yasār, Abū ʿAbd Allāh (d. 101/719): distinguished Baṣran jurist.
Muzanī, Ibrāhīm (d. 264/877): Egyptian Shāfiʿite jurist.
Nāfiʿ (d. 118/736): Medinan legal specialist.
Nakhaʿī, Ibrāhīm (d. 96/714): proto-Ḥanafite Kūfan jurist.
Nawfal b. Musāḥiq: Medinan judge around 76/695.
Nīsābūrī, Muḥammad b. al-Mundhir (d. 318/930): leading, semi-independent jurist, later claimed by the Shāfiʿite school.
Nīsābūrī, Yaʿqūb b. Isḥāq (d. 313/925 or 316/928): Egyptian Shāfiʿite jurist who introduced his school to Isfarāʾīn.

Qabīṣa b. Dhu'ayb, Abū Sa'īd (d. 86/705 or 87/706): prominent Medinan legal specialist.

Qaffāl al-Shāshī (d. 336/947): leading Shāfi'ite jurist and student of Ibn Surayj.

Qāsim b. Muḥammad (d. 110/728): Medinan legal specialist.

Qatāda b. Di'āma al-Sadūsī (d. 117/735): leading Baṣran legal specialist.

Rabī' b. Sulaymān: see Murādī.

Rabī'a (Rabī'at al-Ra'y) b. Abī 'Abd al-Raḥmān (d. 136/753): Medinan legal authority.

Ru'aynī, Abū Khuzayma: judge in Egypt between 144/761 and 154/770.

Sa'īd b. Jubayr (d. 95/713): Kūfan legal specialist.

Sa'īd b. al-Musayyab (d. 94/712): Medinan legal authority.

Sakhtiyānī: see Abū Ayyūb.

Ṣāliḥ b. Kaysān: Medinan traditionist (fl. ca. 100/718–120/737).

Sawwār b. 'Abd Allāh: Baṣran judge serving during the late 130s/750s.

Ṣayrafī, Abū Bakr (d. 330/942): leading Shāfi'ite jurist and student of Ibn Surayj.

Sha'bī, 'Āmir (d. 110/728): distinguished Kūfan legal specialist.

Shāfi'ī, Muḥammad b. Idrīs (d. 204/819): leading jurist and eponym of the Shāfi'ite legal school.

Sharīk b. 'Abd Allāh: Kūfan judge during the 160s/780s.

Shāshī: see Qaffāl.

Shāshī, Abū 'Alī (d. 344/955): Ḥanafite jurist and legal theoretician.

Shaybānī, Muḥammad b. al-Ḥasan (d. 189/804): leading Kūfan jurist and co-founder of the Ḥanafite legal school.

Shurayḥ: proto-*qāḍī* of Kūfa (d. sometime between 63/682 and 78/705).

Sufyān b. 'Uyayna (d. 198/814): distinguished traditionist and teacher of Shāfi'ī.

Sulamī, 'Umar b. 'Āmir: Baṣran judge during the 130s/750s.

Sulaym b. 'Itr: Egyptian proto-*qāḍī* between 40/660 and 60/680.

Sulaymān b. Yasār (d. 110/728): Medinan legal specialist.

Ṭabarī, Muḥammad b. Jarīr (d. 310/922): leading Baghdadian jurist whose nascent school did not survive.

Ṭalḥa b. 'Abd Allāh b. 'Awf: proto-*qāḍī* of Medina between 60/679 and 72/691.

Tamīmī, Manṣūr (d. before 320/932): Shāfi'ite jurist and student of Anmāṭī.

Ṭāwūs (d. 106/724): Yemenite legal specialist.

Thaljī, Muḥammad b. Shujā' (d. 267/880): leading Iraqian Ḥanafite jurist.

Thawrī, Sufyān (d. 161/777): leading Kūfan jurist and an eponym of an extinct legal school.

'Ubayd Allāh b. Bakara: commander and proto-*qāḍī* of nascent Baṣra.

'Udharī, 'Abd al-Raḥmān: military commander and *qāḍī* of Damascus around 100/718.

'Umar I, b. al-Khaṭṭāb: the second caliph after the Prophet (r. 13/632–23/644) and one of his Companions.

'Umar II, b. 'Abd al-'Azīz: Ummayad caliph (r. 99/717–101/720).

'Umarī, 'Abd Allāh: judge in Egypt between 185/801 and 194/809.

'Urwa b. al-Zubayr (d. 94/712): Medinan legal specialist.

ʿUthmān b. ʿAffān: the third caliph of Islam (r. 23/644–35/655) and a Companion of the Prophet.
Yaḥyā b. Saʿīd: judge of Baghdad during Manṣūr's reign (136/754–158/775).
Yaḥyā b. Yaḥyā: see Laythī.
Yazīd b. ʿAbd al-Malik: Umayyad caliph (r. 101/718–105/723).
Yazīd b. Bilāl (d. 140/757): Egyptian judge.
Zayd b. Thābit: the Prophet's scribe.
Ziyād b. ʿAbd al-Raḥmān (d. ca. 200/815): Medinan Mālikite jurist who introduced Mālikism to Andalusia.
Zufar b. Hudhayl (d. 158/774): leading Kūfan jurist and student of Abū Ḥanīfa.
Zuhrī, Abū Muṣʿab (d. 242/857): Medinan jurist.
Zuhrī, Ibn Shihāb al-Dīn (d. 124/742): leading Medinan jurist.
Zuraqī, ʿUmar b. Khalda: judge of Medina around 80/699.

Bibliography

In classifying entries no account is taken of the letter *ʿayn* or the Arabic definite article *al-*.

PRIMARY SOURCES

Abū Zurʿa, see Dimashqī.
ʿAsqalānī, Ibn Ḥajar, *Rafʿ al-Iṣr ʿan Quḍāt Miṣr*, ed. Ḥāmid ʿAbd al-Majīd, 2 vols. (Cairo: al-Hayʾa al-ʿĀmma li-Shuʾūn al-Maṭābiʿ al-Amīriyya, 1966).
Rafʿ al-Iṣr ʿan Quḍāt Miṣr, printed with Kindī, *Akhbār*.
Baghdādī, al-Khaṭīb, *Tārīkh Baghdād*, 14 vols. (Cairo: Maṭbaʿat al-Saʿāda, 1931).
Bājī, Abū al-Walīd, *Iḥkām al-Fuṣūl fī Aḥkām al-Uṣūl*, ed. ʿAbd al-Majīd Turkī (Beirut: Dār al-Gharb al-Islāmī, 1986).
Dhahabī, Shams al-Dīn, *Siyar Aʿlām al-Nubalāʾ*, ed. B. Maʿrūf and M. H. Sarḥān, 23 vols. (Beirut: Muʾassasat al-Risāla, 1986).
Tārīkh al-Islām, ed. ʿUmar Tadmurī, 52 vols. (Beirut: Dār al-Kitāb al-ʿArabī, 1987–2000).
Dimashqī, Abū Zurʿa, *Tārīkh*, ed. Shukr Allāh al-Qawjānī, 2 vols. (n.p., n.p., 1970).
Hāshimī, Sayyid Aḥmad, *Jawāhir al-Adab fī Adabiyyāt wa-Inshāʾ Lughat al-ʿArab*, 2 vols. (Beirut: Muʾassasat al-Risāla, n.d.).
Ḥaṭṭāb, Muḥammad, *Mawāhib al-Jalīl li-Sharḥ Mukhtaṣar Khalīl*, 6 vols. (Ṭarāblus, Libya: Maktabat al-Najāḥ, 1969).
Ḥusām al-Shahīd, Ibn Māza, *Sharḥ Adab al-Qāḍī lil-Khaṣṣāf* (Beirut: Dār al-Kutub al-ʿIlmiyya, 1994).
Ibn ʿAbd al-Barr, Abū ʿUmar Yūsuf, *Jāmiʿ Bayān al-ʿIlm wa-Faḍlihi*, 2 vols. (Beirut: Dar al-Kutub al-ʿIlmiyya, n.d.).
Ibn ʿAbd Rabbih, Aḥmad b. Muḥammad, *al-ʿIqd al-Farīd*, ed. Muḥammad al-ʿAryān, 8 vols. (Cairo: Maṭbaʿat al-Istiqāma, 1953).
Ibn Aʿtham, Abū Muḥammad Aḥmad, *al-Futūḥ*, 8 vols. (Beirut: Dār al-Kutub al-ʿIlmiyya, 1986).
Ibn al-Farrāʾ, Muḥammad b. Abī Yaʿlā, *Ṭabaqāt al-Ḥanābila*, ed. Muḥammad al-Fiqī, 2 vols. (Cairo: Maṭbaʿat al-Sunna al-Muḥammadiyya, 1952).

Ibn Ḥazm, Muḥammad, *Muʿjam al-Fiqh*, 2 vols. (Damascus: Maṭbaʿat Jāmiʿat Dimashq, 1966).
Ibn Ḥibbān, Muḥammad, *Kitāb Mashāhīr ʿUlamāʾ al-Amṣār*, ed. M. Fleischhammer (Cairo: Maṭbaʿat Lajnat al-Taʾlīf wal-Tarjama wal-Nashr, 1379/1959).
Kitāb al-Thiqāt (Hyderabad: ʿAbd al-Khāliq al-Afghānī, 1388/1968).
Ibn Kathīr, Ismāʿīl b. ʿUmar, *al-Bidāya wal-Nihāya*, 14 vols. (Beirut: Dār al-Kutub al-ʿIlmiyya, 1985–88).
Ibn Khallikān, Shams al-Dīn Aḥmad, *Wafayāt al-Aʿyān*, 4 vols. (Beirut: Dār Iḥyāʾ al-Turāth al-ʿArabī, 1417/1997).
Ibn Māza, see al-Ḥusām al-Shahīd.
Ibn al-Nadīm, *al-Fihrist* (Beirut: Dār al-Maʿrifa lil-Ṭibāʿa wal-Nashr, 1398/1978); trans. B. Dodge, *The Fihrist of al-Nadim: A Tenth-Century Survey of Muslim Culture* (New York: Columbia University Press, 1970).
Ibn al-Najjār, Taqī al-Dīn, *Muntahā al-Irādāt*, ed. ʿAbd al-Mughnī ʿAbd al-Khāliq, 2 vols. (Cairo: Maktabat Dār al-ʿUrūba, 1381/1962).
Ibn Naqīb al-Miṣrī, *ʿUmdat al-Sālik*, trans. N. H. M. Keller, *The Reliance of the Traveller* (Evanston: Sunna Books, 1993).
Ibn Qāḍī Shubha, Taqī al-Dīn, *Ṭabaqāt al-Shāfiʿiyya*, 4 vols. (Hyderabad: Maṭbaʿat Majlis Dāʾirat al-Maʿārif al-ʿUthmāniyya, 1398/1978).
Ibn al-Qāṣṣ, Aḥmad b. Muḥammad, *Adab al-Qāḍī*, ed. Ḥusayn Jabbūrī, 2 vols. (Ṭāʾif: Maktabat al-Ṣiddīq, 1409/1989).
Ibn Qudāma, Muwaffaq al-Dīn, *Mughnī*, 14 vols. (Beirut: Dār al-Kutub al-ʿIlmiyya, 1973).
Ibn Quṭlūbughā, Zayn al-Dīn, *Tāj al-Tarājim* (Baghdad: Maktabat al-Muthannā, 1962).
Ibn Saʿd, Muḥammad, *al-Ṭabaqāt al-Kubrā*, 8 vols. (Beirut: Dār Bayrūt lil-Ṭibāʿa wal-Nashr, 1958).
Jammāʿīlī, ʿAbd al-Ghanī b. ʿAbd al-Wāḥid, *al-ʿUmda fī al-Aḥkām*, ed. Muṣṭafā ʿAṭāʾ (Beirut: Dār al-Kutub al-ʿIlmiyya, 1986).
Jaṣṣāṣ, *Sharḥ Adab al-Qāḍī*, see Ḥusām al-Shahīd.
Kindī, Muḥammad b. Yūsuf, *Akhbār Quḍāt Miṣr*, ed. R. Guest (Cairo: Muʾassasat Qurṭuba, n.d.).
Laknawī, ʿAbd al-Ḥayy, *al-Fawāʾid al-Bahiyya fī Tarājim al-Ḥanafiyya* (Benares: Maktabat Nadwat al-Maʿārif, 1967).
Mālik b. Anas, *al-Muwaṭṭaʾ* (Beirut: Dār al-Jīl, 1414/1993).
Nawawī, Muḥyī al-Dīn Sharaf al-Dīn, *Tahdhīb al-Asmāʾ wal-Lughāt*, 2 vols. (Cairo: Idārat al-Ṭibāʿa al-Munīriyya, n.d.).
Niẓām, al-Shaykh, et al., *al-Fatāwā al-Hindiyya*, 6 vols. (repr.; Beirut: Dār Iḥyāʾ al-Turāth al-ʿArabī, 1400/1980).
Qalqashandī, Aḥmad b. ʿAlī, *Ṣubḥ al-Aʿshā fī Ṣināʿat al-Inshā*, 14 vols. (Beirut: Dār al-Kutub al-ʿIlmiyya, 1987).
al-Qurʾān al-Karīm (Kuwait: Wizārat al-Awqāf, 1981), trans. M. M. Pickthall, *The Meanings of the Glorious Koran* (New York: Mentor, n.d.).

Saḥnūn b. Saʿīd al-Tanūkhī, *al-Mudawwana al-Kubrā*, ed. Aḥmad ʿAbd al-Salām, 5 vols. (Beirut: Dār al-Kutub al-ʿIlmiyya, 1415/1994).
Samarqandī, Abū Naṣr, *Rusūm al-Quḍāt*, ed. M. Jāsim al-Ḥadīthī (Baghdad: Dār al-Ḥurriyya lil-Ṭibāʿa, 1985).
Shāfiʿī, Muḥammad b. Idrīs, *al-Risāla*, ed. M. Kīlānī (Cairo: Muṣṭafā Bābī al-Ḥalabī, 1969), trans. M. Khadduri, *Islamic Jurisprudence: Shafiʿi's* Risala (Baltimore: Johns Hopkins University Press, 1961).
Shāshī, Abū ʿAlī, *Uṣūl* (Beirut: Dār al-Kitāb al-ʿArabī, 1402/1982).
Shaybānī, Muḥammad b. al-Ḥasan, *al-Aṣl*, 5 vols. (Beirut: ʿĀlam al-Kutub, 1990).
Shīrāzī, Abū Isḥāq Ibrāhīm, *Sharḥ al-Lumaʿ*, ed. ʿAbd al-Majīd Turkī, 2 vols. (Beirut: Dār al-Gharb al-Islāmī, 1988).
Ṭabaqāt al-Fuqahāʾ, ed. Iḥsān ʿAbbās (Beirut: Dār al-Rāʾid al-ʿArabī, 1970).
Simnānī, Abū al-Qāsim, *Rawḍat al-Quḍāt*, ed. Ṣalāḥ al-Dīn Nāhī, 4 vols. (Beirut and Amman: Muʾassasat al-Risāla, 1404/1984).
Subkī, Tāj al-Dīn b. Taqī al-Dīn, *Ṭabaqāt al-Shāfiʿiyya al-Kubrā*, 6 vols. (Cairo: al-Maktaba al-Ḥusayniyya, 1906).
Suyūṭī, Jalāl al-Dīn ʿAbd al-Raḥmān, *al-Radd ʿalā man Akhlada ilā al-Arḍ wa-Jahila anna al-Ijtihāda fī Kulli ʿAṣrin Farḍ*, ed. Khalīl al-Mays (Beirut: Dār al-Kutub al-ʿIlmiyya, 1983).
Tanūkhī, ʿAlī b. al-Muḥassin, *Nishwār al-Muḥāḍara*, 8 vols. (n.p., n.p., 1971–).
Ṭūfī, Najm al-Dīn Sulaymān, *Sharḥ Mukhtaṣar al-Rawḍa*, ed. ʿAbd Allāh al-Turkī, 3 vols. (Beirut: Muʾassasat al-Risāla, 1407/1987).
Wakīʿ, Muḥammad b. Khalaf, *Akhbār al-Quḍāt*, 3 vols. (Beirut: ʿĀlam al-Kutub, n.d.).

SECONDARY SOURCES

Abbott, Nabia, *Studies in Arabic Literary Papyri*, vol. II: *Qurʾānic Commentary and Tradition* (Chicago: University of Chicago Press, 1967).
Abu-Lughod, Janet L., *Cairo: 1001 Years of the City Victorious* (Princeton: Princeton University Press, 1971).
ʿAlī, Jawād, *al-Mufaṣṣal fī Tārīkh al-ʿArab Qabl al-Islām*, 10 vols. (Beirut: Dār al-ʿIlm lil-Malāyīn, 1970–76).
Ansari, Zafar I., "The Authenticity of Traditions: A Critique of Joseph Schacht's Argument *e silentio*," *Hamdard Islamicus*, 7 (1984): 51–61.
"Islamic Juristic Terminology before Šāfiʿī: A Semantic Analysis with Special Reference to Kūfa," *Arabica*, 19 (1972): 255–300.
ʿAthamina, K., "Al-Qasas: Its Emergence, Religious Origin and its Socio-Political Impact on Early Muslim Society," *Studia Islamica*, 76 (1992): 53–74.
"The ʿUlama in the Opposition: The 'Stick and the Carrot' Policy in Early Islam," *Islamic Quarterly*, 36, 3 (1992): 153–78.
Azami, M. M., *On Schacht's Origins of Muhammadan Jurisprudence* (New York: John Wiley, 1985).
Studies in Early Ḥadīth *Literature* (Beirut: al-Maktab al-Islami, 1968).

Bakar, Mohd D., "A Note on Muslim Judges and the Professional Certificate," *al-Qanṭara*, 20, 2 (1999): 467–85.

Ball, Warwick, *Rome in the East: The Transformation of an Empire* (London and New York: Routledge, 2000).

Beeston, A. F. L., "Judaism and Christianity in Pre-Islamic Yemen," *L'Arabie du sud*, vol. I (Paris: Editions G.-P. Maisonneuve et Larose, 1984), 271–78.

"The Religions of Pre-Islamic Yemen," *L'Arabie du sud*, vol. I (Paris: Editions G.-P. Maisonneuve et Larose, 1984), 259–69.

Black's Law Dictionary, 5th ed. (St Paul: West Publishing Co. 1979).

Bligh-Abramsky, Irit, "The Judiciary (Qāḍīs) as a Governmental-Administrative Tool in Early Islam," *Journal of the Economic and Social History of the Orient*, 35 (1992): 40–71.

Bravmann, M. M., *The Spiritual Background of Early Islam* (Leiden: E. J. Brill, 1972).

Brock, S. P., "Syriac Views of Emergent Islam," in G. H. A. Juynboll, ed., *Studies on the First Century of Islamic Society* (Carbondale: Southern Illinois University Press, 1982), 9–21.

Brockopp, J., *Early Mālikī Law: Ibn ʿAbd al-Ḥakam and his Major Compendium of Jurisprudence* (Leiden: Brill, 2000).

Burton, J., *The Collection of the Qurʾān* (Cambridge: Cambridge University Press, 1977).

Caspers, E. C. L. During, "Further Evidence for 'Central Asian' Materials from the Arabian Gulf," *Journal of the Economic and Social History of the Orient*, 37 (1994): 33–53.

Cohen, Hayyim, "The Economic Background and the Secular Occupations of Muslim Jurisprudents and Traditionists in the Classical Period of Islam (Until the Middle of the Eleventh Century)," *Journal of the Economic and Social History of the Orient*, 13 (1970): 16–61.

Coulson, N. J., *A History of Islamic Law* (Edinburgh: Edinburgh University Press, 1964).

Crone, Patricia, "Two Legal Problems Bearing on the Early History of the Qurʾān," *Jerusalem Studies in Arabic and Islam*, 18 (1994): 1–37.

Crone, Patricia and M. Cook, *Hagarism: The Making of the Muslim World* (Cambridge: Cambridge University Press, 1977).

Crone, Patricia, and M. Hinds, *God's Caliph: Religious Authority in the First Centuries of Islam* (Cambridge: Cambridge University Press, 1986).

Donner, Fred, "The Role of Nomads in the Near East in Late Antiquity (400–800 C.E.)," in F. M. Clover and R. S. Humphreys, eds., *Tradition and Innovation in Late Antiquity* (Madison: University of Wisconsin Press, 1989), 73–88.

Dussaud, René, *La Pénétration des arabes en Syrie avant l'Islam* (Paris: Paul Geuthner, 1955).

Dutton, Yasin, "*ʿAmal* v. *Ḥadīth* in Islamic Law: The Case of *Sadl al-Yadayn* (Holding One's Hands by One's Sides) When Doing Prayer," *Islamic Law and Society*, 3, 1 (1996): 13–40.

The Origins of Islamic Law: The Qur'an, the Muwaṭṭa' *and Medinan* ʿAmal (Richmond: Curzon, 1999).

Edens, C. and Garth Bawden, "History of Taymā' and Hejazi Trade During the First Millennium B.C.," *Journal of the Economic and Social History of the Orient*, 32 (1989): 48–97.

Goitein, S. D., "The Birth-Hour of Muslim Law," *Muslim World*, 50, 1 (1960): 23–29.

Studies in Islamic History and Institutions (Leiden: E. J. Brill, 1966).

"A Turning Point in the History of the Islamic State," *Islamic Culture*, 23 (1949): 120–35.

Goldziher, I., *The Ẓāhirīs: Their Doctrine and their History*, trans. Wolfgang Behn (Leiden: E. J. Brill, 1971).

Hallaq, Wael, "The Authenticity of Prophetic Ḥadīth: A Pseudo-Problem," *Studia Islamica*, 89 (1999): 75–90.

Authority, Continuity and Change in Islamic Law (Cambridge: Cambridge University Press, 2001).

ed., *The Formation of Islamic Law*, The Formation of the Classical Islamic World, edited by L. Conrad, no. 27 (Aldershot: Ashgate Publishing, 2004).

"From *Fatwā*s to *Furūʿ*: Growth and Change in Islamic Substantive Law," *Islamic Law and Society*, 1 (1994): 17–56.

A History of Islamic Legal Theories (Cambridge: Cambridge University Press, 1997).

"'Muslim Rage' and Islamic Law," *Hastings Law Journal*, 54 (August 2003): 1–17.

"On the Authoritativeness of Sunni Consensus," *International Journal of Middle East Studies*, 18 (1986): 427–54.

"On Dating Mālik's *Muwaṭṭa'*," *UCLA Journal of Islamic and Near Eastern Law*, 1, 1 (2002): 47–65.

"On Inductive Corroboration, Probability and Certainty in Sunnī Legal Thought," in N. Heer, ed., *Islamic Law and Jurisprudence* (Seattle: University of Washington Press, 1990), 3–31.

"*Qāḍī*s Communicating: Legal Change and the Law of Documentary Evidence," *al-Qanṭara*, 20, 2 (1999): 437–66.

"The *Qāḍī*'s *Dīwān* (*sijill*) before the Ottomans," *Bulletin of the School of Oriental and African Studies*, 61, 3 (1998): 415–36.

"The Quest for Origins or Doctrine? Islamic Legal Studies as Colonialist Discourse," *UCLA Journal of Islamic and Near Eastern Law*, 2, 1 (2002–03): 1–31.

"A Tenth–Eleventh Century Treatise on Juridical Dialect," *The Muslim World*, 77, 2–3 (1987): 189–227.

"Use and Abuse of Evidence: The Question of Roman and Provincial Influences on Early Islamic Law," *Journal of the American Oriental Society*, 110 (1989): 79–91; reproduced in W. Hallaq, *Law and Legal Theory in Classical and Medieval Islam* (Aldershot: Variorum, 1994), article IX, 1–36.

"Was al-Shafiʿi the Master Architect of Islamic Jurisprudence?" *International Journal of Middle East Studies*, 25 (1993): 587–605.

Halm, Heinz, *Die Ausbreitung der šāfiʿitischen Rechtsschule von den Anfängen bis zum 8./14. Jahrhundert* (Wiesbaden: Dr. Ludwig Reichert Verlag, 1974).

Hennigan, P., "The Birth of a Legal Institution: The Formation of the *Waqf* in Third Century AH Ḥanafī Legal Discourse" (Ph.D. dissertation, Cornell University, 1999).

Hodgson, M., *The Venture of Islam: Conscience and History in a World Civilization*, 3 vols. (Chicago: University of Chicago Press, 1974).

Hoyland, R. G., *Seeing Islam as Others Saw it: A Survey and Evaluation of Christian, Jewish and Zoroastrian Writings on Early Islam* (Princeton: The Darwin Press, 1997).

Juynboll, G. H. A., *Muslim Tradition: Studies in Chronology, Provenance and Authorship of early Ḥadīth* (Cambridge: Cambridge University Press, 1983).

ed., *Studies on the First Century of Islamic Society* (Carbondale and Edwardsville: Southern Illinois University Press, 1982).

King, G. R. D., "Settlement in Western and Central Arabia and the Gulf in the Sixth-Eighth Centuries AD," in G. R. D. King and A. Cameron, eds., *The Byzantine and Early Islamic Near East*, vol. II (Princeton: The Darwin Press, 1994), 181–212.

Kister, M. J., "al-Ḥīra: Some Notes on its Relations with Arabia," *Arabica*, 15 (1968): 143–69.

"*...lā taqraʾū l-qurʾāna ʿalā l-muṣḥafiyyīn wa-lā taḥmilū l-ʿilma ʿani l-ṣaḥafiyyīn...*: Some Notes of the Transmission of *Ḥadīth*," *Jerusalem Studies in Arabic and Islam*, 22 (1998): 127–62.

"The Market of the Prophet," *Journal of the Economic and Social History of the Orient*, 8 (1965): 272–76.

Landau-Tasseron, Ella, "The Cyclical Reform: A Study of the *Mujaddid* Tradition," *Studia Islamica*, 70 (1989): 79–117.

Lapidus, Ira M., "The Arab Conquests and the Formation of Islamic Society," in Juynboll, ed., *Studies on the First Century of Islamic Society*, 49–72.

Lecker, Michael, "On the Markets of Medina (Yathrib) in Pre-Islamic and Early Islamic Times," in M. Lecker, *Jews and Arabs in Pre- and Early Islamic Arabia* (Aldershot: Variorum, 1998), 133–46.

Levenson, J., *European Expansion and the Counter-Example of Asia, 1300–1600* (Englewood Cliffs, N.J.: Prentice Hall, 1967).

Lowry, Joseph, "The Legal–Theoretical Content of the *Risāla* of Muḥammad b. Idrīs al-Shāfiʿī" (Ph.D. dissertation, University of Pennsylvania, 1999).

Madelung, Wilferd, "The Early Murjiʾa in Khurāsān and Transoxania and the Spread of Ḥanafism," *Der Islam*, 59, 1 (1982): 32–39.

Maghen, Z., "Dead Tradition: Joseph Schacht and the Origins of 'Popular Practice'," *Islamic Law and Society*, 10, 3 (2003): 276–347.

Makdisi, George, "The Significance of the Schools of Law in Islamic Religious History," *International Journal of Middle East Studies*, 10 (1979): 1–8.

Melchert, Christopher, *The Formation of the Sunni Schools of Law* (Leiden: E. J. Brill, 1997).

Mohammed, Khaleelul Iqbal, "Development of an Archetype: Studies in the Shurayḥ Traditions" (Ph.D. dissertation, McGill University, 2001).

Motzki, Harald, *Die Anfänge der islamischen Jurisprudenz: Ihr Entwicklung in Mekka bis zur Mitte des 2./8. Jahrhunderts* (Stuttgart: Franz Steiner, 1991); trans. Marion H. Katz, *The Origins of Islamic Jurisprudence: Meccan Fiqh before the Classical Schools* (Leiden: Brill, 2002).

"Der Fiqh des–Zuhrī: die Quellenproblematik," *Der Islam*, 68, 1 (1991): 1–44.

"The Role of Non-Arab Converts in the Development of Early Islamic Law," *Islamic Law and Society*, 6, 3 (1999): 293–317.

Piotrovsky, Mikhail B., "Late Ancient and Early Medieval Yemen: Settlement, Traditions and Innovations," in G. R. D. King and Avril Cameron, eds., *The Byzantine and Early Islamic Near East*, vol. II (Princeton: The Darwin Press, 1994), 213–20.

Potts, D. T., *The Arabian Gulf in Antiquity*, 2 vols. (Oxford: Clarendon Press, 1990).

Powers, David, "The Exegetical Genre *Nāsikh al-Qurʾān wa-Mansūkhuh*," in Andrew Rippin, ed., *Approaches to the History of the Interpretation of the Qurʾān* (Oxford: Clarendon Press, 1988), 117–38.

"On Judicial Review in Islamic Law," *Law and Society Review*, 26 (1992): 315–41.

Organizing Justice in the Muslim World 1250–1750, Themes in Islamic Law, edited by Wael B. Hallaq, no. 2 (Cambridge: Cambridge University Press, in progress).

Rashid, Saad, *Darb Zubayda: The Pilgrim Road from Kufa to Mecca* (Riyadh: Riyadh University Libraries, 1980).

Rippin, Andrew, "al-Zuhrī, *Naskh al-Qurʾān* and the Early *Tafsīr* Texts," *Bulletin of the School of Oriental and African Studies*, 47 (1984): 22–43.

Rubin, Uri, "*Ḥanīfiyya* and Kaʿba: An Inquiry into the Arabian Pre-Islamic Background of *Dīn Ibrāhīm*," *Jerusalem Studies in Arabic and Islam*, 13 (1990): 85–112.

Sālim, Sayyid, *Tārīkh al-ʿArab fī ʿAṣr al-Jāhiliyya* (Alexandria: Muʾassasat Shabāb al-Jāmiʿa, 1990).

Sartre, Maurice, *L'Orient romain* (Paris: Seuil, 1991).

Schacht, Joseph, "From Babylonian to Islamic Law," in *Yearbook of Islamic and Middle Eastern Law* (London and Boston: Kluwer Law International, 1995), 29–33.

An Introduction to Islamic Law (Oxford: Clarendon Press, 1964).

The Origins of Muhammadan Jurisprudence (Oxford: Clarendon Press, 1950).

Schoeler, Gregor, *Charakter und Authentie der muslimischen Überlieferung über das Leben Mohammeds* (Berlin: W. de Gruyter, 1996).

Serjeant, R. B., "The Constitution of Medina," *Islamic Quarterly*, 8 (1964): 3–16.

Shahid, Irfan, *Byzantium and the Arabs in the Fifth Century* (Washington, D.C.: Dumbarton Oaks Research Library and Collection, 1989).

Byzantium and the Arabs in the Sixth Century (Washington, D.C.: Dumbarton Oaks Library and Collection, 1995).

"Pre-Islamic Arabia," in *The Cambridge History of Islam*, ed. P. M. Holt et al., vol. I A (Cambridge: Cambridge University Press, 1970), 3–29.

Spectorsky, Susan, "*Sunnah* in the Responses of Isḥāq B. Rāhawayh," in Weiss, ed., *Studies in Islamic Legal Theory*, 51–74.

Stol, M. , "Women in Mesopotamia," *Journal of the Economic and Social History of the Orient*, 32, 2 (1995): 123–44.

Sudairī, ʿAbd al-Raḥmān, *The Desert Frontier of Arabia: al-Jawf through the Ages* (London: Stacey International, 1995).

Thung, Michael, "Written Obligations from the 2nd/8th to the 4th Century," Islamic Law and Society, 3, 1 (1996): 1–12.

Tsafrir, N., "The Beginnings of the Ḥanafī School in Iṣfahān," *Islamic Law and Society*, 5, 1 (1998): 1–21.

. "The Spread of the Ḥanafī School in the Western Regions of the ʿAbbāsid Caliphate up to the End of the Third Century AH." (Ph.D. dissertation, Princeton University, 1993).

Tyan, E., *Histoire de l'organisation judiciare en pays d'Islam*, 2 vols. 2nd ed. (Leiden: E. J. Brill, 1960).

"Judicial Organization," in M. Khadduri and H. Liebesny, eds., *Law in the Middle East* (Washington, D.C.: The Middle East Institute, 1955), 236–78.

VerSteeg, Russ, *Early Mesopotamian Law* (Durham, N. C.: Carolina Academic Press, 2000).

Wansbrough, J., *Qurʾānic Studies* (Oxford: Oxford University Press, 1977).

The Sectarian Milieu (Oxford: Oxford University Press, 1978).

Watt, Montgomery, "The Arabian Background of the Qurʾān," *Studies in the History of Arabia*, vol. I (Riyadh: University of Riyadh Press, 1399/1979), 3–13.

The Formative Period of Islamic Thought (Edinburgh: Edinburgh University Press, 1973).

Weiss, Bernard, "Knowledge of the Past: The Theory of *Tawātur* According to Ghazālī," *Studia Islamica*, 61 (1985): 81–105.

ed., *Studies in Islamic Legal Theory* (Leiden: Brill, 2002).

Young, Walter, "*Zinā*, *Qadhf* and *Sariqa*: Exploring the Origins of Islamic Penal Law and its Evolution in Relation to Qurʾānic Rulings" (MA thesis, McGill University, in progress).

Zaman, Muhammad Qasim, *Religion and Politics under the Early ʿAbbāsids* (Leiden: Brill, 1997).

Suggested further reading

CHAPTER 1

Ball, Warwick, *Rome in the East: The Transformation of an Empire* (London and New York: Routledge, 2000).

Berkey, Jonathan, *The Formation of Islam: Religion and Society in the Near East, 600–1800* (Cambridge: Cambridge University Press, 2003), 3–53.

Coulson, N. J., *A History of Islamic Law* (Edinburgh: Edinburgh University Press, 1964), 9–20. Otherwise, largely dated for the classical and medieval periods; but also see relevant pages under chapter 2, below.

King, G. R. D. and A. Cameron, eds., *The Byzantine and Early Islamic Near East*, vol. II (Princeton: The Darwin Press, 1994), 181–212.

Kister, M. J., "Mecca and Tamīm," *Journal of the Economic and Social History of the Orient*, 3 (1965): 113–62.

Lecker, M., *Jews and Arabs in Pre- and Early Islamic Arabia* (Aldershot: Variorum, 1998).

Peters, F. E., ed., *The Arabs and Arabia on the Eve of Islam*, The Formation of the Classical Islamic World, edited by L. Conrad, no. 3 (Aldershot: Variorum, 1999).

Rubin, Uri, ed., *The Life of Muhammad*, The Formation of the Classical Islamic World, edited by L. Conrad, no. 4 (Aldershot: Variorum, 1998).

Schacht, Joseph, "From Babylonian to Islamic Law," in *Yearbook of Islamic and Middle Eastern Law* (London and Boston: Kluwer Law International, 1995), 29–33.

Shahid, Irfan, *Byzantium and the Semitic Orient before the Rise of Islam* (London: Variorum, 1988).

Smith, Sidney, "Events in Arabia in the 6th Century AD," *Bulletin of the School of Oriental and African Studies*, 16, 3 (1954): 419–68.

VerSteeg, Russ, *Early Mesopotamian Law* (Durham, N. C.: Carolina Academic Press, 2000).

CHAPTER 2

ʿAthamina, K., "al-Qasas: Its Emergence, Religious Origin and its Socio-Political Impact on Early Muslim Society," *Studia Islamica*, 76 (1992): 53–74.

Bravmann, M. M., *The Spiritual Background of Early Islam* (Leiden: E. J. Brill, 1972), 123–98.
Coulson, N. J., *A History of Islamic Law* (Edinburgh: Edinburgh University Press, 1964), 21–35. Otherwise, largely dated for the classical and medieval periods.
Hallaq, Wael B., ed., *The Formation of Islamic Law*, The Formation of the Classical Islamic World, edited by L. Conrad, no. 27 (Aldershot: Ashgate Publishing, 2004).
Juynboll, G. H. A., ed., *Studies on the First Century of Islamic Society* (Carbondale and Edwardsville: Southern Illinois University Press, 1982).
Tyan, E., *Histoire de l'organisation judiciare en pays d'Islam*, 2 vols., 2nd ed. (Leiden: E. J. Brill, 1960).

CHAPTER 3

Azami, M. M., *On Schacht's Origins of Muhammadan Jurisprudence* (New York: John Wiley, 1985).
Goldfeld, Y., "The Development of Theory on Qur'ānic Exegesis in Islamic Scholarship," *Studia Islamica*, 67 (1988): 5–27.
Hallaq, Wael, "Use and Abuse of Evidence: The Question of Roman and Provincial Influences on Early Islamic Law," *Journal of the American Oriental Society*, 110 (1989): 79–91; reproduced in W. Hallaq, *Law and Legal Theory in Classical and Medieval Islam* (Aldershot: Variorum, 1994), article IX, 30–31.
Maghen, Z., "Dead Tradition: Joseph Schacht and the Origins of 'Popular Practice'," *Islamic Law and Society*, 10, 3 (2003): 276–347.
Masud, M. K., "Procedural Law between Traditionalists, Jurists and Judges: The Problem of *Yamīn maʿ al-Shāhid*," *al-Qanṭara*, 20, 2 (1999): 389–416.
Mitter, Ulrike, "Unconditional Manumission of Slaves in Early Islamic Law: A *Ḥadīth* Analysis," *Der Islam*, 78 (2001): 35–72.
Motzki, Harald, *The Origins of Islamic Jurisprudence: Meccan Fiqh before the Classical Schools*, trans. Marion H. Katz (Leiden: Brill, 2002).
"The Role of Non-Arab Converts in the Development of Early Islamic Law," *Islamic Law and Society*, 6, 3 (1999): 293–317.
Nawas, J., "The Birth of an Elite: *Mawālī* and Arab Ulama," *Israel Oriental Studies* (forthcoming).
"The Emergence of *Fiqh* as a Distinct Discipline and the Ethnic Identity of the *Fuqahā*ʾ in Early and Classical Islam," in S. Leder, *et al.*, eds., *Studies in Arabic and Islam* (Leuven and Paris: U. Peeters, 2002), 491–99.
Powers, David, *Studies in Qur'ān and* Ḥadīth: *The Formation of the Islamic Law of Inheritance* (Berkeley: University of California Press, 1986).

CHAPTER 4

Nielsen, J., *Secular Justice in an Islamic State:* Maẓālim *under the Baḥrī Mamlūks: 662/1264–789/1387* (Leiden: Nederlands Historisch-Archaeologisch Instituut, 1985), 1–33.

Tyan, E., *Histoire de l'organisation judiciare en pays d'Islam*, 2 vols. 2nd ed. (Leiden: E. J. Brill, 1960).

"Judicial Organization," in M. Khadduri and H. Liebesny, eds., *Law in the Middle East* (Washington, D.C.: The Middle East Institute, 1955), 236–78.

CHAPTER 5

Dutton, Yasin, "*'Amal* v. *Ḥadīth* in Islamic Law: The Case of *Sadl al-Yadayn* (Holding One's Hands by One's Sides) When Doing Prayer," *Islamic Law and Society*, 3, 1 (1996): 13–40.

The Origins of Islamic Law: The Qur'an, the Muwaṭṭa' *and Medinan* 'Amal (Richmond: Curzon, 1999).

Hallaq, Wael, "From Regional to Personal Schools of Law? A Reevaluation," *Islamic Law and Society*, 8, 1 (2001): 1–26.

Spectorsky, Susan, "*Sunnah* in the Responses of Isḥāq B. Rāhawayh," in Bernard Weiss, ed., *Studies in Islamic Legal Theory* (Leiden: Brill, 2002), 51–74.

CHAPTER 6

Calder, Norman, "*Ikhtilāf* and *Ijmā'* in Shāfi'ī's *Risāla*," *Studia Islamica*, 58 (1983): 55–81.

Hallaq, Wael, *A History of Islamic Legal Theories* (Cambridge: Cambridge University Press, 1997).

Law and Legal Theory in Classical and Medieval Islam (Aldershot: Variorum, 1994).

"Was al-Shafi'i the Master Architect of Islamic Jurisprudence?" *International Journal of Middle East Studies*, 25 (1993): 587–605.

Lowry, Joseph, "Does Shāfi'ī Have a Theory of Four Sources of Law?" in Bernard Weiss, ed., *Studies in Islamic Legal Theory* (Leiden: Brill, 2002), 23–50.

Melchert, C., "Traditionist-Jurisprudents and the Framing of Islamic Law" (MS).

CHAPTER 7

Conrad, Gerhard, *Die Quḍāt Dimašq und der Maḏhab al-Auzā'ī* (Beirut: Franz Steiner, 1994).

Halkin, A. S., "The Ḥashwiyya," *Journal of the American Oriental Society*, 54 (1934): 1–28.

Hallaq, W. B., *Authority, Continuity and Change in Islamic Law* (Cambridge: Cambridge University Press, 2001).

Hurvitz, Nimrod, *The Formation of Ḥanbalism: Piety into Power* (London: Routledge Curzon, 2002).
Melchert, Christopher, *The Formation of the Sunni Schools of Law* (Leiden: E. J. Brill, 1997).
"The Formation of the Sunni Schools of Law," in Wael B. Hallaq, ed., *The Formation of Islamic Law*. The Formation of the Classical Islamic World, edited by L. Conrad, no. 27 (Aldershot: Ashgate Publishing, 2003), article XIII. In part a revision of findings in his *Formation*.

CHAPTER 8

Hinds, Martin, "Miḥna," in Jere Bacharach et al., eds., *Studies in Early Islamic History* (Princeton: The Darwin Press, 1996), 232–45.
Melchert, Christopher, "Religious Policies of the Caliphs from al-Mutawakkil to al-Muqtadir, AH 232–295/AD 847–908," *Islamic Law and Society*, 3, 3 (1996): 316–42.
Zaman, Muhammad Qasim, *Religion and Politics under the Early ʿAbbāsids* (Leiden: Brill, 1997).

ON DATING EARLY LEGAL TEXTS

Calder, Norman, *Studies in Early Muslim Jurisprudence* (Oxford: Oxford University Press, 1993).
Dutton, Yasin, "*ʿAmal* v. *Ḥadīth* in Islamic Law: The Case of *Sadl al-Yadayn* (Holding One's Hands by One's Sides) When Doing Prayer," *Islamic Law and Society*, 3, 1 (1996): 13–40.
Hallaq, Wael, "On Dating Mālik's *Muwaṭṭaʾ*," *UCLA Journal of Islamic and Near Eastern Law*, 1, 1 (2002): 47–65.
Lowry, Joseph, "The Legal Hermeneutics of al-Shāfiʿī and Ibn Qutayba: A Reconsideration," *Islamic Law and Society*, 11, 1 (2004; forthcoming).
Motzki, Harald, "The Prophet and the Cat: On Dating Mālik's *Muwaṭṭaʾ* and Legal Traditions," *Jerusalem Studies in Arabic and Islam*, 22 (1998): 18–83.
Muranyi, M., "Die frühe Rechtsliteratur zwischen Quellenanalyse und Fiktion," *Islamic Law and Society*, 4 (1997): 224–41.
Zaman, Muhammad Qasim, *Religion and Politics under the Early ʿAbbāsids* (Leiden: Brill, 1997), 91–101.

Index

In classifying entries no account is taken of the letter *ʿayn* and the Arabic definite article *al-*.